Japanese Economic Development

# Japanese Economic Development
## Third Edition

YOSHIHARA KUNIO

KUALA LUMPUR
**OXFORD UNIVERSITY PRESS**
OXFORD  SINGAPORE  NEW YORK
1994

Oxford University Press

Oxford  New York  Toronto
Delhi Bombay Calcutta Madras Karachi
Kuala Lumpur Singapore Hong Kong Tokyo
Nairobi Dar es Salaam Cape Town
Melbourne Auckland Madrid
and associated companies in
Berlin Ibadan

Oxford is a trade mark of Oxford University Press

Published in the United States
by Oxford University Press, New York

© Oxford University Press 1977, 1986, 1994
First published 1977
Third edition 1994

British Library Cataloguing in Publication Data
Data available

Library of Congress Cataloging-in-Publication Data
Yoshihara, Kunio, 1939–
Japanese economic development/Yoshihara Kunio.—3rd ed.
Includes bibliographical references.
ISBN 967 65 3052 2
1. Japan—Economic conditions—1868–    I. Title.
HC462.Y66    1994
330.952'03—dc20
94-15913
CIP

Typeset by Typeset Gallery Sdn. Bhd., Malaysia
Printed in Singapore by Kyodo Printing Co. (S) Pte. Ltd.
Published by Oxford University Press,
19–25, Jalan Kuchai Lama, 58200 Kuala Lumpur, Malaysia

*To the memory of*
*Mr and Mrs Nakamura Shigeichi*

# Preface

It was in the early 1960s that the Japanese economy began attracting international attention. At that time, Japan resembled the Newly Industrializing Economies of Asia today. The country had begun exporting steel, ships, transistor radios, and other industrial products, and prospects for becoming an industrial nation seemed bright. For those who remembered the collapse of the Japanese economy after the Pacific War, its resurgence was astonishing.

From the perspective of the United States, which was engaged in the Cold War with the Soviet Union in the early 1960s, Japan's economic achievements and promising future were not a politically neutral development; they were worth exploiting in the American anti-Communist ideological campaign. Particularly in Asia, Japan could be useful as an anti-Communist development model. Its basic economic system was capitalism, and economic development was propelled by a mixture of innovations and traditions. Japan was showing the world that capitalistic development was not unique to the West and that it was the most effective way to promote economic development. In subsequent years, as Japan continued to grow while Socialist economies stagnated, the Japanese model became increasingly attractive. This was especially so because post-war Japanese capitalism was not accompanied by the usual excesses of capitalism, such as exploitation of workers and inequality of income.

Apart from the Cold War rhetoric, the continued growth of Japan began posing intellectual challenges to social scientists. To the economists, one pertinent question was what accounted for the high level of savings in Japan, as this was a major factor in high capital accumulation, which, in turn, was a major factor in the country's ability to sustain economic growth. Another growth-related question was what accounted for the ability to create one export after another in the 'flying-geese' fashion. This enabled Japan to increase exports, which, in turn, enabled it to increase imports which were indispensable for sustained economic growth. The social scientists who used a multi-disciplinary approach to studying Japanese economic growth were interested in the relations between the state and the economy, the place of traditional values in business development, the importance of community or national interest in economic development—the kinds of questions which relate economic performance to institutional structure and interrelations.

In the 1980s, as Japanese industry began surpassing the West in a number of high-tech products, the Japanese case was clearly no longer that of a late starter catching up with the West. Japan had become a model for the West in certain areas. The most important area where Japan excelled—and continues to excel—is in regulating individual interest for the sake of group interest. The group can be a community, a corporation, or a nation. In the capitalist economy, there has to be individual freedom, but as is often the case in the West, particularly in the United States, if there is too much emphasis on individual rights, the group to which individuals belong tends to become divisive, and it therefore becomes difficult to build a community out of it. High productivity in a Japanese corporation is due, at least in part, to the fact that it is a community of workers, managers, and stockholders; they all have a common interest and share in the prosperity of the corporation. This clearly makes for higher productivity than in a situation where stockholders hire or fire managers on the basis of their ability to earn short-term profits and have little interest in the welfare of employees.

Japan offers to developing countries a different development model from that of the West whose model combines liberal democracy with capitalism. Despite political democracy, Japan retains a strong bureaucracy and hierarchical social structure, both of which have facilitated collective action. A more egalitarian and diversified society would weaken the country's ability to act effectively in the national interest. Although critics may contend that the Japanese model leads to authoritarian excesses or is used to justify poorly performing authoritarian regimes, liberal democracy has its own inherent problems. For example, restoring power to the people, as posited by the advocates of liberal democracy, may create too divisive a society. Although it may allow people to broaden the sphere of their personal freedom, it may also weaken their ability to act in the national or community interest. For many developing countries, the Japanese model often works better since it accommodates traditional institutions and tries to improve on them, while attaching importance to the ability to act collectively. The Japanese model assumes that individual welfare cannot be promoted unless national—or community—interest is advanced. Although the term 'collective interest' may conjure up the image of an authoritarian state, the Japanese model actually allows a great deal of personal freedom. It cannot be unfavourably compared to the liberal democratic model in view of Japanese success in promoting economic growth, literacy, economic equality, and law and order. In fact, the balance has been tipping in Japan's favour in recent years. According to the United Nations' human development index, Japan ranks number one.

This book has been written to serve two purposes. One is to give the student or general reader a short introduction to the transformation of the Japanese economy and its characteristics. The other is to relate Japanese development to social institutions and cultural values. Typically, long-term economic growth is regarded as the result of change in economic variables, but in explaining why those variables change in certain ways at a certain stage, one cannot avoid discussing how non-economic institutions change and interact with the economy. For example, in explaining why Japan does better than the United States in a number of manufacturing industries, one often looks to schools and the kinship institution for an answer. Undoubtedly, non-economic institutions change over time as the result of economic change, but are not uniquely determined by the level of income. The same thing can be said about cultural values which determine, as well as are determined by, the working of institutions. One major thesis of this book is that Japan's success in economic development has greatly depended on the ability to blend modern values and institutions with those from the pre-modern period.

Chapter 1 gives an overall view of the development process since the Meiji Restoration of 1868. Chapter 2 puts Japanese economic development in a comparative framework and discusses its distinguishing features. Chapter 3 deals with trade and development, more specifically, how trade patterns have changed over time, what accounts for these changes, and the degree to which trade has stimulated Japanese development. Chapter 4 looks closely at conditions in the mid-nineteenth century, and contrasts Japan's preparedness for development with that of two other Asian countries. Chapter 5 discusses the institutional reforms of the early Meiji era and the Allied occupation after the Pacific War—the reforms which produced significant impact on economic development in subsequent years. Chapter 6 discusses the overall business environment created by government, the organization of workers in a company and inter-corporate arrangements to reduce business risk, and the work ethic and level of education of workers and other agents of production. Chapter 7 deals with the negative aspects of Japanese economic development, a subject which has been completely ignored by one group of scholars but given almost exclusive emphasis by another (especially leftist scholars). The recent success of Japan in economic development has put the leftists on the defensive and is threatening to overshadow the negative side. But the negative side should be given due weight so that the dangers in the Japanese model can be well understood. The final chapter briefly summarizes the major implications of Japanese economic development for developing countries. For the reader's convenience, specialized terms relating to Japanese history are listed in the Glossary, and major historical events since the early 1850s in the Chronology. Those who want to read more on the subject of each chapter should consult Further Reading at the end of the book.

The first two editions of this book, published in 1977 and 1986, were favourably received, but a new edition has become necessary in the light of recent economic changes as well as new perspectives on economic development. To understand Japanese economic development, it is important to study three aspects. The first is to know how economic variables changed over time. This is less of a problem in the post-war period when the availability of statistical data significantly improved, but for the pre-war period, the quantification of economic changes is often not satisfactory. The second is how non-economic variables, such as institutions and cultural values, affected economic variables in Japan. For this, one has to understand Japanese institutions and cultural values, preferably in a comparative framework. The third is to understand new economic theories and use them to re-examine development issues in Japan. In this edition, I have made efforts to incorporate recent writings in the last two areas, so that we can better understand Japanese development, in particular, its ability to sustain economic growth and productivity increase.

*Center for Southeast Asian Studies*                    YOSHIHARA KUNIO
*Kyoto University*
*May 1993*

## Note

In this book, Japanese names are presented in the usual Japanese order: surname first and given name second.

All references to dollars ($) are to US dollars, unless otherwise specified. The word 'billion' is used to mean a thousand million.

# Contents

# 1
# The Historical Course of Development

ECONOMIC development, which transformed Japan into an industrial country, is sometimes regarded as a post-Pacific War phenomenon, but its beginnings go back several decades. In this chapter, discussion of the Japanese development process begins with 1868, the year when an important political change known as the Meiji Restoration[1] took place and a new government, which was determined to carry out modernization measures, was born. To start with 1868 does not mean, however, that Japan suddenly emerged from a primitive state in that year. Prior to 1868, there were social developments and a degree of economic progress (see Chapter 4). Since it was after the Meiji Restoration, however, that industrial progress and other qualitative changes in the economic life of Japan began in earnest, it is justifiable to take the year 1868 as the great watershed.

## Laying the Foundations for a Modern Economic System, 1868–1885

In the first 17 years of the Meiji era, Japan broke out of the fetters of feudalism and made the transition into a new economic age. In the first few years, social and political reforms were carried out to dispose of various feudal institutions of the Tokugawa period (1603–1867). First, the decentralized Tokugawa political system was abolished to bring about the political integration of the country, and then feudal restrictions and privileges were revoked in order to establish a new order of society based on merit and individual initiative.[2] It was also necessary to modernize monetary and fiscal systems, and to educate people in the necessity of adopting modern Western technology. Since these tasks took some time, it was not until the mid-1880s that a new economic system was firmly established and the economy was set on a path of long-term growth.

The Tokugawa fiscal system was too cumbersome for a modern state: the rice tax (which accounted for the bulk of government revenue in the period) was paid in kind; tax rates varied from province to province, and were subject to the size of the harvest. In order to create a monetary tax whose rate was uniform throughout the country, the Meiji government instituted a tax reform which led to the establishment of a new land tax. Besides being a uniform monetary tax, as required of a modern form of taxation, the land tax was also important in that it accounted for the bulk of the tax revenue in the first few decades of the Meiji era and was the major financial source of government expenditure for development purposes. Furthermore, by making a taxpayer the legal owner of the land on which he paid tax, the land tax conferred alienability on the land and laid the foundation for the private property system.

The Tokugawa monetary system was also an obstruction to the economic integration which the Meiji government wished to achieve. Under the late Tokugawa system, there was no central control over the issue of money. Paper money was issued by local governments, and coins were minted by the shogunate. There were, as well, some regional differences in the monetary standard. In Osaka, prices were expressed in terms of the weight of silver, whereas in Edo,[3] merchants used different units[4] to express the price of commodities, and these depended primarily on gold coins. Furthermore, the difference in the relative prices of gold and silver in Japan and the West caused a large outflow of gold from Japan after trade with the West began in the 1850s.[5]

In 1871, monetary reform established a standardized and sound currency for the country. For this purpose, the Meiji government withdrew the power of issuing money from local governments, and brought it under its sole control. The cumbersome Tokugawa monetary standard was then replaced by the decimal system with the yen as the basic monetary unit, and money carrying the new denomination was issued for use throughout the country.[6] Furthermore, the gold standard was adopted, and paper notes were issued on a convertible basis.

The last task, however, was especially difficult to implement. The gold standard was already collapsing in the mid-1870s. The government designated the gold coin as the standard, but also minted 1 yen silver coins, which were to be circulated in restricted areas in order to facilitate foreign trade transactions. The silver coin had the same metallic content as the Mexican dollar, which was widely accepted as a means of payment among foreign traders in Asia, and was made equivalent to the 1 yen gold coin at the ratio of 16 units of silver to 1 unit of gold. For a number of reasons, including a large discovery of silver in the United States, the price of silver began to decline in 1875, and the price ratio of silver to gold became 20 to 1 in the following year. Since the conversion rate remained the same in Japan, silver coins were brought into the country to exchange for gold coins, and there was a renewed outflow of gold from Japan. To make up for the scarcity of gold coins, the government had to approve the unrestricted use of silver coins, and thus adopted, *de facto*, the silver standard.

The convertibility of paper notes was fraught with difficulties for internal reasons. Because political instability limited the ability of the government to collect taxes in the first few years of the Meiji era, expenditure exceeded revenue by a large margin. The bulk of expenditure had to be met by issuing paper notes, especially in the mid-1870s when the government was compelled to increase military expenditure in order to suppress rebellions by opponents of modernization measures. The situation was exacerbated towards the end of the 1870s because the government allowed national banks to use government bonds[7] as the reserve for their notes. As a consequence, paper notes circulated at discount values.

In 1881, Matsukata Masayoshi became Minister of Finance. He immediately began to withdraw paper notes from circulation by creating surpluses in the government budget, thereby causing the so-called 'Matsukata deflation'.[8] He was able to reduce government expenditure, create new taxes, and redeem paper notes with the surpluses thus created, a policy he continued until his retirement in 1885 when the convertibility of notes was virtually restored. During his term as Minister of Finance, the Bank of Japan was established as the only note-issuing bank, and thus the basis for monetary management was laid.[9]

One major economic activity of the Meiji government in this period was the building of the country's infrastructure. In 1869, the government decided to construct railways and, in 1872, the first line was completed between Tokyo and Yokohama. In subsequent years, railway mileage increased fairly rapidly: from 18 miles in 1872 to 212 miles in 1885, and to 580 miles in 1889 when the Tokaido line from Tokyo to Kobe was completed. Sea transportation was also modernized by importing steamships from the West. The government did not operate shipping lines directly, but gave large subsidies to Iwasaki Yataro to build a fleet of modern merchant vessels to meet the increasing demand for sea transport.[10] The government also modernized the network of communications by introducing postal and telegraphic services. At the end of this period, there were over 5,000 post offices handling about 100 million items of mail per year. Major telegraph lines in the country had been completed and the number of private messages handled per year approached 3 million. In addition, overseas telegraph communications became possible when Nagasaki, on the island of Kyushu, was linked to the undersea cable from Shanghai which was, in turn, connected to London through Singapore and India. In contrast, however, to the rapid development of the telegraph system, there was little progress in telephone communications in this period.

Since the scale of modern enterprises often required more capital than one merchant or one family could command, a joint-stock company, which pools capital from different people, was promoted as a form of enterprise suitable for the new period. In 1871, for the first time, joint-stock companies were formed in the fields of transportation, finance, and land reclamation. In manufacturing, the first joint-stock company was established in 1873 for silk-reeling.[11] It was around this time that men like Shibusawa Eiichi and Godai Tomoatsu resigned their government posts in order to enter business as private individuals, and to persuade tradition-bound merchants of the merits of the new form of enterprise. Consequently, from the mid-1870s, more and more people became convinced of the value of joint-stock companies. By 1885, there were 1,279 such companies with capital amounting to 50 million yen.

A new dynamic economy necessitated the wide use of machines in industrial production, and the government took various measures to lead the economy in this direction. By importing machinery from the West and inviting foreign technicians to Japan, the government operated mines and factories in textiles, metals, cement, glass, and shipbuilding.[12] Government production itself was not great, but it showed investors the potential of the new methods of production. Spinning, which the government envisaged as the first industry to undergo an industrial revolution, was given first priority. Spindles were leased out on favourable terms, and low-interest loans were given to those wishing to establish spinning mills. In the period 1880–2, the government used 350,000 yen for this purpose, and an additional 100,000 yen was spent on experiments in spindle production. Furthermore, a number of delegations were sent to industrial exhibitions abroad to give them the opportunity to observe industrial progress in the West.

Despite these government-initiated measures, no great progress was achieved during this period in introducing machines. Even in spinning, the highest priority industry, machine-spun yarn comprised only a small part of total yarn production—about 25 per cent in 1882-4. Domestic yarn, which was therefore mostly hand-spun, barely survived under the pressure of import competition from the West (imports accounted for about 75 per cent of total yarn consumption in the early 1880s); yet, with about 60,000 modern spindles installed by the end of 1885, machine-based production gradually grew in importance. In paper, steel, and shipbuilding, the proportion of machine-based production rose. Although its overall impact was small, its rise in those industries signalled the beginning of the machine age in Japan.

## Economic Take-off, 1886–1911

In the remaining 25 years of the Meiji era, a 'miracle' was achieved. Japan, which had previously attracted little attention, astonished the world by winning two major wars and thus earned the right to join the ranks of the Great Powers. When miracles are spoken of in the context of Japan, the economic successes of the period after the Pacific War come most quickly to mind. But the first 'miracle' in Japan's history was the increase in the country's power during the latter years of the Meiji era.

Japan's military strength was first demonstrated by its victory in the Sino-Japanese War (1894–5), after which China ceded Taiwan to Japan. Then, in 1905, Japan defeated Russia in a war fought over the question of control over Korea and China. The fact that it was a victory over a Western country raised Japan's reputation in the eyes of the world. After this, Japan began to be accepted for the first time as a respectable nation by the Western Powers, and the last inequality in the treaties signed in 1858, which restricted the Japanese tariff rate to a maximum of 5 per cent, was removed. But this did not satisfy the Japanese military, for they now wanted to establish supremacy over all of East Asia, and in 1910, Korea fell prey to their expansionist policy.

Behind the Meiji miracle was solid economic development. As in the 1870s, the government continued to play an active role in building the infrastructure of the country. From 1885 to 1911, the government-operated railways increased from 212 to 4,775 miles; the number of post offices from about 5,000 to 7,000, and the amount of mail handled per year from about 100 million to 1,500 million items; the number of telegraph offices from about 50 to 4,500, and the number of telegrams handled per year from about 3 million to 25 million. In addition, the telephone service began to grow after 1892, and by 1911, about 180,000 households and offices had telephones. With government encouragement, private capital was also invested in the building of infrastructure. In 1911, there were about 1,400 miles of private railway lines and about 1,800 privately owned steamships with a total tonnage of 1.4 million tons. Also, the supply of electricity began to increase in the early 1900s, and by 1911, had reached a capacity of 322,000 kWh.

The most remarkable aspect of economic development in this period was the rise of the cotton textile industry. In the mid-1880s, yarn spun by machine comprised only a small part of domestic production. Soon after, however, large-scale spinning mills were established, and hand-spinning gradually disappeared. The next task was to eliminate imports, but this was to take another decade. In 1891, Japan began exporting yarn to China, and then in 1897, for the first time, exports exceeded imports. By the end of this period, spinning was firmly established as an export industry. In addition, the establishment of a Japanese spinning mill in Shanghai in 1911 foreshadowed the growing importance of Japanese textile investment abroad.

Import substitution of cotton fabric was delayed until 1909. Because the superiority of imported power looms over hand-operated looms was not very obvious in early years, production with hand-operated looms remained important until relatively late in Japan. But eventually, it became inevitable that a shift to power looms was necessary if the fabric industry was to survive. The first machine production was undertaken by spinners who were also engaged in weaving. By the 1890s, some had even begun to export to China. The rapid increase of machine production did not occur until about 1905 when higher wages, as a result of past growth, and the increased availability of electric power made the use of power looms attractive for small-scale hand-weavers. After this date, both production and exports increased at a rapid pace, and imports declined dramatically.

One of the most significant characteristics of the textile industry was its resilience. With the commercial treaty signed at the end of the Tokugawa period, foreign merchants could bring in cheaper textiles from abroad by paying a maximum 5 per cent tariff. This greatly disrupted the traditional Japanese textile industry, although it did not succumb to the import challenge. By adopting new technology, the Japanese textile industry gradually recovered its share of the domestic market and finally succeeded in phasing out imports. This was done without the aid of trade protection. Furthermore, soon after import substitution was completed, the textile industry became a leading export industry.

Mechanization and technological progress also took place in other industries. Several modern sugar mills were set up in Taiwan after it became Japan's colony, and the government also took measures to increase sugar-cane production there. In 1898, Japan built a steel ship of about 6,000 tons which was the first Japanese ship to be underwritten by Lloyd's of London, known for the strictness of its insurance standards. Then in 1908, two steel ships of 13,000 tons each were built. By 1910, Japan had developed a capacity to build most of its naval ships and more than half of its civilian steamships.[13] Mechanized silk-reeling became increasingly common and, in the mid-1890s, factory production exceeded household production. In iron and steel, a large-scale steel mill (Yahata Steel Mill) began operation in 1901, and pig iron production, which had been about 20,000 tons per year before the opening of the mill, increased to about 200,000 tons a few years later. By 1910, domestic production accounted for about half of pig iron consumption and about a third of steel consumption.

The increased use of machines in industrial production in this period is reflected in the following figures. The number of factories utilizing steam or electric power leapt from 53 to 7,745. The increase was partly due to the appearance of private power companies. The imports of industrial machinery from the West increased. In the previous period, the annual import value of industrial machinery had been about 300,000 yen, but in this period, it increased to 12 million yen. Furthermore, the paid-up capital in industrial companies reached 500 million yen by the end of the period—50 times the amount at the beginning of the period. It would be reasonable to assume that a large part of this increase was used to finance the purchase of machinery.

In agriculture, changes took place within a traditional setting, and were not as revolutionary as in manufacturing. None the less, development was quite impressive, as can be seen from the index of agricultural production, which rose at an annual rate of about 2 per cent in this period. This increase was, of course, slower than in industry, but it was a significant break from the stagnation of the Tokugawa period.[14] The production of rice (the major agricultural crop) increased by about 30 per cent over the period. Among the most important factors of this increase was the introduction of new strains of rice which were responsive to the application of fertilizer and resistant to cold. The new varieties more resistant to cold spread rice production to northern Japan where winter comes early, or increased productivity in the areas where rice had been cultivated but frequently destroyed by an early winter. In addition, many agricultural households went into silk production, and total production rose about six times. Towards the end of this period, silk was second in importance to rice.

Since agriculture was still the most important sector of the economy, its growth affected overall economic performance. Furthermore, with economic development, more and more people moved from the agricultural to the non-agricultural sector. Consequently, an increasingly large percentage of the population was forced to purchase food. If this demand had not been met by domestic production, food imports would have caused a drain on foreign exchange and constrained industrialization. Agricultural production increased rapidly enough in this period, however, to meet food requirements. Moreover, the land tax revenue made an important contribution to the government budget, and enabled the allocation of funds for the promotion of industry. Increased production of tea and, especially, raw silk made it possible to earn the foreign exchange necessary to buy machinery and industrial raw materials from abroad. In short, agriculture played an important supportive role in Japanese industrialization; without agricultural development, the rapid pace of industrialization in this period would have been impossible.[15]

## The Rise of Heavy Industry, 1912–1936

Agriculture continued to play a supportive role in industrialization between 1912 and 1936 although its significance was greatly reduced for a number of reasons. First, the industrial sector became less dependent on agriculture for the supply of food simply because the colonies acquired in the previous period—Taiwan and Korea—became Japan's food suppliers. In 1925, imports from these colonies amounted to 18 per cent of rice, 67 per cent of wheat, 126 per cent of soy bean, and 44 per cent of adzuki bean production in Japan.[16] Secondly, agriculture declined in importance as an earner of foreign exchange. Exports of raw silk increased until the end of the 1920s, and continued to be the major foreign exchange earner, but cotton fabric emerged to overtake it. Raw silk finally lost its position as the leading foreign exchange earner in the early 1930s when the demand for raw silk declined as a result of the economic depression in the United States and the invention of nylon, which could be used as a substitute for silk in the production of stockings and other products. Thirdly, the financial contribution from agriculture to industry decreased; despite the increased tax burden per agricultural household, agricultural income formed an increasingly smaller percentage of national income. By the late 1920s, it was exceeded by industrial income, and in 1936 it comprised less than 20 per cent of the national income.[17]

In exports, the rise of light industrial goods was impressive. First, there was a rapid increase in cotton fabric production. During this period—the most glorious age in the history of the cotton textile industry in Japan—Japan dethroned Manchester from its position as the world centre of textile production. Silk fabric also became an important export commodity as part of the raw silk produced began to be woven and exported in the form of fabric. In the 1930s, the exports of garments and rayon fabric expanded rapidly—more than compensating for the decline in silk exports. By the mid-1930s, the products of light industry began to dominate Japanese exports. Supported by the increase in export demand, yarn production increased 3.2 times, cotton fabric 6.2 times, silk fabric 8.6 times, and light industry as a whole 3.6 times.

From the above, it might be inferred that light industry became the dominant sector of manufacturing industry but, on the contrary, there was a significant decline in its importance relative to heavy industry. At the beginning of this period, light industry employed 85 per cent of factory workers, but by 1936, the percentage had declined to 60. In terms of production, the percentage declined from 80 to 50. Thus, despite a remarkable performance in exports and a large absolute increase in production, light industry was ceding its predominant position to heavy industry.

The beginnings of heavy industry can be traced to the end of the Tokugawa period, when the shogunate and provincial governments introduced Western technology to produce modern weapons. From that time, industrialization was promoted, at least in part, for development of the armaments industry.[18] In the early phase of industrialization, the government directly operated factories in such areas as iron and steel, weapons, shipbuilding, and precision machinery; but, from the mid-1880s onwards, through subsidies and protection from foreign competition—the latter was possible only after Japan regained tariff autonomy in 1911—the government encouraged the private sector to enter heavy industry. The only major exception to the government's hands off policy was the establishment of the Yahata Steel Mill in the 1890s. In other words, heavy industry did not suddenly appear in the period 1912–36, but in earlier periods it had been much less noticeable, and its foundation was still fragile. In this period, overall economic progress and the accelerated military build-up in the 1930s led to rapid expansion of the heavy industry sector. As a result, by the end of the period, a fairly well-developed industrial complex had emerged in Japan.

In the development of heavy industry, it is important to note the impact of the First World War. Japan was a participant in the war on the side of the Allies but, since there was no prospect of serious fighting in Asia, there was also no strong need to expand the production of weapons and their related products. The impact of the war on heavy industry was, rather, indirect. The war brought unprecedented prosperity to Japan which became the supplier of manufactured goods for Asian countries which had formerly depended on the West. This was generally conducive to investment in heavy industry. In addition, the halt of imports of machinery, parts, and intermediate goods from the West brought about a sharp increase in their prices and created a favourable economic environment for their production in Japan.

The war boom did not, however, last long. The war ended in late 1918 and within a few years the Western countries returned to re-capture former markets in Japan. This time, though, they had to face high tariff barriers erected by the Japanese government to protect the import substitution industry, primarily heavy industry, created during the war. It was, in fact, the first time that Japan used the tariff autonomy it had regained in 1911 to give protection to its domestic industry.

One characteristic of this period was that the economy was subject to serious cyclical disturbances. The years 1914–19 were the most prosperous the Japanese economy had so far experienced. The First World War reduced the economic capacity of the West and brought about an overall shortage of goods, allowing Japan to take advantage of the situation. During the period 1914–18, a surplus of 1,475 million yen was recorded in the trade account and, from

1915 to 1920, a surplus of 2,207 million yen was recorded in the invisible account. Because of such a huge surplus, the supply of money increased sharply and, consequently, prices increased 2.7 times from 1915 to 1920. In this inflationary setting, with cost increase lagging behind price increase, healthy profits were generally achieved, and companies recording profit rates of over 100 per cent were not exceptional. Stimulated by such increased profitability, a large number of new companies were formed, and most existing companies expanded their production capacity. As a result, the amount of industrial capital increased from 644 million yen to 2,829 million yen between 1913 and 1920.

The boom continued for about 18 months after the war but, in the spring of 1920, the first reaction set in. The 1920s became a gloomy decade for the Japanese economy, in contrast to a prosperous decade for the American economy. The Japanese economy suffered, not in the sense that indicators of the real sector of the economy declined in the decade, but in the sense that many companies went bankrupt and large numbers of people became indebted or unemployed. In 1923, a severe earthquake hit the Tokyo area and further set back the economy which had begun to show signs of recovery. In 1927, there was a financial crisis which shook public confidence in banks. Then, in 1929, the crash of the American stock market led to the depression of the 1930s in the West. The resultant shrinkage of the American market adversely affected Japan's exports of raw silk and silk fabric. The economic gloom continued until 1932 when the Japanese government took expansionary measures and prices, which had been declining since 1920, began to rebound.

The progress of heavy industry and the recession of the 1920s intensified economic concentration, most notably in the area of finance. The number of banks, which had been increasing up to 1901, declined after that point, partly reflecting the government policy of encouraging mergers. Until the end of the First World War, however, the rate of decline was slow; it was in the 1920s that there was a significant increase in concentration. In this decade, because of numerous company bankruptcies, banks accumulated large bad debts, and some became financially insolvent. The difficulties the banks were facing culminated in the financial crisis of 1927 when approximately 30 banks, including a few large ones, closed their doors, and the government declared a moratorium on debts. The closure of badly managed banks continued in the following years and, by the end of the period, a small number of better managed large banks, such as Mitsui, Mitsubishi, Sumitomo, and Yasuda, had established their dominance.[19]

In heavy industry, output concentration in a few big companies is to be expected, since the relatively high level of technology and the large amount of capital necessary for entry acts as barriers. Shipbuilding, iron and steel, and general machinery, which had shown some progress in earlier periods, were oligopolies dominated by a few giant companies. At that time, however, output concentration did not attract much attention, since light industry was relatively more important and its structure less oligopolistic, with a large number of small companies competing in the same industry. The spinning industry was the exception since large companies occupied an important position in the market. But even in this case, barriers to entry were not as high as in a typical heavy industry, as reflected in the existence of a large number of small spinning companies. As heavy industry progressed, the competitive structure of light industry receded into the background, and the oligopolistic structure of heavy industry established itself as the typical structure of industry as a whole.

The intensification of output concentration is an important development in this period, but it is not a characteristic unique to the Japanese economy; it may be observed in any capitalistic country. What became alarming in Japan, however, was that several zaibatsu—family-controlled conglomerates—began to exert a large influence on the economy in the latter part of the period. Among them, Mitsubishi, Mitsui, and Sumitomo were the most diversified and powerful. Through holding companies, they controlled enterprises in finance, mining, industry, and other modern sectors of the economy. These zaibatsu did not appear suddenly; some even predated the Meiji era and, before the First World War, operated banks, mining companies, and other enterprises. Yet, it was not until after the war that they became particularly noticeable. In the 1920s, they aggressively moved into heavy industry, took over businesses which were suffering from heavy losses, and used holding companies to extend control over a large number of firms through partial ownership. The government, far from taking measures to reduce the economic power of the zaibatsu, aided their growth by means of subsidies, protective tariffs, and the approval of cartel formation. In the 1930s, when the government desired further expansion in heavy industry for military purposes, the relationship between the government and the zaibatsu became particularly close, and the latter evolved into powerful politico-economic organizations.

## War and Occupation, 1937–1951

This period covers what may be termed the 'abnormal' years of modern Japanese economic history. The first phase of the period comprised the war years, beginning with the outbreak of war against China in June 1937, which continued for eight years, until the end of the Pacific War. The second phase, the Allied occupation, began with Japan's surrender on 15 August 1945 and lasted until April 1952, when sovereignty was restored. The last year of this period, 1951, is the last full year of the occupation.

The year 1937 marked an important turning-point in Japanese economic development. First, the financial orthodoxy which had been established by Matsukata in the mid-1880s, and which had been instrumental in maintaining price stability in the following years, was abandoned. Although government expenditure had been increasing since 1931, the increment was still moderate prior to 1936 because people like Takahashi Korekiyo, a financial conservative, objected to sharp increases in military expenditure through the issue of government bonds to cover the resultant deficits in the government budget.[20] By 1937, however, most influential conservatives had been assassinated or forced to modify their views under the pressure of the military, and government expenditure had begun increasing rapidly. From 1936 to 1937, government spending more than doubled, and in the following three years, it doubled again.

The second major event of 1937 was the passage of laws empowering the government to impose direct controls on the economy. Soon after war broke out, three important decisions were made. The Armament Mobilization Law, which had been passed during the First World War, was extended to the present war (the China Incident which started in 1937), and the government was authorized to set up armament production. The Law Relating to Temporary Measures for Export and Import Control was enacted to give the government the power to control exports and imports, and the Temporary Adjustments Law was passed to funnel capital and credit to war-related industries and to stop the flow to non-essential industries.

Not satisfied with these measures alone, the military exerted pressure on the government to enact the National Mobilization

Law in April 1938. This gave the government power to control prices and wages and to institute distribution control. Thus, in less than one year after the China Incident broke out, all the legal measures necessary to move the economy on to a war footing were completed.

One might argue that to take 1937 as a turning-point is too arbitrary since the government had begun to enact control measures in the early 1930s with the Major Industries Control Law in 1931 and the Foreign Exchange Control Law in 1933. These laws increased the scope of government intervention, but they were not designed to prime an economy for mobilization. The Foreign Exchange Control Law gave the government the power to restrict the allocation of foreign exchange in order to deal with the deteriorating balance of payments. Initially, it was used mainly to control non-essential imports, and it was not until early 1937 that all imports became subject to approval by the government. The main intention of the Major Industries Control Law was to encourage the formation of cartels and to create 'order' in the major industries, rather than to let the government control production directly. The passage of this law permitted a number of important mergers—Oji Paper, Japan Steel Manufacturing, and others were born at this time—and *zaibatsu* increased their economic power. This law changed the competitive structure of industry and made major industries more oligopolistic. Certainly, it was a step towards government control of industrial production and distribution, although it was still a preliminary emergency measure.

Because of the havoc caused to the economy by the Pacific War, it is tempting to think that income declined during the war. However, it was not until the last year of the war that real GNP declined and, in fact, there was a 25 per cent increase over the period 1940–4. This does not mean, however, that general economic welfare improved over those years, for the main component of the increase was military expenditure, which increased by about 430 per cent over this period. Consumption, on the other hand, decreased by 30 per cent. Furthermore, the increase in real GNP was maintained by scrapping non-military hardware and mobilizing people who did not work under normal circumstances. It seems, therefore, that in terms of all possible indices, there was a substantial decline in individual welfare over the period.

Changes in the industrial structure during the war are worthy of note. Production in light industry, which consisted primarily of non-essential goods, declined absolutely as well as relatively. The two laws passed to restrict production of non-essential goods after the war broke out in 1937 were, for the most part, responsible for initiating this decline. For example, cotton textile production, which had recorded remarkable growth by the end of the previous period, declined sharply after September 1937 when the Law Relating to Temporary Measures for Export and Import Control restricted the importation of raw cotton to production of textiles for export. Cotton textile production declined still further after the outbreak of the Pacific War as it cut off Japan from most of its major sources of cotton supply. In 1944, the level of textile production stood at about 90 per cent below the peak of mid-1937. On the other hand, production of heavy industry rose prior to mid-1944 because of the government policy of concentrating available resources on steel, non-ferrous metals, and machinery essential to the war effort. As a result, the share of heavy industry in total industrial production continued to rise from 50 per cent in 1936 to more than 70 per cent in 1942.

Another important development occurred as government control of the economy tightened. In order to establish more effective economic control and obtain greater efficiency in the utilization of scarce resources, the government preferred to deal with only a small number of large companies in each industry and pressed for mergers by resorting to mobilization measures. This policy further increased the economic power of the *zaibatsu*. They were in a favourable position to take advantage of it, not only because their companies could, as leading companies in their respective fields, initiate mergers, but also because they could use the political power they had acquired to influence the government committees or industry associations which administered the mergers. By the end of the war, in terms of paid-up capital, the share of the 4 largest *zaibatsu* had increased to 50 per cent in finance, 32 per cent in heavy industry, and 11 per cent in light industry; the share of the 10 largest in the three areas amounted to 53, 49, and 17 per cent.[21]

Although industrial production increased from 1943 to 1944, the procurement of raw materials for production of steel and non-ferrous metals became increasingly difficult. As a result, production of basic materials declined slightly over the same period despite various efforts to bolster it. The overall increase from 1943 to mid-1944 was made possible by utilizing available stocks and increasing the production of machinery and other final goods.

By mid-1944, Japan had lost its naval supremacy and had been cut off from its overseas territories, a major source of raw materials. As a result, the production of basic materials began to decline sharply, affecting, in turn, the production of final goods. By the beginning of 1945, acute shortages of oil, bauxite, iron ores, and other essential raw materials had developed. The intensified bombing in the last several months of the war delivered the final blow to the already tottering economy.[22]

At the time of Japan's surrender, the economy was in a complete shambles. In August 1945, industrial production was reduced to a fraction of what it had been a year earlier; it amounted to only about 10 per cent of the 1934–6 level. Food production, which had been maintained at a relatively high level despite the shortage of manpower and fertilizer, declined by about 30 per cent in 1945. As a consequence, a food crisis developed towards the end of the year which continued into the first half of 1946. The shortage of goods was made more acute by the breakdown of the government machinery for collecting and distributing goods at fixed prices. Naturally, the surrender caused a loss of confidence in government, and brought about a state of near anarchy.

Economic recovery had to be undertaken under difficult conditions. Bombing by the Allies had destroyed about 25 per cent of the national wealth.[23] Among other things, it had caused an acute shortage of housing in the major cities. The loss of the colonies, Taiwan and Korea, meant not only that their natural resources could no longer be obtained at concessionary rates, but also that several million Japanese had to return to look for jobs and houses in the already crowded home market. Japanese overseas assets, which had provided income as well as bases for overseas operations in the pre-war period, were confiscated. The demands of the occupation forces for such services as housing and transportation also had to be met. Furthermore, changes in the political environment in the Asian countries which had been important markets for Japanese exports before the war dramatically reduced their importance as the export markets essential for economic recovery.

The chaos of the post-war economy is reflected in the hyperinflation which occurred from mid-1945 to early 1949. For a few months before the surrender, the tempo of price increase quickened and became somewhat alarming, but it was nothing compared with what took place thereafter. The consumer price index—with 1945 as the base—rose to 515 in 1946, 1,655 in 1947, 4,857 in 1948, and

7,889 in 1949—a total increase of approximately 8,000 per cent. Fortunately, despite this hyper-inflationary setting, production increased. In 1948, industrial production improved to 50 per cent of the 1934–6 level, while food production made a full recovery.

In 1949, the government undertook a new stabilization policy. Top priority was given to curbing inflation through expenditure cuts and tax increases in the government budget. This anti-inflationary measure was reinforced by the adoption, in April 1949, of the single exchange rate of 360 yen per dollar. It then became necessary for the government to monitor the movement of prices and to adjust monetary policy accordingly in order to maintain the fixed exchange rate. As these measures became effective in securing economic stability, the government removed various measures of direct control. By mid-1950, the market economy had been basically restored.

Although the stabilization measures adversely affected companies which were poorly managed or overextended, on the whole they had a favourable effect on the economy. Economic recovery progressed smoothly in 1949 and in the first half of 1950. After June 1950, when the Korean War[24] broke out, Japan became a supply base as well as a place of 'rest and recreation' for American soldiers. The demand for Japanese goods and services rose sharply as a consequence, and the economy experienced the first post-war boom. It gave a final push to economic recovery, and allowed many companies to reap large profits. Much of this profit was retained in companies and used later for plant renewal and expansion, and for the introduction of technology from abroad.

Economic recovery was greatly influenced by occupation policy. At first, the Allies followed a policy of non-responsibility, as indicated in a directive of November 1945 to the Supreme Commander for the Allied Powers (SCAP): 'You will make it clear to the Japanese people that you assume no obligation to maintain any particular standard of living in Japan.'[25] In 1946, food aid began as a means of forestalling a famine which threatened the country. By this time, the SCAP had assumed responsibility for preventing disease and unrest and, by the end of the year, had decided to allow the economy to return to the pre-war level. In line with this policy, aid in the form of oil, iron ore, coal, and other raw materials necessary for Japanese industry began. By the end of 1948, the SCAP was strongly encouraging the Japanese government to take measures to stabilize the economy and to promote development beyond the pre-war level. Thus, within three and a half years, there had been a dramatic change in occupation policy: a shift from an attitude of non-responsibility to the promotion of economic development.

The main reason behind this change was that the United States, which controlled the SCAP, was compelled to modify its policy as the Cold War with the Soviet Union intensified. The United States now wanted to use Japan as an American ally to maintain the security of Asia and, at the same time, promote it as a non-Communist model of development. As the civil war in China progressed in favour of the Communists (their final victory occurred in 1949), the United States realized the danger of Japan becoming another Communist state. If both Japan and China became Communist states, it could threaten the whole East, destabilizing South-East Asia as well. For Japan to develop economically was also useful ideologically, because such development could become a counter-model to Communism.

In line with this new policy, the United States not only pursued a more favourable economic policy towards Japan, but also initiated a move to end the occupation. Initially, the United States faced objections from its allies, but finally succeeded in persuading them to come to the conference table. Under the auspices of the United States, the San Francisco Peace Conference was held in September 1951, and in April of the following year, the occupation of Japan formally ended. The fact that the United States dominated occupation policy and restored Japan's sovereignty greatly influenced the nature of the framework of the Japanese economy in the post-war period.

## Post-war Economic Expansion, 1952–1973

No overall increase in GNP or per capita income occurred during the previous period, because the war interrupted the growth trend. There were, however, large differences in growth potential between 1937 and 1951. One such difference lay in the social and political environment. Soon after Japan's unconditional surrender in August 1945, the Allied occupation forces disarmed the country and reorganized the government along democratic lines. To support the new political goals, land reform, labour reform, education reform, and the dissolution of the *zaibatsu* were carried out. Consequently, post-war society became more egalitarian and competitive, and the heavy burden of military expenditure was greatly lightened.

It is essential also to note that industry was better prepared to generate economic growth. During the war years, investment and technical progress took place in many war-related sectors of heavy industry so that, by the end of the war, Japan had reached a high level of technological sophistication. The cessation of military requirements and the pent up demand for consumer goods caused a decline in the importance of heavy industry in the immediate post-war period, but the experiences and experiments of the war years provided a basis not only for developing new products with greater growth potential, but also for absorbing new Western technology. As a result, heavy industry became the driving force of Japan's post-war economic growth.

Changes in the international environment also raised the growth potential of the post-war economy. Because Japan had now become an ally of the United States, economic co-operation between the West and Japan increased. Barriers to the transfer of technology to Japan which had been erected in the 1930s were now removed, and new Western technology became more readily available. This was particularly important because Japan could now take advantage of the backlog of science-based technology which had developed during the 1930s and 1940s. The first major application of basic science had been in the field of chemistry, resulting in the production of synthetics and antibiotics. The post-war period witnessed the industrial applications of physics, stimulated partly by the US government's spending on missile technology and the space programme. Advances in electronics were also made at this time and, since these new discoveries were available to Japanese industry, they made an important contribution to its technical progress.

Closer economic contacts among nations were also made possible by the Bretton Woods system which was established in the early post-war years. One pillar of the system was the General Agreement on Tariffs and Trade (GATT) which promoted free trade among the nations of the world. Although GATT has not yet achieved the goal of free trade, it has been effective in reducing tariff and non-tariff barriers and in making the most favoured nation treatment—in which GATT does not allow discrimination of one member country against another in the application of tariff rates, a discrimination often practised in the pre-war period—a general practice. The International Monetary Fund (IMF), the second pillar of the new system, also contributed to international trade by championing the fixed exchange rate system and freer international transactions, pressing its member countries to remove foreign exchange restrictions on trade. Although the fixed exchange rate system, having been found unworkable, was abandoned in the early 1970s, the IMF has promoted trade liberalization in developing countries by using its loans as a weapon.

For a country like Japan, which depends greatly on international trade for development, this new economic system was particularly valuable. It not only enabled Japan to increase the volume of trade, but also contributed to increased efficiency by forcing Japanese companies to compete in the international market, thus enlarging the size of the market for those who succeeded. Over time, too, the Japanese market became more open, and competition from imports became a problem for certain industries. This problem began in the mid-1960s when foreign exchange control was removed on imports. The impact was felt more as wages increased and further import liberalization measures were taken in the 1970s. Freer international trade strengthened internationally competitive industries and weakened uncompetitive ones, thus contributing to the improved efficiency of the overall economy.

By the end of the occupation, agricultural production, industrial production, national income, per capita GNP, per capita consumption, labour productivity, real wages, and most other indicators of economic development had returned to the 1934–6 level, but there was one exception: trade did not return to the pre-war level until several years later.[26] Exports, for example, stood at less than 40 per cent of the pre-war level in 1952, and did not recover fully until 1960. This was due to various difficulties which faced exports in the post-war environment. Political changes in Korea, Taiwan, and China—which together had accounted for 40 per cent of Japan's exports in the pre-war period—eroded their importance as a Japanese market. Cotton textiles, the major export in the pre-war period, were subject to an import substitution policy in Korea, Taiwan, and South-East Asian countries which had been its major markets in the pre-war period. The export demand for silk, another important export in the pre-war period, virtually dried up after the appearance of a substitute, nylon. The fact that Japan had not yet concluded all the necessary commercial treaties, because the issue of war reparations for the damage caused by Japanese military aggression had not been settled, handicapped exports throughout the early 1950s.[27]

Sustained increase in exports required that heavy industrial goods become major exports since their terms of trade were more favourable and their demand elasticity was higher than other goods. To this end, heavy industry had to be strengthened. Subsidies for plant expansion and renewal were given to encourage the introduction of more up-to-date machinery and technology. To protect the companies which were producing heavy industrial goods, the government restricted import of those goods through foreign exchange control. The construction of large industrial estates along the coast allowed better co-ordination of production and a reduction in transport costs. Furthermore, the policy of protecting and promoting the domestic coal industry was discarded and oil was substituted for coal or, where this was technically unfeasible, better and cheaper coal was imported.[28]

By 1960, the government's industrialization policy began to show returns. Heavy industry had become internationally competitive in such areas as steel, ships, and radios, and was becoming the propelling force of Japanese exports.[29] By the mid-1960s, motor cars, synthetic fibres, and new electronic products such as tape-recorders and television sets had joined the list of major exports, driving total exports to an even higher level. The volume of exports returned in 1960 to the pre-war level, and increased about seven times in the following 13-year period. In this process of rapid export expansion, textile products, which had been so critical in the pre-war period, declined in importance, whereas heavy industrial goods, previously unimportant or non-existent, came to dominate.

The export increase made an important contribution to industrial production. Over this period, industrial production increased by about 2.7 times, recording an annual growth rate of some 13 per cent. By virtue of this rapid increase, in 1972 Japan became the world's largest producer of synthetic fibres, rubber products, pig iron, and passenger cars, and the third largest producer of pulp, nitrogen fertilizer, cement, steel, copper, and aluminum. Industrial production not only increased in volume but also diversified to include synthetic rubber, synthetic fibres, petrochemicals, new electronic goods such as colour television sets, and other newly developed products. By the early 1970s, in terms of both volume and diversity, Japanese industry had become one of the most advanced in the world.

Spurred on by this industrial expansion, GNP recorded a large increase. From 1952 to 1958, GNP expanded at a rate of 6.9 per cent. In 1959, economic growth accelerated, and thus began an annual growth rate of 10 per cent which was to characterize the 1960s—a rate so high at that time that people called it an economic miracle. In the years 1970–3, the growth rate declined slightly, to 7.8 per cent, but even this was high by international standards.

As the Japanese economy grew, it attracted increasing world attention. In 1950, Japanese GNP was about $24 billion, less than that of any major Western country and only a few per cent of American GNP. In the following years, however, Japan's GNP surpassed that of all Western countries except the United States: by 1960, it had exceeded that of Canada; by the middle of the decade, those of Britain and France; and by 1968, that of West Germany. In 1973, Japanese GNP was about $360 billion. While still less than American GNP, the difference had narrowed to three to one—a considerable gain over 1950. Per capita income did not grow as spectacularly during this period as GNP, but nevertheless increased substantially. In terms of exports and also economic aid, Japan's international standing rose significantly during this period.

## Overcoming the Oil Shocks, 1974–1984

The period of rapid growth was brought to a sudden end by the oil crisis which began in October 1973. The first phase of the crisis resulted from an oil embargo imposed by the Organization of Petroleum Exporting Countries (OPEC) on the industrial countries in an effort to exert pressure on them to take a pro-Arab stand on the fourth Middle Eastern War which had commenced a short time earlier. Because the embargo was brief, its effect was temporary, but the decision by OPEC to triple oil prices had a more lasting impact. Since Japan imported almost all of its oil and about 90 per cent of its energy requirements at that time, the price increase was a severe blow to the economy. For the first time since the Pacific War, GNP showed a negative growth rate (–1.3 per cent) in 1974.

In the next year, the economy did a little better, recording a small positive growth rate (2.4 per cent). Although this growth was much slower than in the period preceding the oil crisis, it still exceeded the performance of the Western countries who mostly recorded negative growth at this time; only France recorded slight positive growth. Then, in 1976, Japan's economic growth rose to over 5 per cent, stabilizing at this level for the next two years. The Economic Planning Agency stated in an economic white paper for the fiscal year 1978 that 'the Japanese economy completed the post-oil crisis adjustment process ... for the first time in five years. Now it seems to be entering a new growth period.'[30]

This prediction turned out to be premature. Oil prices began going up again slowly in late 1978; they accelerated in 1979, resulting in a second oil crisis. Although the rate of increase slowed down in 1980, it continued into the next year. This second oil crisis did not adversely affect the growth of GNP immediately, but the increase, which at the highest point almost tripled oil prices, was too large for the economy to withstand. The Japanese economy was, however, better prepared this time as it had been reducing its dependence on oil. There was therefore no decline in GNP, but its growth came down to 4.0 per cent in 1981 and 3.3 per cent in 1982–3. Then, in 1984, it returned to 5 per cent. In the period 1973–84, the Japanese growth rate averaged 4 per cent.

Although the Japanese economy was adversely affected by the worsened terms of trade and the recession of its major overseas markets in the period 1973–84, it performed comparatively better than the industrial economies of the West. Over the same period, the United States recorded an annual growth rate of 2.1 per cent, West Germany 1.6 per cent, France 2.4 per cent, and Britain 1.0 per cent.[31]

In 1983, Japanese GNP amounted to about $1.2 trillion. This formed the second largest GNP after that of the United States, which was $3.3 trillion, and was almost double that of the third largest country, West Germany, which was $0.6 trillion. Japan's per capita performance was less impressive, but in 1983, Japan appeared for the first time in the list of the top 10 countries. The United States and several West European countries—Switzerland, Denmark, Sweden, and West Germany—had higher incomes, but Japan had overtaken France, the Netherlands, and Britain. Japan's advance was due to its better economic performance in the preceding decade *vis-à-vis* the West European countries.

Why was Japan's performance better? One important reason was its ability to change its industrial structure, notwithstanding many difficulties. The increase in oil prices raised the cost of energy, and caused serious problems in the industrial materials sector which is high in energy consumption, particularly in industries such as steel. Japan was successful in saving energy, and in improving methods of resource extraction. In steel, for example, oil consumption per unit of production in Japan halved in the years 1973–80, and the ratio of final steel products to steel ingots improved following the adoption of the continuous casting method.[32] Despite these improvements, however, the industrial materials industry lost its position as Japan's leading industrial sector. The decline of this industry was a major cause of the negative growth of GNP in 1974 and the slow recovery of industrial production, which did not return to the 1973 level until 1977. Steel showed some signs of recovery around 1980, but it went into recession again, and in 1983, its production stood below the 1973 level.

Machinery and equipment replaced industrial materials as Japan's leading industrial sector in the mid-1970s. In particular, the growth of electrical machinery, which includes electronic products, was spectacular. Its production increased by almost 2.5 times in the period 1973–83. In the early 1980s, integrated circuits (ICs), videotape recorders (VTRs), and computers became the growth points of the industry. While production of general and transport machinery increased faster than that of industrial materials, it recorded a less spectacular increase. The result was, however, a shift in the industrial structure towards high-value-added, low-energy-using industries. This shift was was much more pronounced in Japan than in the United States or West Germany.[33]

The shift is reflected in the change in the composition of Japanese exports. In 1970, steel accounted for about 15 per cent of total exports but its share declined to less than 9 per cent in 1983. Conversely, machinery and equipment rose from 45 to 68 per cent in the same period. Particularly noticeable was the percentage increase in car exports—from 7 to 18 per cent. Cars thus became Japan's major export item. In the early 1970s, it seemed likely that the colour television would overtake the motor car but this did not materialize. It was overtaken instead by the VTR in the late 1970s and the IC in the early 1980s. In fact, the VTR almost caught up with steel in 1983.

In order to pursue a strategy of changing the industrial structure in favour of high-value-added, low-energy- and -raw materials-using industries, Japan had to develop so-called high technology industries. Substantial progress was made first in micro-electronics, as reflected in the rise of the semiconductor, the computer, and the VTR. In its application field, mechatronics (industrial robots) became a new growth point. Robots were introduced into the assembling of components and parts, painting, welding, loading and unloading, cutting and grinding materials, and for many other purposes. Today, Japan leads the world in their production and application. In the early 1990s, there were around 200,000 robots working in Japan, compared with about 37,000 in the United

States.[34] Some progress was also made in optoelectronics, new materials, and biotechnology, though at a comparatively slow pace.

## Recent Economic Changes, 1985–1992

With the decline of oil prices after 1982, the Japanese economy recorded a growth rate of a little over 5 per cent. It was as if it had returned to a steady growth trajectory. But another crisis emerged, this time in the form of a sharp yen revaluation. Japan had handled the second oil crisis better than most other Western countries by changing its industrial structure (expanding high-value-added industries and reducing the importance of energy- or raw materials-using industries). Some high-value-added goods became new exports or rose in importance as exports. But, because the prices of oil and other primary imports declined, and despite the recovery of the economy, Japanese imports hardly increased. This gap between exports and imports put strong pressure on the yen to revalue. The exchange rate of the yen, which was about 250 per dollar in mid-1985, began to appreciate after the Plaza Accord of September 1985, and became 165 per dollar a year later and 123 towards the end of 1987.

The rise of the yen was too great for the Japanese economy to absorb smoothly. The growth rate of 1986 thus declined to 2.6 per cent. In the following years, however, the exchange rate of the yen stabilized at the new level or slightly depreciated, and the Japanese economy did rather well. In the years 1987–91, the growth rate ranged between 4 and 6 per cent, which was substantially higher than the 3 per cent recorded by the industrial countries as a whole.

Behind Japan's relatively good economic performance was a massive effort on the part of Japanese companies to overcome the yen revaluation. Production of many goods could no longer be continued in Japan but had to be relocated to South-East Asia and other Asian countries where labour costs were lower. As a result, Japan's overseas investment rose sharply from 1986, reaching a peak in 1989. The amount of overseas investment rose from $12.2 billion to $67.5 billion between 1985 and 1989; in 1990, it declined, but was still high at $56.9 billion. Not all of this went to South-East Asia and other Asian countries.[35] The items which began to be produced with Japanese investment comprised not only light industrial products. Producers of electronic and electrical goods were particularly active investors in this period, relocating production of low-value-added goods abroad. The goods produced there were sent primarily to third countries, but some were brought back to Japan (for example, microwave ovens, household air-conditioners, radio cassette recorders, and small-size colour television sets). If goods produced by foreign producers are added to the imports from Japanese factories abroad, the imports of manufactured goods, as a percentage of total imports, rose sharply, reaching 50 per cent in the late 1980s—a significant increase from the 30 per cent in the mid-1980s. The major reason for this increase was, of course, the yen revaluation.

By transferring the production of low-value-added goods to low-wage countries, many Japanese companies concentrate locally on high-value-added goods (in the case of electronic industries, high-end, multifunctional models using larger numbers of components), a trend started since the first oil shock but accelerated in this period. Part of the exports went to Japanese trans-plants in Asia, for example, ICs and facsimile machines, but the bulk were ordinary exports. As in the previous period, motor cars were the leading export of this period, though the pace of increase slowed down. It was the export of VTRs, ICs, facsimile machines, video cameras, disc players, which started in the previous period, that rose sharply in this period. As a result, in the export composition there was a further shift towards machinery, which accounted for about 75 per cent of total exports in 1991.[36]

With a healthy growth rate and the sharp appreciation of the yen, Japanese per capita GNP rose to $25,430 in 1990, higher than that of the United States ($21,790) or of Germany ($22,320). Only Switzerland and Norway had a higher per capita GNP than Japan in that year.[37] This international comparison of incomes based on the exchange rate does not, however, give a true picture of income differences since the exchange rate, which is primarily determined by capital flows and current account balances, is not a good approximation to a purchasing power parity index. Since the figure based on the exchange rate overestimated real income (based on the purchasing power parity index) by about 50 per cent in 1988,[38] some adjustment has to be made to the 1990 figure.

Clearly, Japan has to reduce the prices of various goods and services for it to catch up with—and surpass—the living standards of the United States and a number of other industrial countries of the West. But it should be pointed out that Japan ranks number one in the United Nations' human development index, which takes into account life expectancy at birth, adult literacy, and the level of education, in addition to income.[39] Japan has also become the top creditor nation (its net overseas assets were nearly $300 billion), as well as the largest donor country of economic aid.

The Japanese economy went into recession in 1992. Though GNP grew at 1.5 per cent in that year, it was the second lowest growth rate since 1955.[40] GDP, which does not include income from abroad, fared even worse; in the last quarter of 1992, it declined at an annual rate of 0.3 per cent. Industrial output also fell by more than 8 per cent in the year, and many large manufacturing companies recorded huge losses (some for the first time in their corporate history). Even the automobile industry, which is widely regarded as the strongest industrial sector in Japan, experienced a 13.5 per cent decline in production in 1992.

In previous recessions, the Japanese economy had returned to a healthy growth path after a while. This time, however, the situation seems to be different. Even after the recession is over, the economy will probably not be able to repeat even the growth rate of the years 1987–91, which was by no means high compared with the East Asian NIEs (Newly Industrializing Economies); it is likely that growth rates will stabilize at 2–3 per cent per annum.

The troubles Japan are facing are twofold. The first is the fact that it has become a high-cost country. Although real income may be lower than the per capita income derived from the exchange rate, as argued above, the latter counts in international competitiveness. With one of the top per capita incomes in the world, the general cost of production is naturally high in Japan, which makes a large number of goods internationally uncompetitive. Japan can export high-value-added goods but they tend to be the goods which Western industrial countries want to produce themselves, and can not be freely exported from Japan because of voluntary quotas and other constraints. Motor cars and ICs are two well-known examples of this. As a result, it is now more difficult for Japan to rely on exports to move out of recession or raise the rate of economic growth.

Aggravating the current recession is the yen revaluation in early 1993. After having depreciated to a little over 140 per dollar in 1989, the yen appreciated somewhat in the following year, and this continued also in 1991. During the first few months of the following year, there was no further revaluation, but as imports of goods and services declined with the economic slow-down while exports remained at roughly the same level, the current account recorded the largest surpluses in history, surpassing the peak of 1987. Since there was no strong drive for overseas investment among the companies (those which had to invest overseas had done so, and many were facing financial problems due to recession), the surpluses put pressure on the exchange rate. Towards the end of February 1993, the yen appreciated to about 117 per dollar. With no immediate prospect for economic recovery, the yen revaluation is taking a toll on some of the most famous companies (such as Matsushita, Nissan, and Nippon Telegraph and Telephone Public Corporation. Many companies are implementing or planning re-structuring, including lay-offs and plant closings.

## Future Prospects

Japan is not alone in having problems; all its Western competitors have problems of their own, some of which are non-economic in nature but which will affect their economies slowly over time, such as moral crises, the rise of crime, and the decline in the standard of education. But since it is unlikely that the next tier of countries—the NIEs—will catch up in the immediate future, economic leadership in the world will remain with the present industrial countries in the forseeable future. The most dynamic economies among these will be the ones which are strong in high technology industries.

Today, Japan is investing considerable time and money in research and development (R&D), but it still lags far behind some Western countries in basic science. This is reflected in the deficits of Japan's technology trade. In the early 1990s, Japan's technology exports were somewhere between $2 billion and $3 billion, but imports were about $6 billion. Around the same time, the United States exported $16 billion worth of technology. The gap between exports and imports was particularly high in Japan for high-tech products.[41]

However, it is possible to develop high-technology industries by importing technology. For example, in the machinery industry—this seems to apply less to the chemical industry—to develop a new product (a product innovation) and to make it a commercial success are two different things. Thus, Japan can buy the patent for a new product and, by improving on its production process, can make it a commercial success. Japanese corporations excel in process innovations. This can be seen, for example, in the fact that Japan is far ahead in the introduction of a flexible manufacturing system, which automates the assembling of different models on the same line and thus enables production to respond quickly to market conditions.

The strength of small- and medium-size companies, which are tied to large assemblers under the *keiretsu* system, also gives flexibility and cost-effectiveness to the Japanese machinery industry. Because of these advantages, Japanese corporations have become world leaders of machinery products which were initially developed in Western countries. In the late 1980s, Japan produced 100 per cent of the video cameras, 95 per cent of the facsimile machines, 90 per cent of the copying machines, 80 per cent of VTRs, and 50 per cent of the ICs made throughout the world.

High-technology industries, of course, do not comprise the machinery and equipment industry alone. In biotechnology, new materials science industries, and other high-technology fields, will Japan repeat the success of the machinery industry? In these areas, the accumulation of gradual process innovations, which give an advantage to the machinery industry, is more difficult. How will Japan do in high-technology industries as a whole then?

Some people believe that in the twenty-first century, Japan will lead the world in high-technology industries. Certainly, the overall environment for Japanese business is good. The institutions of the family and the school have both done a relatively good job in disciplining and educating children. For example, over 90 per cent graduate from high schools, and Japanese students come near the top in any international assessment of achievement. The government has been rather effective in providing public goods to the market economy and preventing its excesses. It has avoided the kind of debt burden plaguing the United States; it has minimized litigations by keeping the number of lawyers low and by making litigations difficult (for example, there is no product liability law in Japan); and it has allowed inter-corporate ownership, including the representation of financial institutions on the board of directors, and made corporate take-overs by financial Vikings difficult.

Japan is also investing heavily in the future. The investment ratio— the ratio of gross domestic investment to GNP—is the highest among the industrial countries. The plant and equipment investment per employee is three times as high as that in the United States and twice as high as in Europe. Civilian R&D spending, as a fraction of GNP, is 50 per cent above that of the United States, slightly above that of Germany, and far above that of Europe as a whole.[42]

On the other hand, critics argue that Japan, being a homogeneous country of one race, one language, and one culture, will not be able to adjust to the future economic climate. Although this homogeneity has been an advantage so far, with the world shrinking with the advance of communications and transportation technology, internationalization will be the trend of the future. They argue that the leaders of high-technology industries will be the multinational corporations who will source scientists and engineers (as well as managers) globally and locate production in those countries which offer the best environment for success.

It is not clear which situation will prevail. In the past, Japanese Marxists were pessimistic about the prospect of Japanese development because they believed that existing traditional institutions had to be removed before modernization could take place. Blindly following the Western paradigm of development, they did not realize that some traditional institutions could be used to advantage for industrialization and economic development. For example, Japanese labour practices, which Japanese Marxists thought feudal, turned out to be very effective in raising productivity. Similarly, the vertical *keiretsu*, consisting of a large assembler and small suppliers, which the Marxists believed was exploitive, turned out to be a useful industrial structure. The most optimistic were Japanese nationalists who had fanatical faith in the future of the country. Even immediately following the defeat of Japan, some of them fervently believed that the country would revive like a phoenix and regain its greatness.

Among the foreign observers of Japan, there were conflicting views of the people. General Douglas MacArthur, who came to occupy Japan after the Pacific War, did not think highly of them. He was not, however, completely negative about the potential of the Japanese after having dealt with the Filipinos—of whom he had an even lower opinion—before and during the war. Possibly influenced by the racist propaganda of the American government during the war, he thought that the Japanese were like 12-year-old boys. On the other hand, another American who had a great impact on the course of Japanese history, Commodore Matthew C. Perry, who came to Japan in the mid-nineteenth century and forced open its doors, had a better appreciation of Japan's potential. Perry's view, expressed more than a century ago when Japan was still a poor, backward country, was that:

In the practical and mechanical arts, the Japanese show great dexterity, and when the rudeness of their tools and their imperfect knowledge of machinery are considered, the perfection of their manual skill appears marvelous. Their handicraftsmen are as expert as any in the world, and, with a freer development of the inventive powers of the people, the Japanese would not remain long behind the most successful manufacturing nations. Their curiosity to learn the results of the material progress of other people, and their readiness in adapting them to their own uses, would soon, under a less exclusive policy of government, which isolates them from national communion, raise them to a level with the most favored countries. Once possessed of the acquisitions of the past and present of the civilized world, the Japanese would enter as powerful competitors in the race for mechanical success in the future.[43]

The American futurologist, Herman Kahn, who predicted that the twenty-first century would be Japan's century, might be considered the modern-day equivalent of Commodore Perry. The latter's predictions turned out to be remarkably accurate, but there is no way, at present, of knowing the accuracy of Kahn's predictions. The social sciences, including economics, are not of much use in predicting the course of events over such a long period. There are too many uncertainties affecting the relative position of Japan in the future. Those who say that the next century will be Japan's century do so as a matter of faith. But it is not wild speculation, given the strength of Japan in the past decade *vis-à-vis* the United States and Europe.

To many Japanese, such a possibility is a cause of great pride. To the world, it gives them something to think about. The fact that Japan is a non-Western country is significant, but the problem is not a matter of racism, although that seems to have subtly crept into the minds of some of those who advocate the Japanese model. What is important is that Japan has created some unique methods and institutions which have enabled it to outperform Western industrial countries. With Japan as a new model, developing countries no longer have to blindly copy Western methods and institutions. The following chapters attempt to delineate the culture and institutions which have characterized Japanese development.

1. The Meiji Restoration refers to the political events of 1868 which overthrew the Tokugawa regime and returned power to the emperor. His reign (1868–1912) is called the Meiji ('enlightened rule') era.

2. The first section of Chapter 5 discusses the Meiji institutional reforms in more detail.

3. Tokyo was called Edo in the Tokugawa period.

4. These units were called *ryo*, *bu*, and *shu*.

5. Foreign trade was virtually prohibited during most of the Tokugawa period.

6. The yen is the unit of Japanese money in the modern period. In the early 1870s, 1 yen was roughly equivalent to 1 US dollar. By 1897, the yen had devalued to 2 yen per dollar. From then until 1931, the rate remained at about the same level (although in the early 1920s there was a tendency for the yen to devalue). In 1932, the yen devalued sharply, and the rate remained for the rest of the 1930s at approximately 4 yen per dollar. In the post-war years, the exchange rate was set at 360 yen to the dollar in 1949, and remained at that level until December 1971. The yen then revalued to 308 to the dollar, and this rate was maintained until February 1973. Since then, a floating exchange rate system has been adopted. The exchange rate became 180 yen per dollar in mid-1978, but the yen then slowly devalued, and the exchange rate had become about 250 yen per dollar by early 1985. After the Plaza Accord in mid-1985, the yen began appreciating. The exchange rate became 165 yen per dollar a year later and 123 yen by the end of 1987. In subsequent years, the yen depreciated a little, but towards the end of 1992, began appreciating again. At the time of this writing (early April 1993), the exchange rate is about 113 yen per dollar.

7. In the Tokugawa period, the samurai (the ruling warrior class) received their salaries in rice. The Meiji government assumed the financial responsibility of supporting the former samurai but, instead of continuing the same system, decided to commute their rice stipends to government bonds bearing interest at rates of 5–6 per cent. At first, commutation was voluntary and then, in 1876, it became compulsory. Government bonds handed to samurai totalled about 190 million yen.

8. The Matsukata deflation is discussed further in the section on price increase in Chapter 2.

9. On the question of Matsukata's encounter with Leon Say, a conservative Minister of Finance in France in the late 1870s, and Say's possible influence on Matsukata's financial orthodoxy, see H. Rosovsky, 'Japan's Transition to Modern Economic Growth, 1868–1885', in H. Rosovsky (ed.), *Industrialization in Two Systems: Essays in Honor of Alexander Gerschenkron*, New York, John Wiley and Sons, 1966, p. 133.

10. Iwasaki Yataro was the founder of Mitsubishi, one of the four largest *zaibatsu* in the pre-war period.

11. Tsuchiya Takao and Okazaki Saburo, *Nihon Shihonshugi Hattatsu-shi Gaisetsu* [Historical Outline of the Development of Japanese Capitalism], Tokyo, Yuhikaku, 1937, pp. 117–21.

12. For government involvement in industry in the early Meiji period, see T. C. Smith, *Political Change and Industrial Development in Japan: Government Enterprises, 1868–1880*, Stanford, Stanford University Press, 1955.

13. Takahashi Kamekichi, *Meiji Taisho Sangyo Hattatsu-shi* [History of Industrial Development in the Meiji and Taisho Eras], Tokyo, Kaizo-sha, 1922, pp. 520–2.

14. See T. C. Smith, *The Agrarian Origins of Modern Japan*, Stanford, Stanford University Press, 1959. Smith argues that there was considerable technological progress in Tokugawa agriculture and challenges the view that it was stagnant. But even if this view is accepted, it would be reasonable to argue that the increase in productivity was slow and not continuous.

15. On the role of agriculture in the period, see K. Ohkawa and H. Rosovsky, 'The Role of Agriculture in Modern Japanese Economic Development', *Economic Development and Cultural Change*, October 1960.

16. Takahashi, *Meiji Taisho Sangyo Hattatsu-shi*, p. 411.

17. K. Ohkawa et al., *National Income: Estimates of Long-Term Economic Statistics of Japan Since 1868*, Tokyo, Toyo Keizai Shinpo-sha, 1974, Vol. 1, Table 9.

18. J. Dower (ed.), *Origins of the Modern Japanese State: Selected Writings of E. H. Norman*, New York, Pantheon Books, 1975, pp. 225–34.

19. Mitsui, Mitsubishi, Sumitomo, and Yasuda were the four largest *zaibatsu* before the Pacific War. Mitsubishi and Sumitomo were diversified *zaibatsu*, involved in finance, manufacturing, and mining (Mitsubishi was also involved in trading, but not Sumitomo). On the other hand, Yasuda *zaibatsu* concentrated on finance, and Mitsui was strong in finance, trading, and mining but weak in heavy industry.

20. Takahashi Korekiyo held various Cabinet posts, including that of Minister of Finance, from the mid-1910s to 1936 when he was assassinated.

21. E. Hadley, *Anti-Trust in Japan*, Princeton, Princeton University Press, 1969, Chapter 3.

22. J. Cohen, *Japan's Economy in War and Reconstruction*, Minneapolis, University of Minnesota Press, 1949, pp. 104–9. Also consult this source for Japan's war preparation in the 1930s and the state of the economy during the war.

23. Keizai Kikaku-cho [Economic Planning Agency], *Sengo Keizai-shi; Sokan-hen* [History of the Post-war Economy: Overview], Tokyo, Printing Bureau, Ministry of Finance, 1957, pp. 9–12.

24. Although the Korean War lasted until July 1953, major hostilities ended in July 1951 when truce talks began.

25. Cohen, *Japan's Economy*, p. 417.

26. Keizai Kikaku-cho [Economic Planning Agency], *Keizai Hakusho 1952* [White Paper on the Economy], Tokyo, Printing Office, Ministry of Finance, 1952.

27. Keizai Kikaku-cho [Economic Planning Agency], *Keizai Hakusho 1953* [White Paper on the Economy], Tokyo, Printing Office, Ministry of Finance, 1953, p. 32.

28. Keizai Kikaku-cho [Economic Planning Agency], *Keizai Hakusho 1960* [White Paper on the Economy], Tokyo, Printing Office, Ministry of Finance, 1960, p. 42.

29. Light industrial goods include food products, textiles, wood products, ceramics and glass products, printing and publishing, and miscellaneous manufactured goods, whereas heavy industrial goods include chemicals, iron and steel, non-ferrous metals, and machinery (including electronic products).

30. Economic Planning Agency, *Economic Survey of Japan 1978/79*, Tokyo, Japan Times, 1979, p. 3.

31. These are GNP growth rates for the years 1973–83.

32. M. Shinohara, *Industrial Growth, Trade, and Dynamic Patterns in the Japanese Economy*, Tokyo, University of Tokyo Press, 1982, p. 141.

33. Tsusho Sangyo-sho [Ministry of International Trade and Industry], *Tsusho Hakusho 1984* [White Paper on International Trade], Tokyo, Printing Office, Ministry of Finance, 1984, p. 110.

34. L. Thurow, *Head to Head: The Coming Economic Battle among Japan, Europe and America*, New York, William Morrow and Co., 1992, p. 127.

35. Tsusho Sangyo-sho [Ministry of International Trade and Industry], *Tsusho Hakusho 1992; Soron* [White Paper on International Trade 1992: Survey], Tokyo, Printing Office, Ministry of Finance, 1992, p. 124.

36. Tsusho Sangyo-sho [Ministry of International Trade and Industry], *Tsusho Hakusho 1992: Kakuron* [White Paper on International Trade 1992: Discussion by Topic], Tokyo, Printing Office, Ministry of Finance, 1992, p. 3.

37. World Bank, *Development Report 1992*, New York, Oxford University Press, 1992, pp. 218–9.

38. United Nations Development Programme, *Human Development Report 1991*, New York, United Nations, 1991, p. 174. One might say that Japanese prices were 50 per cent higher than American prices in 1988 when compared using the exchange rate.

39. Ibid., p. 119.

40. The GNP series computed by the present method is available from 1955 (published in Keizai Kikaku-cho [Economic Planning Agency], *Keizai Hakusho 1992* [White Paper on the Economy], Tokyo, Printing Office, Ministry of Finance, 1992, p. 73 in the data appendix section). The worst year in the period was 1974 when GNP declined as a result of the first oil shock.

41. Kagaku Gijutsu-cho [Science and Technology Agency], *Kagaku Gijutsu Hakusho 1992* [White Paper on Science and Technology], Tokyo, Printing Office, Ministry of Finance, 1992, pp. 202–21.

42. Thurow, *Head to Head*, pp. 247–8.

43. Quoted in S. Morison, *'Old Burin': Commodore Matthew C. Perry, 1794–1858*, Boston, Little, Brown & Co., 1967, p. 428.

# 2
# The Characteristics of Development

WHILE Chapter 1 traced the historical course of Japanese development, this chapter puts it in a comparative framework. Japan's economic development is compared both with the West and with the developing countries which are presently trying to overcome their own specfic development problems. This chapter attempts to answer three questions. In what respects has Japanese development differed from that of the West? What advantages did Japan enjoy over the developing countries today in pursuing economic development? How were the obstacles they are facing overcome by Japan?

## High Economic Growth

Simon Kuznets defines modern economic growth as a long-term upward trend in income which results in a dramatic change in economic life.[1] Modern economic growth in this sense began first in Britain in the second half of the eighteenth century, and then spread within the next century to other Western European countries and their overseas offshoots. In view of the similarity of key institutions and values, the fact that the British growth caused a chain reaction among Western countries is not surprising, but it is more striking that it triggered modern economic growth in Japan, a distant country which does not share a common cultural background with the West.

As shown in Table 1, Japan's modern economic growth started relatively late—not until the fourth quarter of the nineteenth century—but once it started, the pace of growth was remarkably fast. The rate of growth of total product per decade was 48.3 per cent, the highest among the countries listed and more than twice that of Belgium, Britain, and France. In terms of the growth of per capita income, Japanese performance was also remarkable: 32.3 per cent per decade, higher than in any other country.

TABLE 1
Modern Economic Growth

| Period | Rates of Growth per Decade (%) | | | Coefficients of Multiplication in a Century | | |
|---|---|---|---|---|---|---|
| | Total Product | Population | Product Per Capita | Total Product | Population | Product Per Capita |
| Great Britain 1765/85 to 1963-7 | 23.7 | 10.1 | 12.4 | 8.4 | 2.6 | 3.2 |
| France 1831-40 to 1963-6 | 21.8 | 3.2 | 18.1 | 7.2 | 1.4 | 5.3 |
| Belgium 1900-4 to 1963-7 | 20.3 | 5.3 | 14.3 | 6.3 | 1.7 | 3.8 |
| Netherlands 1860/70 to 1963-7 | 27.7 | 13.4 | 12.6 | 11.5 | 3.5 | 3.3 |
| Germany 1850-9 to 1963-7 | 31.0 | 10.8 | 18.3 | 14.9 | 2.8 | 5.4 |
| Switzerland 1910 to 1963-7 | 26.3 | 8.8 | 16.1 | 10.4 | 2.3 | 4.5 |
| Denmark 1865-9 to 1963-7 | 32.5 | 10.2 | 20.2 | 16.6 | 2.6 | 6.3 |
| Norway 1865-9 to 1963-7 | 31.4 | 8.3 | 21.3 | 15.3 | 2.2 | 6.9 |
| Sweden 1861-9 to 1963-7 | 37.4 | 6.6 | 28.9 | 23.9 | 1.9 | 12.6 |
| Italy 1895-9 to 1963-7 | 31.4 | 6.9 | 22.9 | 15.3 | 2.0 | 7.8 |
| Japan 1874-9 to 1963-7 | 48.3 | 12.1 | 32.3 | 51.4 | 3.1 | 16.4 |
| United States 1834-43 to 1963-7 | 42.4 | 21.2 | 17.5 | 34.4 | 6.9 | 5.0 |
| Canada 1870-4 to 1963-7 | 41.3 | 19.0 | 18.7 | 31.8 | 5.7 | 5.6 |
| Australia 1861-9 to 1963-7 | 36.4 | 23.7 | 10.2 | 22.3 | 8.4 | 2.7 |

Source: S. Kuznets, Economic Growth of Nations, Cambridge, Harvard University Press, 1971, pp. 4–14.

Note: When years in stubs are connected by a slash (/), data are for the single years indicated; when connected by a dash (–), they are for all years in the interval.

One unique feature of Japanese growth is that the rate of growth increased over time or, as Ohkawa and Rosovsky have put it, there was 'a trend acceleration'.[2] At first, the growth rate was relatively modest; it stepped up in 1910 and reached its peak after the Second World War. This is in contrast to the time pattern of growth in other countries. In Britain, the time pattern is an inverted V-shape: growth peaked in the second half of the nineteenth century and then declined. In France, the pattern is the opposite of Britain's: the growth rate at first declined, reaching its lowest point in the early twentieth century, and then rose in the following years. Unlike these two cases, Japanese growth accelerated over time, with growth literally feeding growth.

Japanese modern economic growth began from a subsistence level of income. Western countries, on the other hand, started from a higher level of income. As shown in Table 2, per capita income in the West at the beginning of the period of modern economic growth ranged, in 1965 prices, from Britain's $227 to Australia's $930. Even the lowest British level was about three times as high as per capita income in Japan, whose figure of $74 is comparable to that of low-income countries in Africa and South Asia today. The figure of $74 implies that there was practically no increase in per capita income in the period before the beginning of modern economic growth.

In the subsistence-income equilibrium model, output and population can increase without affecting the level of income. If agricultural output increases over time as a result of increases in acreage or technological innovation, it may temporarily increase per capita income, but it induces population increase by reducing the death-rate with better nutrition or by making early marriage possible. Population increase in turn brings down per capita income to the original subsistence level. That is, there is a well-defined relationship between population and output which makes the subsistence level a stable equilibrium.

Why was the income level of Western Europe higher than subsistence at the beginning of modern economic growth? This is not known precisely, but one possible scenario is as follows. Up to the end of the Middle Ages, income was at subsistence levels; and there was a built-in economic mechanism which restored a temporarily displaced income to its original level. Then, for some reason, the economy broke away from this mechanism and income started to increase, although the increase was so slow and uneven that it does not qualify as modern economic growth. By the time

TABLE 2

Approximate Product Per Capita at the Beginning of Modern Growth
(Developed Countries)

| | *Extrapolation to Initial Date* | | |
| | GNP Per Capita, 1965 (US$) (1) | Date[1] (2) | Reduction Factor (growth) (3) | GNP Per Capita, Initial Date, 1965 Prices[2] (4) |
|---|---|---|---|---|
| Great Britain | 1,870 | 1765–85 | 8.23 | 227 |
| France | 2,047 | 1831–40 | 8.46 | 242 |
| Belgium | 1,835 | (1865) | 3.80 | 483 |
| | | (1831–40) | 5.63 | 326 |
| Netherlands | 1,609 | (1865) | 3.27 | 492 |
| | | (1831–40) | 4.64 | 347 |
| Germany[3] | 1,939 | 1850–9 | 6.41 | 302 |
| Switzerland | 2,354 | (1865) | 4.45 | 529 |
| Denmark | 2,238 | 1865–9 | 6.05 | 370 |
| Norway | 1,912 | 1865–9 | 6.65 | 287 |
| Sweden | 2,713 | 1861–9 | 12.64 | 215 |
| Italy | 1,100 | 1895–9 | 4.06 | 271 |
| | | 1861–9 | 4.22 | 261 |
| Japan | 876 | 1874–9 | 11.88 | 74 |
| United States | 3,580 | 1834–43 | 7.56 | 474 |
| Canada | 2,507 | 1870–4 | 4.94 | 508 |
| Australia | 2,023 | 1900–4 | 2.18 | 930 |
| | | 1861–9 | 2.66 | 760 |

*Source*: S. Kuznets, *Economic Growth of Nations*, Cambridge, Harvard University Press, 1971, p. 24.

*Notes*:  1.  Dates in parentheses are conjectural.
2.  Column 4 = column 1/column 3.
3.  In 1936, per capita income in the Federal Republic and in the territory Germany held before the Second World War differed by only 2 per cent.

modern economic growth began, however, the level of income had become substantially higher than mere subsistence.

It would seem, then, that in the economic development of Western Europe, there was a long period of transition from subsistence income to the beginning of modern economic growth. In Britain, for example, if it is assumed that the economy broke away from the low-income equilibrium towards the end of the Middle Ages, about 200 years passed before modern economic growth began. In contrast, there was no such lengthy transition period in Japanese economic development. The four-century path of Britain was telescoped into one century for Japan.

## Low Population Growth

Population remained stable at about 30 million throughout the last 150 years of the Tokugawa period, but began to increase soon after the Meiji Restoration of 1868. Annual growth during the 1870s was somewhere around 0.5 per cent, increasing gradually in the next five decades. It peaked in the 1920s at 1.4 per cent and then declined to 1.0 per cent in the 1960s, though the downward trend was temporarily interrupted during the baby boom in the late 1940s. The rate of population growth in the modern period as a whole has averaged about 1.1 per cent per annum.

Compared with population growth during the period of modern economic growth in Western countries, the Japanese rate is not high by any means, but the pressure created even by this rate was felt strongly in Japan because of the unfavourable ratio of population to available land. As shown in Table 1, Australia, the United States, and Canada—the offshoots of Western Europe—recorded much higher growth, and a few West European countries experienced about the same rate as Japan. But these countries did not face the same population pressure as Japan, for the offshoots of Western Europe had vast frontier land and served also as a safety valve for West European countries.

Although much of the growing population in Japan was absorbed into gainful employment by expanding the economy, not all could be fully employed. A percentage of the working population was continually unemployed, or forced into menial work. The increase in open and disguised unemployment during times of economic downturn became an important source of social discontent, and it is sometimes argued that it was an important factor for Japan's military expansion to Korea and China.

Although population pressure was a more serious concern in Japan than in Western countries, it was never as serious as in many of the developing countries of today. Most of them have experienced annual population increases of more than 2 per cent in the past few decades, with some over 3 per cent. There has been some success in the 1980s in bringing down population growth, but many countries are still facing high growth. Large population increases have caused serious problems, such as unemployment, a housing shortage, a decline in the quality of education, etc.; indeed, population growth has been the most disequilibrating force in those countries. From this comparative perspective, the population problem faced by Japan in its developing stage has been much less serious.

The rapid population growth of developing countries began to be a problem when the equilibrium between birth- and death-rates was disturbed by external factors which brought about a sharp decline in the death-rate. The first disturbance occurred in the early decades of this century when progressive techniques in medical science, which had been developed in the West, were introduced to developing countries. The effect at this time was still relatively modest. A more dramatic effect occurred after the Second World War when antibiotics, DDT, and other synthetic materials which destroy germs or their carriers were introduced. Japan also benefited from the fruits of Western scientific progress, although their impact on the death-rate was less. By the time they were introduced, the Japanese death-rate was already fairly low because of improvements in nutrition, medicine, and hygiene made possible by past economic development.

## Development with One's Own Resources

During the early decades of industrial development, European countries depended heavily on foreign capital. For example, France relied on British capital in the post-Napoleonic period, Belgium on French capital in the 1830s, and West Germany on French, Belgian, and Swiss capital in the 1840s and 1850s. Even Russia, often considered to be a classic example of internally generated development, depended heavily on foreign capital for building railways and modern industries during the Tsarist period.[3]

The Japanese case was quite different. From the Meiji Restoration to the early years of the twentieth century, the only major foreign loan was the 5 million yen borrowed in 1870 to build the railway between Tokyo and Yokohama—and this was only a small section of the railway line constructed in the period.

Why was there so little dependence on foreign capital in Japan? One reason was that Japan was not particularly attractive to potential investors. The difference between the interest rates in Japan and the West was not large, and the profit from the difference which did exist could be easily wiped out by the continual devaluation of the yen. Furthermore, there were no mineral resources particularly attractive to Western capital. Conversely, Japan was also cautious about borrowing foreign capital, having witnessed the unhappy experiences of Egypt and Turkey which had mismanaged foreign capital and thus invited foreign intervention.[4]

The situation changed in the early 1900s. Japan now wanted to borrow money from abroad. At the same time, European investors became more willing to invest in Japan. After the gold standard was adopted in 1897 and the exchange rate stabilized, there was no exchange risk in investing in Japan. The Anglo-Japanese Treaty of 1902 and Japan's victory in the war with Russia also served to increase the country's potential as an investment market. From about 1904, foreign capital began to surge into Japan, and in 1913, foreign capital in Japan amounted to approximately 2 billion yen ($1 billion or a quarter of the GNP in that year).

Foreign borrowing in this period was undoubtedly necessary for the Japanese economy. It is important to note, however, that the borrowing was not directly related to industrial development. The government was responsible for 85 per cent of the foreign borrowing, and a large percentage of the funds so acquired were used to finance the Russo-Japanese War and to pay the interests of the bonds issued for this purpose. It should be noted also that Japan was in debt to foreign countries for only a short period. During the First World War, large surpluses in the balance of payments turned Japan into a creditor country. In subsequent years, Japan maintained its position as a net creditor.

Also striking is Japan's cautious approach to direct foreign investment. At the beginning of the Meiji period, direct foreign investment in mining was prohibited. In building an infrastructure, Japan depended at first on foreign technicians and, in one case (the railway between Tokyo and Yokohama), on foreign loans, but the country never left the management and ownership of its infrastructure to foreigners. In foreign trade and shipping, Japan quickly promoted its own companies, Mitsubishi and Mitsui, in particular. In the early phase of economic development, because of long isolation and inexperience, Japan depended on Western trading and shipping companies, but soon reduced its dependence on them.

Japanese manufacturing industry was, however, more subject to foreign penetration, although this did not begin until the early twentieth century. First, foreign firms manufacturing electrical machinery, such as Siemens, General Electric, and Westinghouse, began to invest in Japan in the early 1900s.[5] In the remaining years before the Pacific War, there was a continuous rise in the amount of direct investment. By the mid-1930s, Shell, Nestle, IBM, and other Western multinational companies had set up operations in Japan.[6] Nevertheless, direct foreign investment amounted to only about 200 million yen (or $60 million) at that time, and the dependence of the modern sector of the Japanese economy on foreign capital was small. This was in sharp contrast with other Asian countries which were developing with Western capital as the supply source of primary products and the market for industrial products.

The role played by multinational enterprises in the Japanese economy after the Pacific War continued to be negligible. Originally, Japan prohibited direct foreign investment, and any investment that was approved was an exception. For example, in 1960, IBM was allowed to start production, but only as a yen-based company, so that there were no remittances overseas. IBM had to agree to sell all of its patents to Japanese companies wanting to use them. This restrictive policy was modified later and various steps were also taken to liberalize direct foreign investment, especially after Japan joined the Organization for Economic Co-operation and Development (OECD) in 1964. Yet, only a small number of Western companies have succeeded in establishing manufacturing operations in Japan. When their Japanese competitors were weak, the government's restrictive policy discouraged them from investing in Japan. Conversely, when the policy was liberalized, Japanese companies had become strong and it was difficult for foreign companies to start operations.

Since direct investment bestows various benefits on the host country, Japanese policy may not always seem justifiable from an economic viewpoint. It is sometimes argued that multinational enterprises are the most likely generators of an industrial revolution in the Third World. This argument is more convincing if one considers the positive effects of regional diversification of industry: production and income generally improve in an area of a country where new factories are built. In the southern states of the United States, for example, industrial production rose and wages increased after large corporations moved to that part of the country. Since there is no intrinsic difference between the economic impact of regional diversification and multinational spread, the same case can be made for direct foreign investment.

This argument was, however, unknown to Japanese leaders until relatively recently; even if it had been known, they would not have been persuaded. In the nineteenth century—a high point of imperialism—they were afraid that the Western Powers might use their companies as a *point d'appui* for gaining territorial concessions and eventually colonizing the country. Even after this threat became remote, Japan's nationalistic leaders found it distasteful to rely on Western companies for the country's development.

The reason was partly economic. They felt that the benefits to Japan would be greater if the Japanese could emulate foreign companies. For example, in the area of foreign trade, the Japanese government promoted local companies such as Mitsui Bussan because it felt that to depend on Western trading companies would mean less profit for Japan.[7] In the area of mining, it was felt that the mineral resources were the patrimony of the nation and should be guarded carefully. As early as 1873, the government included in the mining law a clause stating that 'the mineral resources of the Divine Land [Japan] all belong to the Japanese government and their exploration and extraction are not allowed to anyone except Japanese'.[8] More recently, in the 1950s and 1960s, the Ministry of International Trade and Industry (MITI) promoted and protected Japanese companies on the assumption that they would create externality and bring greater benefits to the national economy. In the minds of Japanese government leaders, control over the economy was an integral part of national sovereignty.

Technology was one Western item which Japan desperately needed for industrialization, and thus scientific and technical education was given priority from the beginning of the modern period. Machinery which incorporated the most recent technological improvement was imported. Foreign experts were invited to Japan. Many Japanese were sent abroad for training and education. If technology was patented, Japanese corporations drew up licensing agreements for its use in Japan. Sometimes, Western products were merely examined and the technology behind them learned.

Japan has continued to be a heavy borrower of technology from the West, as is reflected in the large deficits in the balance of technology trade. Indeed, until very recently, Japan has concentrated on applying the basic technology developed in the West to industrial production rather than producing its own.

Advocates of multinational enterprises argue that if investment is allowed freely, it will be accompanied by the introduction of new technology and will contribute to technological progress in the host country. This, however, is not the only way to introduce technology from abroad. The Japanese approach has been to 'unbundle' the package of technology and capital which direct investment entails, and to borrow technology alone, with no strings attached. In general, this approach works only if the domestic capital market can raise the necessary capital, and if there is a strong indigenous base for technology. If it does work, the conflict between industrial development and nationalism is minimized.

Although many developing countries restricted foreign capital after winning independence in the post-war years, this did not lead to industrial progress, as in Japan. The latter's success, as in the case of its 'unbundling' of technology from capital, heavily depended on the ability to create companies which could efficiently undertake the activities of Western enterprises. Why could Japan do this?

First, the business tradition which had developed during the Tokugawa period meant that the creation of large companies was not a completely alien concept. There was also the tradition of co-operation and joint-undertaking beyond the village level, which meant that to pool resources, especially capital, from a large number of people (for example, in setting up joint-stock companies) was not an impossible task. Moreover, Japan's educational tradition made it feasible to spread learning to the masses and create a large pool of educated manpower in a relatively short time. All these factors made it possible for many companies, large and small, to be set up and to start performing various new economic activities, some competing with Western companies without protection, others after an initial period of protection.

The development strategy of restricting foreign enterprise, however, works only if good domestic substitutes can be produced without imposing too much cost on the economy. The major reason why this does not work in many developing countries is that such substitutes can not be easily established. Those which are set up are usually protected for a long time and impose a heavy burden on the economy.

## Building on Traditions

In many ways, industrialization is incompatible with traditional society since it requires new institutions and values. The place of production must be moved to a factory, for example. Moreover, an understanding of the principles of industrial technology necessitates the development of rational thinking. Yet, in Japanese industrialization, the break with traditional society was far from complete. Many traditional values and institutions were retained during the course of industrial progress. Even today, traditional values can be observed in business organization and practice.

One obvious explanation for this is that the post-traditional period was short in Japan. In contrast with Britain, which had a transition period of about two centuries, the transition accomplished in the Meiji era was so rapid as to be almost non-existent. Furthermore, since growth was rapid, a level of development comparable to that in the West was reached quite soon. There was insufficient time for society to digest this enormous economic growth, and therefore many traditional values and institutions survived intact.[9]

This is not, however, the only reason for the continued existence of traditional values and institutions. It is important to note the conscious efforts of the Japanese government to preserve them.[10] Under the Meiji modernization plan to create a rich and militarily strong nation—with greater emphasis on the latter—Japanese society had to be geared for modernization, but there was no desire on the part of government leaders to make Japan a liberal democracy. Instead, they made sure that certain parts of traditional society remained intact; for example, the government retained and promoted the traditional authoritarian political system, though it became more unified and rationalized by vesting sovereignty in the emperor. After the Pacific War, sovereignty was transferred to the people, and the political system became more democratic, but in many respects the government has remained supreme over the people. The role of the government in accelerating economic development (as discussed later in this chapter) was possible in such a political setting.

The traditional family system was another institution which the Meiji government retained and promoted. Although the government's motives were largely non-economic, the effects of this action reverberated in the economic field. Despite some modernization, in many areas the family remained the basic social unit around which economic activities were organized. This was true for practically all small businesses, and also, before the Pacific War, for many large ones, such as *zaibatsu* companies. A *kacho* (family head) headed a *zaibatsu* company and, when the *kacho* died or retired, the *zaibatsu* was passed down to his eldest son. Before the Pacific War, a modern joint-stock company was not necessarily more dynamic than a family enterprise. The opposite often tended to be true, since joint ownership led to disputes among the shareholders and this adversely affected management.

One should not assume, however, that *zaibatsu* and other large family companies were run in an entirely traditional way. Various innovations were made in the area of management. For example, efforts were made to hire and promote competent people from outside, and responsibility was delegated to those who were found to be trustworthy through many years of service. Sometimes, management was left almost completely to them, especially in the case of large *zaibatsu*. There were numerous family companies, large as well as small, which did not prosper because there was too much family involvement in management, or because management was delegated to incompetent or untrustworthy managers. Delegation of power is a matter of art rather than science.

One factor which helped Japanese family business was the right of primogeniture which was incorporated into the civil code as the basic inheritance pattern by the Meiji government. It prevented family wealth from being split up and simplified the power structure of the family by concentrating power in the *kacho*.

Another feudal heritage was traditional values, especially those governing social relations. They are reflected in various facets of the Japanese economy today, such as management. Japanese management is known for such unique features as lifetime employment, seniority-graded wages, promotion based on seniority, small-group activities, for example, Quality Control or QC circles, and group decision-making and responsibility. Traditional values are reflected in these features. For example, the Confucian respect for older people undoubtedly had an influence on the evolution of the seniority-graded wage system. The group co-operation which existed in a traditional village persisted into the modern period, partly because values emphasizing group co-operation were kept alive through education, making it easier for small-group activities to produce good results. Strong commitment to a particular group in the feudal period, whether the *ie* (family), village, or *han* (provincial) government, probably made it difficult for people to shift their loyalty from one group to another in the modern period, and contributed to the establishment of lifetime employment.[11] Since a corporation is a profit-based organization, traditional values would not have been used if they had worked against productivity. This is probably the reason they were rejected in the West when large corporations were formed. In Japan, however, although some traditional values had to be abandoned or demoted, some were retained because the people, having just emerged from the feudal period, were not yet completely ready for individualistic, predominantly pecuniary values.

Some other traditional values remain strong in Japan. For example, the place of women is still largely in the home, although there has been some change in recent years. Typically, women may work after finishing school, but are usually expected to stop after marriage or pregnancy. There is thus a division of work in the family: the wife takes care of the household and children while the husband works outside and earns money for the family, although the wife may work part-time and supplement the family income after the children have grown up. Although such Japanese corporate practices are discriminatory from the viewpoint of women who want to have careers, this division of work in the family between husband and wife has undoubtedly contributed to Japan's economic growth. It has kept the divorce rate low, made the family stable, and enabled children (who are Japan's investment in the future) to be better disciplined and educated. But clearly, in the future, Japanese women will have to be accepted and given greater opportunities in the corporate world as more and more opt for careers outside the home.

## Dualistic Development

It is not surprising that there is a structural gap in the economy of any country undergoing industrial development. Such an economy has a modern sector and a traditional sector. The former consists of large, monopolistic companies which use capital-intensive techniques of production, in contrast to the latter which is small and uses labour-intensive techniques of production. The structural gap arises because, although much of modern technology is capital-intensive, the degree of substitution between capital and labour is so limited that modern technology has to be introduced without much modification even in countries which lack capital but have abundant labour.

Such a dual structure has been observed in Japan, but the unique feature of Japanese development is the large contribution made by the traditional sector. Although today the modern sector is the largest foreign exchange earner, for quite some time in the past, it was the traditional sector which was the largest foreign exchange earner. In the Meiji period, for example, the agricultural sector exported raw silk and earned the foreign exchange necessary to import machinery and raw materials for industry. In addition, the agricultural sector fed the expanding urban population and bore the major tax burden via the land tax of the Meiji government.

Silk remained the largest foreign exchange earner until the early 1930s. After that, until the early 1960s, small-scale labour-intensive industry took over. Japan exported such labour-intensive products as garments, toys, plastic goods, rubber products, and ceramic wares to the United States and West European countries, who were unable to compete in labour-intensive production because of high wages. Since the 1960s, small-scale industry has declined in importance as a foreign exchange earner, but has nevertheless indirectly supported the exports of the modern sector as the supplier of parts and components. The competitive strength of large assemblers like car makers, for instance, has been made possible by the ability of their small subcontractors to improve the quality of parts and to reduce their prices.

Many factors contributed to the dynamism of the traditional sector in Japan. The relatively high level of education and the strong work ethic of the Japanese have been particularly important factors.[12] Until quite recently, when the Japanese began enjoying the rewards of economic prosperity, they had been taught that life was hard; that it was a struggle to eke a living out of the country's poor natural endowment; and that if they did not work hard and be careful in planning their future, they would not survive. This outlook on life contributed to the strong work ethic. At the same time, this ethic was incorporated into the education system, thus spurring children on to study so that they would be better prepared in their economic struggle. In spreading education to the masses and raising their level of education, Japan had the advantage of being monolingual. It was also helped by the education progress during the Tokugawa period which created the literary class, especially the samurai, throughout Japan, a progress facilitated by the decentralized political system.

In any economy, numerous decisions are made and carried out. Naturally, performance depends on how good these decisions are and how they are implemented. This is where the spread of education, the level of education, and the work ethic are critical. The strength of the traditional sector is possible only with better informed, more skilled, and hard-working people. In a developing country, such a pool of people may be available for the modern sector of the economy, but not for the traditional sector. This seems to be the major reason for the weakness of its traditional sector.

Another reason for the high contribution of the traditional sector in Japan is the *keiretsu* system. If one looks into the production system of motor cars, for example, one finds a hierarchical structure. At the top of the hierarchy is an assembler, for example, Honda. For the various parts which are assembled into a car, the assembler depends heavily on outside suppliers or subcontractors. Each subcontractor, in turn, usually has his own subcontractors who supply the necessary parts and raw materials. Although the *keiretsu* can degenerate into an exploitive system by the assembler, it most often works, and contributes to higher productivity in a number of industries. When it does work, it is because the company at the helm of the hierarchy (like a motor car assembler) helps its subcontractors with capital, technology, and information, maintains the policy to co-prosper with the subcontractors, and the subcontractors are strongly committed to productivity increase (for example, by reducing nepotism and rewarding workers properly). Undoubtedly, the help of the assembler is crucial if the *keiretsu* system is to work, but what is also important is the ability of its subcontractors to adjust to economic changes and raise productivity. The latter is possible only with a large pool of better educated, more skilled, and conscientious people. But also interesting is the fact that Japanese society can make a mutually beneficial system out of a potentially exploitive one. There is no doubt that competitive pressure contributes to this, but it is also helped by a track record of mutually beneficial long-term relations in Japanese society (although undoubtedly, the more powerful gained more).

A slightly different relation can be found between small producers and large trading companies, the so-called *sogo shosha*. It was through these trading companies that small-scale producers exported goods such as silk and textiles before the Pacific War. Trading companies did not simply perform marketing operations; they bought raw materials and machinery, obtained marketing and technological information, and raised finance; that is, they acted as the organizers of small-scale producers. In the case of textiles, for example, they imported raw cotton for the spinners, sold the yarn that the spinners produced to the weavers, and marketed the fabric that the weavers produced. Although spinning was carried out by big companies, weaving was done mostly by small companies and so, in order to be able to export, the latter needed finance and marketing information.

Trading companies were able to act as the organizers of small companies because the Japanese environment enabled them to continue to grow, instead of to decline, as happened in the West in the past century. What made up this environment? The most basic condition must have been Japan's cultural isolation. In order to trade with foreign countries, Japan required a select group of people who could handle foreign trade. The trading companies which provided this service were able to act as agents for small as well as large companies in Japan. Then, after the Pacific War, as major commercial banks began accumulating large excess liquidity, they loaned much of it to the large trading companies. Regulations and restrictions imposed by the Ministry of Finance, for example, the requirement of collateral in lending to small companies and the restriction on the opening of branches of large national banks for the protection of regional banks, prevented the banks from pursuing aggressive lending to small companies. The trading companies thereby gained enormous financial power and strengthened their control over small-scale industry by means of loans. Small-scale industry could not raise enough capital from financial institutions, as they were considered a poor credit risk.[13] Thus, the trading companies became a financial intermediary as well. In recent years, as the pattern of international linkage has diversified and capital has become a less significant constraint, the importance of trading companies has declined, but previously they were indispensable as a channel to the capital and product markets for small-scale industry.

## Government Involvement

The Japanese government's economic policy has been far from *laissez-faire*. Free market economists who believe that an economy performs best without government intervention give the impression that all countries which have succeeded in economic development had a *laissez-faire* government or a government which was not actively involved in the economy. This, however, was not true of Japan. In the early Meiji era, the government pioneered industrialization by setting up model factories. Although most of these were transferred to the private sector in the 1880s, until the Pacific War state enterprises remained important in the production of iron and steel, machinery, and armaments. Furthermore, the government took major responsibility for the construction of railways, communications facilities, and other infrastructure projects. These government activities are reflected in their relatively large share of total investment, which often exceeded 40 per cent in the pre-war period.[14]

Government intervention was not confined to direct involvement in the economy. Until the Pacific War, for example, it gave subsidies and incentives to certain industries, it provided heavy industry with protection from foreign competition in the 1920s and 1930s, and it aided the *zaibatsu* in establishing a dominant position in the economy in the mid-1920s.

After the Pacific War, the nature of the government's involvement changed, although it continued to play an active role.[15] Until the early 1960s, the government controlled imports by quotas and exchange control. It also influenced the structure of industry by allowing only a small number of firms access to foreign technology and by controlling the construction and expansion of plants on the pretext of avoiding 'excess competition'. Furthermore, by channelling the investment funds of government and quasi-government financial institutions into industries which were considered to have high growth potential, the government shaped the pattern of Japan's industrial development.[16] In particular, MITI was instrumental in changing the industrial structure in favour of heavy industry during the 1950s and 1960s.[17]

The main reason for the involvement of the Meiji government in economic development is related to the way in which it came to power.[18] Its leaders, dissatisfied with the social and economic conditions prevailing in the latter Tokugawa period, led the Restoration Movement to establish a new society. The new government they subsequently created was not intended to preserve the *status quo*, but was rather to be the agent of their modernization goals.

One might argue that it would have been sufficient for the nation's leaders simply to have designated the direction in which the economy should evolve without getting directly involved in the process of development. The social and economic conditions which the Meiji government inherited were, however, so unfavourable that the government could not rely solely on private initiative. The merchant class had become too accustomed to feudal protection and were unlikely to play a pioneering role. The capital market was so fragmented that it was difficult to mobilize sufficient private capital to build a nation-wide system of communications and transportation or to construct large-scale factories for shipbuilding, integrated steel production, or other modern industries. Under such circumstances, the government was forced to take measures to enlighten the public about the power of modern industry, to develop public financial institutions, to promote joint-stock companies, and to assume the primary responsibility for projects which required large capital investment.[19]

The difference between what the government wanted and what the private sector could accomplish was made more acute by the threat of Western imperialism. Having seen how Japan's neighbour, China, had been victimized by the Western Powers, for example, during the Opium War, the Meiji leaders were convinced of the need for military modernization and for building up the supporting economy. If Japan were to avoid China's fate, both military modernization and economic development had to be carried out immediately. Since the response of the private sector was expected to be slow and limited in scope for quite some time, the government was forced to play an active role as educator, institutional innovator, and financier.

To a people accustomed to liberal democracy, the idea of a government having independent goals would normally be objectionable. The Japanese people, however, readily accepted such a government, having known only the feudal Tokugawa regime. Although there were people who wanted to promote democracy at that time, they did not become an influential political force. The Meiji government was run by people who felt it natural for the government to establish new goals for the country and to direct the public to attain them. Generally, the public did not find the supremacy of a governing élite objectionable, for it was in accordance with a long-established tradition.[20]

When there was no urgency for a military build-up, for example, in the early 1920s, the government loosened its control of the economy somewhat, but its interventionist nature never changed. In the 1930s, when the military build-up was renewed with great intensity, the economy became gradually a 'command economy'. After the Pacific War, the military backbone of the country was crushed, and Japan became a democracy. But it was only slowly that the concept of democracy took root in society. Meanwhile, the supremacy of the government enabled it to lead the reconstruction of the devastated economy and to restructure it into a dynamic economy.

### A Conservative Monetary Policy

One might say that Japanese economic development took place in an inflationary setting. From the mid-1880s to mid-1930s, despite some fluctuations, consumer prices increased about 4.5 times, an annual rate of slightly over 2 per cent. The pace of increase quickened from the mid-1930s when Japan accelerated its military build-up, and then developed into the hyper-inflation of the immediate post-war years. By the early 1950s, prices had stabilized, but the rate of increase in the following years was even faster than in the pre-war period: from 1950 to 1973, the consumer price index increased slightly more than three times. Even if the war years and the immediate post-war years are excluded, the rate of increase was much faster in Japan than in Western countries.[21] In the relatively stable period of the mid-1880s to mid-1930s, prices increased twice as fast as in the United States or Britain.

Did the price increases stimulate economic growth? Those who hold the Keynesian view will argue that, since the initial impact of inflation is an increase in the price of output while wages and interest remain constant, inflation increases profits. Increased profits subsequently increase total savings by redistributing income in favour of capitalist entrepreneurs who have a higher propensity to save, and who, in turn, stimulate investment by raising its rate of return. On the other hand, those who accept the quantity theory of money will argue that, since inflation distributes income from the holders of cash balances to the government which issues money—that is, inflation imposes a 'tax' on holdings of money—inflation stimulates growth only as long as the government uses the additional income for investment. Whichever view is accepted, inflation is often considered a favourable condition for growth.[22]

Although inflation accompanied and may have even contributed to Japanese economic growth, it is not accurate to say that the government consistently pursued an inflationary policy. At various times the government made serious efforts to keep down price increases, and in two periods it resorted to deflationary measures in order to bring down prices. Sharp deflationary measures were taken to restore the convertibility of paper notes in the years 1881–6. Again, in the years 1920–31, such measures were taken in order to revert to the pre-war exchange rate. These deflationary measures prevented prices from rising excessively.

One might criticize the deflationary measures of the 1920s on the grounds that they were unrealistic. During the First World War, Japan experienced a large balance of payments surplus which led to an increased money supply and, consequently, a price increase of approximately 250 per cent. It is quite possible that the level of prices after the First World War was too high for the original exchange rate to be maintained, so it might have been better to let the rate depreciate. Instead, efforts were made to maintain the original rate by deflationary measures and by reducing the level of prices to those of the United States and Britain. The government finally achieved this objective in January 1931 when the gold standard was reinstated at the pre-war exchange rate. Unfortunately, however, this demanded sacrifice within the economy and made the 1920s a gloomy decade of high unemployment and many bankruptcies. In retrospect, it seems that the maintenance of the original exchange rate after major economic changes had occurred was not only impractical but also harmful.

Nevertheless, the Japanese financial authorities can be given credit for having had the courage and determination to take deflationary measures. They can be favourably contrasted with financial authorities in developing countries today who often mismanage monetary affairs. In these countries, the issue of paper notes need not be backed up with bullion or foreign exchange. Thus, their financial authorities often tend to relax their control over the money supply, for example, by financing the deficits of the government budget with note issue, thereby contributing to inflation. The basic problem is that the government is under pressure to spend but reluctant to tax people. Whether under a democracy or an authoritarian regime, spending pleases people but taxation does not. The end result is that the government budget tends to run into deficit.

A fixed exchange rate is a potential check on inflation but, once inflation starts, devaluation is often the only solution, because measures to reduce the level of prices are usually politically unpalatable, since it requires a reduction of government spending or an increase of taxation. The result is a vicious cycle of inflation and devaluation.

A slow rate of inflation may have some positive effects but, beyond a certain rate—possibly a few per cent—inflation is more likely to be harmful because of the uncertainty it creates for future investment and the distortion of credit allocation this uncertainty, in turn, creates. Furthermore, inflation weakens the currency and stimulates capital flight, since those who have capital find it more attractive to hold assets denominated in a stronger currency, such as the US dollar. This takes place in the very countries where capital is scarce. Especially in the past few decades when the progress of communications and transportation technology has made the world 'smaller', capital flight has become a serious problem. Of course, if interest rates are raised high enough, capital flight can be prevented, or the reversal of capital flight can even take place, but rarely are interest rates allowed to increase to that level.

After the Pacific War, there was a peculiar development in the relationship between the movement of prices and the exchange rate. According to the theory of purchasing power parity, if Japan wants to maintain the dollar–yen exchange rate, its prices must change at the same rate as prices in the United States; that is, the fixed exchange rate is inconsistent with a disparate movement of prices in the two countries. But what happened was that, although the consumer price index increased much faster in Japan than in the United States in the post-war period, the same exchange rate was maintained until almost the end of 1971 when the yen was revalued instead of devalued. In the following two decades, the same phenomenon took place: despite the faster increase of the consumer price index in Japan than in the United States, the yen became stronger.

The main reason for this is that economic growth, which has been almost consistently faster in Japan than in the United States in the post-war period, caused a divergence in the movement of prices in the tradable (goods) and the non-tradable (services) sectors in Japan. After surplus labour began to diminish in the late 1950s, high growth pushed up prices in the non-tradable sector. Because production was labour intensive in this sector, there was little room for the introduction of cost-saving technology. Consequently, the consumer price index, which includes prices in the non-tradable sector, increased. On the other hand, prices in the tradable sector, which enter into the balance of payments and thus influence the exchange rate, increased much more slowly in Japan than in the United States because productivity increase was faster in Japan. This made it possible not only to maintain the fixed exchange rate of 360 yen per dollar over two decades—until the early 1970s—but also to revalue the yen in subsequent years.[23]

1. See S. Kuznets, *Modern Economic Growth: Rate, Structure, and Spread*, New Haven, Yale University Press, 1966, Chapter 1.

2. See K. Ohkawa and H. Rosovsky, *Japanese Economic Growth: Trend Acceleration in the Twentieth Century*, Stanford, Stanford University Press, 1973.

3. D. Landes, 'Japan and Europe: Contrast in Industrialization', in W. Lockwood (ed.), *The States and Economic Enterprise in Japan*, Princeton, Princeton University Press, 1965, pp. 95–7.

4. J. Dower (ed.), *Origins of the Modern Japanese State: Selected Writings of E. H. Norman*, New York, Pantheon Books, 1975, p. 223. In the early 1890s, Japan negotiated a revision of the treaties with the Western Powers in order to abolish the extra-territoriality which Japan had granted them earlier. Japan seems to have considered, as a 'bait' for the revision, the opening up of the country to foreign

investment. Herbert Spencer, who was asked his views on this question by Kaneko Kentaro, a close adviser to the then prime minister, Ito Hirobumi, advised Japan to keep the Western Powers as much as possible at arm's length. To what extent his advice was heeded is not, however, clear. Spencer's letter to Kaneko is reproduced in Lafcadio Hearn, *Japan: An Interpretation*, Tokyo, Charles E. Tuttle Co., 1959, pp. 481–4.

5. W. Lockwood, *The Economic Development of Japan: Growth and Structural Change*, Princeton, Princeton University Press, expanded edition, 1968, pp. 322–3.

6. Tsusho Sangyo-sho [Ministry of International Trade and Industry], *Gaishi-kei Kigyo: Sono Jittai to Eikyo* [Foreign-affiliated Firms: Their Realities and Influences], Tokyo, Printing Office, Ministry of Finance, 1968, p. 15.

7. Yoshihara Kunio, *Sogo Shosha: The Vanguard of the Japanese Economy*, Tokyo, Oxford University Press, 1982, p. 189.

8. Nippon Koho [Japan's Mining Law] of 1873.

9. Nakayama Ichiro, *The Industrialization of Japan*, Honolulu, University Press of Hawaii, 1965, p. 38.

10. For this view, see Sakata Yoshio, 'Nihon Kindaika no Shuppatsu to Tenkai' [The 'Take-off' and Expansion of Japan's Modernization], *Jinbun Gakuho*, March 1970.

11. For further discussion of this, see Chapter 6.

12. The Japanese work ethic is examined further in Chapter 6.

13. For further discussion on the evolution of Japanese trading companies and their role in industrialization, see Yoshihara, *Sogo Shosha*, Chapters 5 and 6.

14. H. Rosovsky, *Capital Formation in Japan*, Glencoe, Illinois, Free Press, 1961, p. 23.

15. For the role of the government in the economy after the Pacific War, see P. Trezise, 'Politics, Government, and Economic Growth in Japan', in H. Patrick and H. Rosovsky (eds.), *Asia's New Giant*, Washington, Brookings Institution, 1976.

16. The major source of funds the government and quasi-government financial institutions used for this purpose was postal savings. Even today, commercial banks are complaining about too much competition from postal savings, which account for about a third of total household savings. Until recently, the rates of interest for postal savings were higher than in commercial banks.

17. For further discussion of this, see Chapter 6.

18. It might be suggested that, in general, the more backward a country is, the greater the role of the government in economic development. The American economic historian, A. Gerschenkron, found this tendency among the Western countries. See A. Gerschenkron, *Economic Backwardness in Historical Perspective*, Cambridge, Harvard University Press, 1962.

In developing countries today, especially in former colonial countries, their governments played an active role in economic development after independence. But in recent years, in view of the poor results of government activism in many of these countries, a large number of economists have begun arguing for less government involvement (privatization, deregulation, and liberalization). But government activism can stimulate economic growth. Japan seems to be a case in point. Whether it will work or not depends partly on the capability of the bureaucracy and the degree of intervention.

19. Dower, *Origins of the Modern Japanese State*, p. 221, and Lockwood, *The Economic Development of Japan*, pp. 505–7.

20. Dower, *Origins of the Modern Japanese State*, p. 154.

21. K. Ohkawa et al., *Prices: Estimates of Long-Term Economic Statistics of Japan Since 1868*, Tokyo, Toyo Keizai Shinposha, 1967, Vol. 8, p. 12.

22. For a more detailed discussion of inflation and economic growth, see Harry Johnson, 'Is Inflation the Inevitable Price of Rapid Development or a Retarding Factor in Economic Growth?', *Malayan Economic Review*, April 1966.

23. For further discussion of this point, see R. McKinnon, 'Monetary Theory and Controlled Flexibility in the Foreign Exchanges', *Essays in International Finance*, Department of Economics, Princeton University, April 1971, No. 84.

# 3
# Trade and Development

In Chapter 1, we looked at Japanese development from the historical perspective, and in Chapter 2 from the international comparative perspective. In this chapter, we shall look at Japanese development from yet another perspective—that of international trade—for Japanese development did not take place in isolation. It was inextricably interwoven with international trade, and it is difficult to conceive how, without such trade, the high standard of living that Japan enjoys today could have been reached and maintained. The chapter first discusses trade expansion, trade patterns, and their changes over time, then tries to explain these in terms of trade models, and finally considers the impact of trade on development.

## Trade Patterns and Expansion

The Tokugawa period was a period of relative economic isolation. The only foreign trade was with the Dutch and Chinese through the port of Nagasaki, and with the Koreans through the island of Tsushima in the Korean Straits. The volume of trade was restricted and small, however, and had little influence on the economic and social affairs of the country. Thus, the period up to the mid-nineteenth century may be considered one of virtual seclusion.

A dramatic change in Japan's foreign policy took place in 1854 when Matthew C. Perry, an American naval commodore, threatened to besiege the city of Edo and forced the shogunate to sign the Treaty of Kanagawa. This treaty stipulated that two ports were to be opened to American ships for provisions; that shipwrecked Americans were to be well treated; and that an American consular agent was to be allowed to reside in Japan. It was not, however, until 1859 that the Western Powers succeeded in opening trade with Japan. A year earlier, the Tokugawa shogunate was persuaded by the first American Ambassador, Townsend Harris, to sign commercial treaties with the West—the treaties known collectively in Japan as the 'Treaties with Five Nations'.

In the first few years of the 1860s, exports increased. The most popular of the goods bought by Western merchants was silk. Difficulties in increasing the silk supply, together with a variety of political factors,[1] however, caused exports to stagnate in the remaining years of the Tokugawa period. It was not until the early Meiji period that trade expansion became a built-in feature of the Japanese economy.

As shown in Table 3, the growth of trade was spectacular in the succeeding period. From the mid-1870s to the mid-1930s, both exports and imports increased at an annual rate of about 7 per cent. This rate was 2–3 times greater than the growth rate of world trade in the same period. From the late 1930s to the mid-1940s, as a consequence of the Pacific War, trade declined sharply. Then, in the post-war years, as the Japanese economy recovered from war-time destruction and dislocation, trade expanded again. Nevertheless, the pre-war level of trade was not reached again until the late 1950s, a point which should be contrasted with the recovery of other economic indicators, such as industrial production, agricultural output, and per capita income, which had returned to the pre-war level by the early 1950s.

This late recovery of trade was due to the difficulties Japan faced in exporting its goods. Silk, a major export commodity before the Pacific War, lost its foothold because of the appearance of nylon. Cotton textiles, another major export in the pre-war period, faced trade barriers erected by newly emergent countries which had decided to industrialize through import substitution. China, the major market before the Pacific War, became a Communist state and restricted its trade with capitalist countries. Despite these difficulties, however, Japan succeeded in creating new markets and new export goods by the late 1950s. In the next decade, the growth of exports continued at an annual rate of increase of about 17 per cent, with the volume of exports increasing about five times. This rapid export expansion continued until the oil crisis in late 1973. After the Pacific War, imports were initially constrained by the lack of foreign exchange but, as exports increased, this constraint was eased, and imports also increased rapidly during the same period.

The rapid expansion of exports over a long period of time was possible because new export commodities were created before the old ones began to decline. This pattern is shown in Figure 1. At

### TABLE 3
Export and Import Quantity Index, the Terms of Trade,
and the Ratios of Exports and Imports to GNP

|  | Export Quantity Index | Import Quantity Index | Terms of Trade | Exports to GNP | Imports to GNP |
|---|---|---|---|---|---|
| 1873–7 | 1.4 | 1.6 | 111.3 | 4.5 | 5.1 |
| 1878–82 | 2.0 | 2.4 | 129.2 | 4.2 | 4.6 |
| 1883–7 | 2.8 | 2.6 | 137.9 | 5.0 | 3.9 |
| 1888–92 | 4.5 | 4.9 | 131.3 | 6.3 | 6.1 |
| 1893–7 | 5.7 | 7.9 | 135.4 | 7.4 | 8.6 |
| 1898–1902 | 8.4 | 11.8 | 134.8 | 11.8 | 12.3 |
| 1903–7 | 11.6 | 16.4 | 144.9 | 13.2 | 15.3 |
| 1908–12 | 15.5 | 17.7 | 125.2 | 13.3 | 14.4 |
| 1913–17 | 26.1 | 21.5 | 110.0 | 20.2 | 16.9 |
| 1918–22 | 26.8 | 31.2 | 112.2 | 17.3 | 19.0 |
| 1923–7 | 32.2 | 43.4 | 121.3 | 16.9 | 21.2 |
| 1928–32 | 44.4 | 45.2 | 104.2 | 16.5 | 18.1 |
| 1933–7 | 73.5 | 53.0 | 76.1 | 21.6 | 22.9 |
| 1948–52 | 19.2 | 22.8 | 82.7 | 7.1 | 11.1 |
| 1953–7 | 50.2 | 56.9 | 88.4 | 10.7 | 15.6 |
| 1958–62 | 99.0 | 101.1 | 97.7 | 12.0 | 13.6 |
| 1963–7 | 219.3 | 193.6 | 96.4 | 10.9 | 10.7 |
| 1968–72 | 471.4 | 367.4 | 98.6 | 11.5 | 9.9 |
| 1973–7 | 801.4 | 521.7 | 70.0 | 12.6 | 12.2 |
| 1978–82 | 1,130.0 | 584.3 | 52.0 | 13.3 | 12.8 |
| 1983–7 | 1,563.9 | 668.4 | 53.8 | 13.0 | 9.9 |
| 1988–91 | 1,823.8 | 990.9 | 70.6 | 10.3 | 8.8 |

*Source*: Economic Planning Agency, *Nihon no Keizai Tokei* [Japanese Economic Statistics]. Volume 1, and Office of the Prime Minister, *Japan Statistical Yearbook*.

*Notes*:   1. 1960 = 100 for the export and import quantity index.

        2. The terms of trade are derived from the ratio of the export price index to the import price index. The base year for both indexes is 1960.

first, Japan exported silk, a primary product in the sense that it was produced by farm households. In about 1900, while exports of silk were growing, Japan completed the import-substitution stage of textile production, and began to export textiles to China. The First World War was a tremendous blessing to Japanese textile exports. Britain, the dominant supplier of textiles until 1914, was forced to withdraw from the Asian scene, for wartime dislocation and the German naval blockade of the British Isles made it impossible for

## FIGURE 1
### Changes in Leading Exports over Time

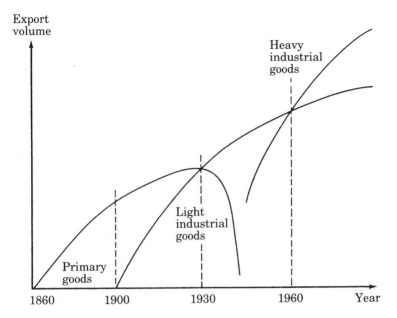

Britain to maintain supply links with Asia. Japanese textiles moved with great vigour into the vacuum created. After 1918, Britain tried to regain the lost markets, but without much success. In the Chinese market, for example, Japan had by then consolidated its position and was able to block British re-entry. Britain was more successful in South-East Asia and India but, even there, Japanese textiles penetrated increasingly in the late 1920s and the 1930s. In about 1930, textile exports surpassed silk exports for the first time, and became a major foreign exchange earner.

Textiles were soon joined by various other light industrial goods, and together they comprise the second product cycle in Figure 1. After being surpassed by textile exports, silk exports declined sharply because of the Depression in the West and the invention of nylon. In place of silk, light industrial products rose in significance to become the propelling force of Japanese exports during this period. Garments, plastic products, and a number of other labour-intensive manufactured goods became significant, especially in the years immediately after the Pacific War. They were exported to the United States and other Western countries where labour costs were much higher than in Japan. It was at the early part of this stage of development, in about the 1930s, that the phrase 'made in Japan' became synonymous with poor-quality products.

In about 1960, the export of light industrial products was surpassed by that of heavy industrial products. As discussed in Chapter 1, heavy industry became more important as Japan developed, particularly in the 1930s when a heavy industrialization programme was deliberately fostered by the government, in preparation for the imminent war. The push towards heavy industry was further accelerated during the years of the Pacific War. In the post-war economic recovery, this industrial imbalance was corrected to a certain extent, but there was still a considerable emphasis on heavy industry. Under the protection and financial assistance of the government, heavy industry expanded its production and eventually became the driving force of Japanese industrialization.

For many years, heavy industry had been of considerable importance in the domestic market, but in the late 1950s, it began to establish itself also as an export industry. Steel and ships were the first major exports, followed by electronic products. The first major electronic product to be exported was the transistor radio, followed by the tape recorder and the black-and-white television set in the early 1960s and the colour television set later in the decade. When cars and synthetic fibres joined the list of major exports in the second half of the 1960s, the growth of the export of heavy industrial products further accelerated. The share of heavy industrial products in total exports increased from 50 per cent in 1960 to 65 per cent in 1965, 76 per cent in 1970, and over 90 per cent in 1983.

The composition of heavy industrial products changed during the 1970s, especially after the oil crisis. Steel, which requires a lot of energy and raw materials for production, declined in significance. In 1970, it was the major export, accounting for about 15 per cent of total exports, but in 1983, its share had fallen to less than 9 per cent. The motor car had taken the place of steel as the major export. In the period 1970–83, its share increased from 7 to 18 per cent. Exports of videotape recorders and semiconductors also grew. In the same period, exports of machinery and equipment, as a percentage of total exports, increased from 45 to 68 per cent. The share of machinery and equipment continued to rise in the following years, and reached 75 per cent in 1991.

As the composition of Japan's exports changed, the direction of exports also changed. In the first period (1860–1900), exports went mostly to Western countries. In this period, Japan exported silk and other primary products to the West. In the second period (1900–30), the developing areas, especially China, became leading Japanese markets, while primary exports to the West continued. In the following few decades, there was no great change in the direction of exports, although the Western share in total exports varied. It declined, for example, in the 1930s as Japan became isolated from the West, and increased in the 1950s and 1960s when Japan aimed its export drive at high-income countries.

In the 1980s, when the income gap between Japan and the West narrowed, partly as a consequence of the economic slow-down in the West, and the East Asian NIEs and ASEAN countries emerged as new export economies, the share of these Asian countries began rising, particularly in the second half of the decade when the Japanese yen revalued. Indeed, their share rose from 20 to 31 per cent between 1986 and 1991. The factories in these countries, including Japanese-affiliated companies there, needed machinery and industrial products as inputs, and an important part of this was supplied from Japan.

As the composition and direction of exports changed, similar changes also took place in imports. Imports of consumer goods occupied an important position in the first period, but lost ground as the domestic production of consumer goods, particularly textiles, increased. In the second period (1900–30) and in the third (1930–60), intermediate goods, capital goods, and primary products (cotton, iron ore, and food) became the principal Japanese imports. Then, in the fourth period (1960–75), as heavy industry became predominant, primary products alone became the principal Japanese imports. However, in the fifth period (1975 to the present), as the Japanese industrial structure shifted to high-value-added, low-energy- and -raw materials-using industries, the importance of primary products declined. In their place, as Japan became a high-cost country with the continuing increase of income in dollar terms, the imports of manufactured goods (especially low-value-added goods) increased their share of total imports. It had reached 50 per cent by the late 1980s.

As the composition of imports changed, the sources of imports also altered. Britain, which had been the major supplier of textiles in the Meiji period, lost its position when textile imports were replaced by domestic production in the early 1900s. The United States, on the other hand, became significant as a supplier of both primary products and capital goods in the years after the First

World War. Developing countries which possessed natural resources gained in importance, especially after 1960, as primary products became increasingly important among Japanese imports. Since the mid-1970s, however, their share has declined as the industrial structure has shifted to high-value-added, low-energy- and -raw materials-using industries. As the share of manufactured goods in total imports rose (from about 20 to 50 per cent between 1981 and 1991; an increase of machinery (for example, airplanes) imports was particularly noticeable), the United States and EC countries have gained importance. The countries in Asia which succeeded in economic restructuring—the East Asian NIEs and some ASEAN countries—also raised their share somewhat by increasing the exports of light industrial goods (textiles in particular) to Japan.

These export and import trends reflect changes in the relationship between Japan and foreign countries. In the first period (1860–1900), Japan imported consumer goods from the West and exported primary products back to the West. The relationship between Japan and the West was, in general, complementary. Japan's relations with developing areas, however, was one of substitution, since the economic structures of Japan and the developing countries were basically similar. In the second and third periods (1900–60), Japan's relationship with the West became both complementary and competitive. It was complementary in the sense that Japan exported primary goods and light industrial goods to the West, and imported capital and intermediate goods from the West. It was competitive in that Japan competed with some Western countries, Britain, in particular, in selling textiles and other light industrial goods. Japan's relationship with the developing areas became complementary during the second and third periods since it exported industrial goods to them and imported primary products from them. The composition of Japan's exports to the developing countries changed over time; the early dominance of consumer goods gave way to heavy industrial goods as these areas began to industrialize, pursuing a policy of import substitution in consumer goods.[2]

In the fourth and fifth periods (1960–the present), Japan's relationship with the developing areas as a whole remained constant, but the degree of complementarity with the oil-producing countries of the Middle East, for example, declined while that with the East Asian NIEs and ASEAN countries increased. On the other hand, the relationship with the West became increasingly competitive after 1960. In the 1960s, as a result of capital accumulation, the factor proportion[3] in Japan became similar to that in the West and, consequently, exports of light industrial goods became less significant. The heavy industrial goods which replaced them were those in which the West had a vested interest. But at this stage, trade frictions were not serious since the United States and other Western countries were willing to let go of some heavy industries, especially those producing not too high-value-added goods, such as steel and colour televisions.

However, the situation was aggravated in the decade after the first oil crisis, since Japan had to offset its trade deficits with the OPEC countries with its trade surpluses with the West. In the following years, as oil prices declined, Japan's surpluses in the balance of trade increased. Although this brought about a sharp rise of the yen relative to the dollar, it did not reduce trade surpluses since Japanese industry succeeded in shifting to more technologically sophisticated goods.

Trade surpluses have become the major source of Japan's overseas investment, including financial investment, which has eased friction with the West to some extent, but large trade surpluses have been a continuing irritation for Western countries which have suffered from the onslaught of Japanese goods in their home markets.

Exacerbating the situation has been the fact that since the second tier of industrial countries—the East Asian NIEs—have gone into low-value-added heavy industrial goods, the only viable strategy for Japan and the Western industrial countries to sustain growth has been to promote high-value-added industries (or high-technology industries). With such high stakes in a narrow range of industries, the free international trade of their goods has become difficult. There are quotas, voluntary as well as mandatory, and other trade restrictions, for example, dumping charges against Japanese exports and the numerical target for the American share of computer chips sold in Japan, which signify the severity of the competitiveness between Japan and Western industrial countries today. There seems to be no alternative to a head-on collision. With the economic decline of the United States, there is no dominant country promoting the free trade of those goods. In this situation, the GATT is powerless. It seems likely that the trade in those goods will continue to be a managed trade for at least some time to come, possibly at an increasing level.

## Trade Models as Explanatory Constructs

The pattern of Japanese trade is so complex that it helps to resort to the theory of international trade as an explanatory construct. Trade models proposed in the past have been built upon rather simple assumptions, but they nevertheless highlight certain features in Japan's pattern of trade that might otherwise go unnoticed. In this section, three major trade models are described in the simplest terms possible; then the ways in which they can be used to explain the Japanese trade pattern are discussed.[4]

The first model is the Ricardian model. It assumes that labour is the only factor of production and that there are only two commodities and two countries in the world. The price ratio of the two commodities is determined by relative labour productivity—the ratio of the labour productivity of one commodity to that of the other. If the price ratio in one country differs from that in the other, trade between the two countries can take place. The first exports the commodity in which it has relatively high labour productivity—the commodity in which it has a comparative advantage—and imports the commodity in which it has relatively low labour productivity. The goods exported by the first country are the goods imported by the second, and vice versa.

Another model is the Heckscher–Ohlin model, which is built upon three basic assumptions: (a) that there are two factors of production (for example, labour and capital); (b) that there are only two commodities and two countries in the world; and (c) that production technology is the same for the two countries. The model predicts that, when trade takes place, the country where capital is abundant (that is, abundant in relation to the capital endowment in the second country) will export the capital-intensive product and the country where labour is relatively abundant will export the labour-intensive product. The two factors of production usually discussed in connection with this model are capital and labour, but they can be any two. For example, they can be non-reproducible (land, including natural resources) and reproducible inputs (some aggregate of labour and capital). The model predicts that, in such a case, the country abundant in the non-reproducible input will export a resource-intensive product and the country abundant in the reproducible input will export a product which is intensive in terms of the aggregate of capital and labour.

Those who are attracted to the theoretical beauty of the Heckscher–Ohlin model argue that differences in technology can be dealt with within the framework of the model by considering technical knowledge as an input. The exports of technologically advanced (technology-intensive) products from industrialized countries to developing countries may be explained by saying that the former have a relative abundance of technical knowledge. This extension of the framework, however, seems to stretch interpretation of the model too far, since it assumes categorically that the two countries have the same level of technology.

The 'technological gap' model assumes explicitly a difference in technology between countries. According to this model, the reason the United States exports aeroplanes is that American aeroplane manufacturers possess the technology and know-how not known to companies in other countries. This technological gap may be temporary but it can be substantial, for two reasons. The new technology may be patented, or the small size of the domestic market for new products may make it difficult for less advanced countries to start production on a very large scale and acquire the new technology involved in the production.

Unfortunately, none of the three models adequately explains the Japanese trade pattern. The technological gap model explains fairly well Japan's import of aeroplanes, but it provides a poor explanation of the imports of primary products. With regard to the latter, the Heckscher–Ohlin model provides a better explanation if land—including natural resources—is considered as an input. The Heckscher–Ohlin model also explains well the imports of garments, toys, and other light industrial goods after 1970, when the factor proportion in Japan changed in favour of capital. It fails, however, to account for the imports of textiles in the early modern period (1860–1900), when there was an abundance of labour; in this case, the technological gap model seems more relevant.

In explaining Japanese export patterns, it is likewise necessary to adopt an eclectic approach towards the application of models. Japanese exports of silk in the first six decades of the modern period, and of garments and other light industrial goods from the early 1930s to early 1960s, can be explained in terms of the Heckscher–Ohlin model. Japan had a comparative advantage in labour-intensive products because wages were relatively low at the time. Exports of textiles to China and other developing countries before the Pacific War are also related to the fact that Japan had a comparative advantage in labour-intensive production *vis-à-vis* Britain. But one should remember that it was only after the Japanese textile industry caught up with the level of British technology that the factor proportion came into play.

It is similarly problematic explaining the export of electronic products. The reason that Japan could export various consumer electronic products in the early 1960s was because their production processes were labour intensive. Japan acquired the technology necessary for the production of consumer electronics, and its low wages gave it a competitive edge over the United States and other high-wage countries. But when Hong Kong, Taiwan, and Korea caught up with Japan in technology, Japan lost this advantage in transistor radios, televisions, and other mature electronic products. The usefulness of the Heckscher–Ohlin model in explaining the exports of such electronic goods is limited as long as there is a technological gap between Japan and its Asian competitors. Only when the gap closes does the model become useful in explaining the decline of Japanese exports of mature electronic products.

Neither the Heckscher–Ohlin model nor the technological gap model provides a satisfactory explanation for the rise of exports of steel, colour television sets, and cars in the 1960s. Production of these goods was not labour intensive as, in general, it employed capital-intensive production techniques. Since it cannot be argued that capital was more abundant in Japan than in the West, where the bulk of the exports went, the Heckscher–Ohlin model cannot be applied. The technological gap model is also inapplicable since it is hardly possible to argue that Japan had more advanced technical knowledge with regard to these products. They were relatively old products, and the technology required for their production was known to all industrial countries.

The only possible explanation for Japan's exports of steel, colour televisions sets, and cars is that Japanese productivity in these products was higher than that in other countries—and therefore the Ricardian model applies. If one objects to the Ricardian assumption that labour is the only factor of production, an aggregate input index constructed from labour and capital can be considered as an input, and the model can be salvaged in terms of total factor productivity (productivity of the aggregate input) instead of labour productivity.

A serious difficulty arises, however, in connection with the Ricardian model. The reasoning involved in explaining the trade pattern by the Heckscher–Ohlin model is relatively straightforward, but the nature of the reasoning is quite different with the Ricardian model. According to this model, productivity in steel, for example, is considered to have been high because it was a major export. Such an argument clearly reverses the logical order of events. If the model is to be useful for predicting future trade patterns, it is necessary to know in advance whether the productivity of the Japanese steel industry is increasing or decreasing in relation to that in other countries.

Even if the productivity trend is known, the problem of explaining it remains. One cannot resort to national characteristics, such as the Japanese work ethic, as an explanation, since not all industries increased productivity uniformly; some became more productive than others. What needs to be explained is the increased productivity of steel, cars, and colour television sets compared with other industries. If this question is to be dealt with satisfactorily, the method of management and technological progress, especially the introduction of new machinery and technical improvements, must be studied, along with government policy and industrial history. At this point, it is necessary to leave the neat field of economic theory.

In general, one can say that as an explanatory construct, the trade models have been losing their value in recent years. Countries have been increasingly integrated through trade and investment, and it has become difficult to explain many trade flows, especially those occurring between industrialized countries. Why those flows take place are as puzzling as why the state of Michigan 'exports' motor cars to another state in the United States, for example, Illinois, or why Shizuoka prefecture 'exports' motor cycles to another prefecture in Japan, for example, Shiga prefecture. In both cases, there were entrepreneurs who pioneered production (motor cars in the case of Michigan and motor cycles in the case of Shizuoka), and an industrial complex, made up of parts suppliers and assemblers, was born. There may have been entrepreneurs in other locations, but those, and their successors, in Michigan or Shizuoka were in command of better technology or were better corporate managers so that their enterprises overwhelmed their competitors in other locations. In the case of the rise of Suzuka City in Mie prefecture, which became a major centre of car production by Honda, the availability of land and possibly the co-operation of local government were important factors for Honda's decision to invest there.

This sort of decision has been taking place internationally for decades, and affects trade flows. For example, the recent export of air-conditioners and other consumer electrical machinery from Thailand to Japan was made possible by Japanese multinationals which had relocated production to Thailand. Japanese (or any other) multinationals could raise capital where its cost was lowest and invest in the country where the investment climate was good. The Philippines, for example, had a similar factor proportion, but it was Thailand's investment climate, consisting of a liberal government policy, political stability, the absence of radical trade union leaders, etc., which attracted Japanese multinationals and generated trade as a consequence.

Another problem with a trade model as an explanatory construct is that its policy prescription is static. For example, the Heckscher–Ohlin model explains perfectly well Japan's exports of garments and labour-intensive products in the 1950s and its imports of the same products in the 1970s and 1980s, but it is a poor model for prescribing the best course for increasing a country's exports. If a country has abundant labour, the model recommends that it specialize in a labour-intensive product. But this recommendation is hardly acceptable for a country which wants to create a comparative advantage in more value-added heavy industrial goods, which is the only way to sustain export increase.

During the preparation of Japan's first long-term plan of the post-war economy, which was drafted in 1949, there was heated discussion concerning which manufacturing industries should be the foci of exports in the future.[5] There were three different views expressed. One view was basically in agreement with the policy prescription of the Heckscher–Ohlin model: since Japan had a comparative advantage in light industrial products, such goods should play a central role in Japanese exports. The second was its opposite: although Japan did not have a comparative advantage in heavy industrial goods, the government should take measures to promote heavy industry and create a comparative advantage in heavy industrial goods, since the demand for such goods in the world market was expected to rise sharply in the future. The third view was that, since Japan was short of capital, it should not aim to export heavy industrial goods; instead, it should make precision machinery the major export in the future.

The Japanese government did not discourage light industry or the precision machinery industry, but it did intervene in the economy to promote heavy industry, thus indirectly discriminating against the other two sectors. The protection and subsidies that heavy industry received from the government contributed to its success in Japan after the Pacific War. In the late 1950s, this policy began to bear fruit, and in the 1960s and 1970s, heavy industrial goods became Japan's major exports. Nevertheless, in the early and mid-1950s, when the outcome of the heavy industrialization policy was still uncertain, the government was criticized by conventional trade theorists. A distinguished American economist argued, for example, that the Japanese government should stop subsidizing the production of cars—a product in which Japan did not have a competitive edge—and reallocate the resources tied up in their production to labour-intensive industry, where Japan did have a comparative advantage. These criticisms were, however, ignored and heavy industrialization continued to be promoted. In retrospect, this was a wise decision, for which the government should be given credit.

This does not imply, however, that heavy industrialization can be promoted in complete disregard of factor proportion. After the Second World War, many developing countries pursued an import-substitution policy and began production of some heavy industrial goods, but the results were often dismal. In heavy industry, in particular, the rate of utilization of machinery was low because of the limited size of the domestic market, and consequently the costs of production tended to be high by international standards. In more recent years, industrial policy in developing countries has been re-evaluated; the immediate post-war enthusiasm for heavy industry seems to have dissipated considerably. But since a shift to heavy industry is essential at some stage of industrialization, and can be promoted by government measures, an industrial plan for developing countries cannot be discussed solely from the viewpoint of factor proportion. The Japanese case suggests that a government can accelerate the move towards heavy industry by taking protective measures, but the success of government inter-vention requires a relatively competent and goal-oriented bureaucracy and a dynamic private sector. Government intervention can harm the economy if it leads to corruption or if the protected industry does not mature.

## The Impact of Trade on Development

There are two opposing views on the relationship between trade and development. The first view is that trade is 'a handmaiden of growth'.[6] The opposing view is that trade is 'an engine of growth'.[7] When the relationship is examined in the Japanese context, it is difficult to subscribe to the first view. Undoubtedly, trade increase was partly a result of economic growth, but to deny it any active role in Japanese economic growth is misleading.

How does trade promote economic growth? According to the theory of international trade, trade increases the income of a participating country by making it possible to exchange goods whose production cost is comparatively low for goods whose cost is comparatively high. This can be better explained by using a diagram. In Figure 2, the curve passing through points D, A, and B is the production possibility curve. This shows various combinations of primary and manufactured goods which can be produced with the available quantity of inputs. Curves $U_1$ and $U_2$ are social indifference curves, which can be interpreted as representing the standard of living.

Before trade begins, the combination of primary and manufactured goods, represented by point A, is produced, and $U_1$, the highest living standard which can be attained given the production possibility curve, is reached. When the country is brought into contact with the world economy, the production combination moves

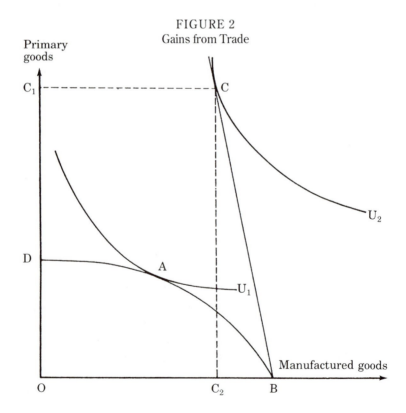

FIGURE 2
Gains from Trade

from A to B, reflecting the fact that it has a comparative advantage in manufactured goods. The international price ratio of the two goods is given, represented by the straight line passing through B and C. Adjusting to this new price ratio, the country now produces only manufactured goods, exports $BC_2$ units of manufactured goods, and imports $OC_1$ units of primary goods. The country consumes $OC_2$ units of manufactured goods and $OC_1$ units of primary goods and enjoys the $U_2$ standard of living. The difference between $U_2$ and $U_1$ is the gain from international trade.

If it is argued that Figure 2 depicts gains from trade accruing to Japan, a number of objections might be raised. In an actual situation, numerous products are traded; to compress them into only two types of goods is unrealistic. Since Japan is a net importer of primary goods and a net exporter of manufactured goods, however, the two-commodity classification can be considered to represent the net balance. Another objection might be that, since some imported goods can not be produced in Japan, it is necessary to treat them separately. Cotton, oil, and coffee, for example, are not produced in Japan. Yet, this does not mean that they cannot be produced in Japan; it is just too expensive to produce them.[8] Thus, it is not absolutely necessary to treat separately the imported goods which are not produced in Japan.

Finally, the objection might be raised that the difference between $U_1$ and $U_2$ can not be measured. It is possible, however, to get a feel of the size of the gap by determining the proportional increase of inputs needed to move from A to C in Figure 2. At this point, it is important to note that the gain from trade is not the ratio of trade to GNP. Today, the ratio of exports or imports to GNP in Japan is about 10 per cent, but this does not mean that if trade were to stop, GNP would decline by 10 per cent. In Figure 2, the ratio of exports to GNP is $BC_2$ divided by OB, but the gain from trade is the difference between $U_2$ and $U_1$, which can be quite large. If trade were to stop now in Japan, part of the productive resources would have to be moved back to primary production, a large part of industrial production would collapse, and the standard of living would decline substantially.

If the economy were to adjust to the international price ratio, a short-term gain would be reaped but, in the course of Japanese economic development, trade gains have accrued over a long period of time. In the Meiji era, specialization in silk and other goods in which Japan had a comparative advantage was handicapped by the existence of a large subsistence sector. The reallocation of

resources to such goods took place over a number of years as the
money economy spread further and the subsistence sector shrank
as a result of improvements in transport and communications.
After the Pacific War, the reallocation of resources away from
primary production was likewise gradual, proceeding as the
government lifted barriers on the import of primary products. One
important step in this direction was the government decision in the
late 1950s to liberalize the import of oil and to phase out coal
production which had hitherto occupied an important position in
the Japanese industrial strategy.[9]

Given the degree of the spread of the money economy, the
terms of trade represented by the slope of the price line in Figure 2
are important in influencing the size of the gain from trade. In
Figure 2, if the slope is steeper (that is, the terms of trade more
favourable), the gain is larger. If it is flatter (or the terms of trade
less favourable), the gain is smaller. When discussing the gain
from trade, therefore, it is important to investigate whether the
terms of trade became favourable or unfavourable over the course
of economic development.

G. Myrdal and R. Prebisch once argued that, with economic
growth, the terms of trade[10] deteriorated for primary producers,
widening the gap between developed and developing countries.[11] If
this is correct, Japan, which has been a net importer of primary
products, should have gained from trade. There is, however, no
empirical evidence of this. As shown in Table 3 earlier, there were
periods in which the terms of trade improved: from the mid-1870s
to the early 1900s they improved by about 30 per cent, and from
the late 1940s to the early 1960s by about 20 per cent. These gains
were offset by the unfavourable trend from the early 1900s to the
mid-1930s, and for a decade after the oil crisis of the early 1970s,
there was a sharp deterioration. In the early 1980s, Japan had to
export twice as much as it did about a century earlier in order to
import the same quantity of goods. In the following years, however, the terms of trade improved with the decline of oil and other
commodity prices. In the years 1988–91, they were back to the
level of the mid-1970s, after the first oil shock, but before the
second one.

The increase of the living standard from $U_1$ to $U_2$ in Figure 2 is a
once-only gain but, when part of the gain is saved, it has dynamic
implications. Behind the production possibility curve in Figure 2 is
the assumption that the quantity of inputs is fixed. However, if part
of the income gain is saved, capital accumulation takes place, and

the production possibility curve is pushed outwards. This creates a new trade gain in the next period.

The dynamic effects of trade are not confined to this capital accumulation effect. A production point—a set of primary and manufactured goods produced in Figure 2—may be pushed outwards to the frontier of the production possibility curve or the curve itself may be pushed outwards by the indirect effects of trade.[12] The first indirect effect occurs when trade improves efficiency by fostering competition and keeping in check potentially inefficient oligopolies; in this case, a production point is pushed outwards to the frontier of the production possibility curve. It is well known that many manufacturing industries in Japan today are oligopolies. In fact, it is difficult to produce an example of an industry in Japan in which many firms compete. Examples of oligopolies, on the other hand, are abundant: the motor car industry, shipbuilding, the manufacture of steel, colour televisions, and aluminium are all oligopolies. Because of the lack of domestic competition, oligopolies are often considered inefficient. When, however, they are subject to international competition, many of the causes of inefficiency are removed. One might even argue that, under free trade, oligopolies are more conducive to technological innovations and they therefore improve efficiency. It is quite conceivable that, because of the competition Japanese oligopolies faced in both export and domestic markets in the years after the Pacific War, and especially after the 1960s when heavy industrial products became important exports, they were more receptive to new ideas to reduce production costs or increase sales.

Trade also contributes to technological progress by making it possible to import machinery and equipment which incorporate the most recent technology; in this case, the production possibility curve is shifted outwards. In the early phase of industrialization, the import of spindles from Britain enabled Japan to catch up with advanced technology and subsequently to outstrip Britain in the Asian market. Later, precision machinery, chemical machinery, electronic products such as semiconductors and computers, and many other new products were imported.

The import of machinery and equipment is not the only way to introduce technical knowledge from abroad. So-called 'disembodied' knowledge has been transferred from Western countries to Japan through international contact, and has, of course, been paid for by export proceeds.[13] Large numbers of Japanese have studied in the West. The rapid technological progress of air transport has made it possible for Japanese corporate executives to travel abroad frequently to assess new investment or technological opportunities themselves. The information network of Japanese trading companies, and to a certain extent banks, which was formed by linking overseas branches by telex and telephone and, more recently, fax and telephone, has also made the most recent information accessible without much delay. Patented knowledge has had to be bought, but it has usually been profitable to the recipient companies since, in some cases, the fees have been modest. For example, the fee charged by Bell Laboratories for the patent of the transistor was only $25,000. By using this knowledge, a small obscure company, set up in the immediate post-war years, Sony, succeeded in producing transistor radios and earned large profits by exporting them to the United States; this laid the foundation for its subsequent evolution into an electronic giant. In many cases, however, the fees were more substantial, for example, those for synthetic fibre (nylon and polyester) technology imported in the early 1950s. Even here, however, the costs were outweighed by the gains which arose from the tremendous growth of production and the export of synthetic fibre in the following years.

Another indirect effect of trade is psychological. (This effect also pushes the production possibility curve outwards by motivating people to work harder for a higher standard of living). Over a century ago, J. S. Mill wrote:

A people (at an early stage of industrial advancement) may be in a quiescent, indolent, uncultivated state, with all their tastes either fully satisfied or entirely undeveloped, and they may fail to put forth the whole of their productive energies for want of any sufficient object of desire. The opening of a foreign trade, by making them acquainted with new objects, or tempting them by the easier acquisition of things which they had not previously thought attainable, sometimes works a sort of industrial revolution in a country whose resources were previously underdeveloped for want of energy and ambition in the people: inducing those who were satisfied with scanty comforts and little work to work harder for the gratification of their new tastes, and even to save, and accumulate capital, for the still more complete satisfaction of those tastes at a future time.[14]

In modern terms, Mill is discussing here the demonstration effect: that is, when a backward people meet an advanced people, it induces them to improve their standard of living. In a way, this concept reflects the feeling of an observer from an advanced country if he were to live the miserable life of a backward people. If a backward people do not respond at all, the notion of the demonstration effect is a mere fantasy. In view of the importance of material motives in human behaviour, however, a complete absence of response is unlikely; the response may not be revolutionary, but it does often take place. In some countries, this response is muted or weak because government control distorts the reward system. Japan, through contact with the West, came to know of the high standard of living in the West, and was stimulated to achieve a similar standard. Otherwise, it is difficult to understand the presence in contemporary Japan of many goods and services, such as colour televisions, cars, stereophonic equipment, and golf, which originated in the West. Mill may have exaggerated the speed of response, but he was essentially right in claiming that contact with an advanced nation can stimulate economic development.

The puzzling question remains as to why, if trade made such a large contribution to Japanese economic development, it did not do the same for other developing countries.[15] Most developing countries that were brought into contact with the world market experienced a rise in exports. Yet, the export sector did not become the propelling force of development in many of these countries.

One possible explanation is that developing countries export primary products whose linkage effects tend to be weak. Japan, on the other hand, exported manufactured goods whose production bestowed a variety of benefits through linkage effects and the training of people. This argument, however, ignores the fact that Japan exported primary products (tea and silk) in the early phase of development.[16]

As a counter-argument, one might say that silk has greater linkage effects than most of the primary products that developing countries export today, but it is difficult to accept this as the major explanation for the difference in economic performance between Japan and many developing countries. As an illustration of this point, contrast Japan with Brazil. The forward linkages of coffee—a major product in Brazil—are weak, since the only production processes which coffee beans require are roasting and grinding. The forward linkage effects of silk are greater, since raw silk goes through the process of reeling, weaving, and needlework before it reaches the consumer. If the backward linkage is considered, however, the opposite conclusions are drawn: coffee requires fertilizer, whereas the basic input in the production of raw silk is the leaves of mulberry trees. Mulberry trees require some fertilizer, but there was little use of chemical fertilizer in the Meiji era, and thus, during that period, the linkage effect of the silk industry on the chemical industry was almost nil. Hence, after both forward and backward linkages are considered, it is not entirely clear which commodity had more beneficial effects on economic development.

Trade can be an engine of economic development if its volume can continue to increase. The maintenance of such an increase essentially depends on a country's ability to increase exports, which earn the foreign exchange necessary to increase imports. How then does a country continue to expand exports? A country cannot do this if it continues to depend on one or a few exports, for competitors are bound to appear and technological changes in the importing countries tend to reduce the demand for such exports. The country which cannot shift to new exports is bound to suffer from deterioration in the terms of trade or from the decline in demand. What is important is to develop one export after another in the 'flying-geese' pattern—the pattern shown in Figure 1. The first major export in Japan was silk. After the invention of nylon reduced the demand for silk, textiles became the main export. After textiles came steel, and after steel, motor cars. In the past decade or so, the videotape recorder, semiconductor, and personal computer have joined the list of major exports.

Japan had to move on to a new product partly because, as in the case of silk, a substitute (nylon) emerged. But, in the case of the shift from textiles to steel, as well as subsequent shifts, a more important reason was that the country could not increase exports with the same product; in fact, it faced the possibility of a decline in demand because, with a rising level of wages brought about by economic growth, the same product was no longer competitive. The only way to keep expanding exports was to shift to more value-added products whose income elasticity was higher and whose supply elasticity was lower. Trade became an engine of economic development in Japan because the country had the ability to shift to new products (which faced less competition) as income rose.

Why was Japan able to develop one export after another? It is not simply a question of international trade. To understand why, consider the following contrast. When nylon was invented, it affected adversely not only Japanese silk but also abaca in the Philippines, which was used for making rope and twine. The immediate effect of nylon was a severe blow to both countries, but the long-term effects differed. Japan absorbed the technology of nylon and other new synthetic fibres and, in the early 1960s, began exporting them. The Philippines was, on the other hand, purely a recipient of this technology and did not commence production of synthetic fibres until the mid-1970s. Even then, production was on a small scale, and was assisted by foreign capital. To understand the difference in response between Japan and the Philippines, one must know the dynamic forces which operated differentially on the two countries.

One major difference between Japan and the Philippines, or any typical developing country which has failed to make trade an engine of development, can be seen in technological capability. Japan could shift to more value-added manufactured products because it had been building the technological base for this. A developing country is often weak in technology. Large, dynamic companies may be found in the field of plantation agriculture, mining, real estate, finance, and service industry, but those in manufacturing are heavily dependent on foreign technology. Car manufacturers are, for example, 'compradore' capitalists—if they are not wholly owned foreign subsidiaries or joint ventures—assembling cars for the domestic market under licence from foreign, now usually Japanese, car makers. Even in such simple industries as textiles, in many developing countries a plant layout is executed by a foreign engineering company, and the ability to independently repair textile machinery is low. Though factories are set up and machine-based production is undertaken on a large scale, industrialization is often ersatz because the technological base to match it is shallow.[17]

In contrast, technology has always been an exceedingly important part of Japanese industrialization. In the pre-war period, this was partly because of the need to build up the armaments industry to strengthen the country's military capability. Japan could not continue to rely on foreign weapons suppliers if it wanted to acquire an independent strike force. To this end, emphasis was put on science and technology education in universities—in contrast to many developing countries where tertiary education tends to be weak in these subjects. In the post-war period, although military require-ments were no longer an important consideration, pre-war experiences with industrialization taught the Japanese that industrialization was synonymous with technology. Since the former was indispensable for economic development, a great deal of emphasis was naturally placed on the latter. Many of the best and the brightest students of high schools were channelled to the science and technology streams in universities and later employed by emerging companies. For example, companies which were founded by technicians as small companies, such as Honda and Matsushita, became successful in the post-war period, not so much because their founders were technically capable but because they could hire the best people graduating from science and engineering faculties.

Technology does not, of course, explain everything. There are numerous other factors to consider in understanding Japan's ability to generate new exports, such as the incentive system in corporations, the investment climate, and government policy, but what makes it particularly difficult for developing countries to replicate the Japanese experience is their weakness in technology. Other factors are also difficult—in varying degrees—to replicate, but technology is the most serious obstacle. Therefore, even very dynamic developing countries today, such as Thailand, still rely on foreign investment as the quickest solution for their technological insufficiency, although this is clearly not a long-term solution. In this way, they have generated new exports and recorded growth of several per cent per annum.

1. Important among these political factors was the shogunate's interference in export activities as well as the anti-foreign sentiments harboured by many discontented samurai who sometimes resorted to terrorism against Japanese merchants undertaking foreign trade.

2. Akamatsu Kaname discusses international trade from the viewpoint of complementarity and substitution. See *Sekai Keizai-ron* [Discourse on the World Economy], Tokyo, Kunimoto Shobo, 1965, Chapter 7.

3. The factor proportion is the ratio of one factor of production to another. In the present context, it is the ratio of capital to labour.

4. For more detailed discussion on the three trade models, consult a standard textbook on international trade, such as R. Jones and R. Caves, *World Trade and Payments: An Introduction*, Glenview, Scott, Foresman & Co., 1985.

5. Kanamori Hisao, *Nihon no Boeki* [Japanese Trade], Tokyo, Shiseido, 1961, pp. 145–6.

6. I. B. Kravis, 'Trade as a Handmaiden of Growth: Similarities between the Nineteenth and Twentieth Centuries', *Economic Journal*, December 1970, and H. G. Johnson, *Economic Policies Toward Less Developed Countries*, Washington, Brookings Institution, 1967, p. 65.

7. Denis Robertson, *Essays in Monetary Theory*, St. Albans, Staples Press, 1948, p. 214.

8. During the Tokugawa period, cotton was grown in Japan. Some oil is produced today, although the quantity is minuscule compared with the quantity consumed. In this case, it may be better to consider that oil can be replaced with coal, with which Japan is more favourably endowed. Coffee can be grown in a

greenhouse, if necessary, or tea can be considered a substitute.

9. The relatively early switch from coal to oil was an important factor for rapid economic growth in the 1960s and early 1970s. Contrast this with Britain, where the switch could not be made easily because of the existence of a powerful trade union of coal-miners.

10. The terms of trade are defined as the ratio of export prices to import prices.

11. R. Prebisch, *Towards a New Trade Policy for Development*, New York, United Nations, 1964, and G. Myrdal, *International Economy*, New York, Harper and Row, 1956.

12. The indirect effects of trade were first discussed by J. S. Mill in his *Principles of Political Economy*, London, Longman, Green and Co., 1923, Book III, Chapter XVII.

13. 'Disembodied' knowledge is knowledge which is not incorporated in any product, such as a machine. If broadly defined, it includes the knowledge which appears in technical and science textbooks and which can be absorbed by schooling. The articles which appear in technical and scientific journals and the papers which are presented in professional meetings constitute the second group of 'disembodied' knowledge. However, in most economic discussions, it is more narrowly defined, and patents and proprietary knowledge are its typical examples.

14. Mill, *Principles of Political Economy*, p. 481.

15. For further discussion of why trade did not lead to development in many developing countries, see G. Meier, *Leading Issues in Economic Development*, 4th edn., New York, Oxford University Press, 1984, pp. 503–9.

16. As explained earlier, silk is here considered a primary product since raw silk was produced by farm households.

17. See Yoshihara Kunio, *The Rise of Ersatz Capitalism in South-East Asia*, Singapore, Oxford University Press, 1988, Chapter 5.

# 4
# Preparedness for Economic Development

To most Western observers who arrived in Asia in the mid-nineteenth century, Japan appeared to be as backward as any other Asian country. Yet, in the next half-century, Japan alone emerged as a modern state. What set it apart from the other Asian countries? This chapter looks at the Japan of the 1850s, and contrasts its preparedness for modernization with that of other countries in the region.

## Colonization Versus Independence

It is sometimes argued that Japan's success at modernization was due solely to the fact that the country was not colonized by the Western Powers, as other Asian countries were. Contrasting Japan with India, Paul Baran, a Marxist economist, contends that Japan developed because it was independent, while India remained backward because of exploitation by the British during the colonial period.[1] Clifford Geertz, an American anthropologist, claims that Japan was similar to Java in many respects in the mid-nineteenth century: both were heavily populated, both were engaged in labour-intensive rice cultivation, and both had roughly the same rice yield per hectare. In attempting to account for the difference in economic performance between the two countries in the following century, Geertz suggests that agricultural surpluses in Java were siphoned off to the mother country, the Netherlands, and were not used, as in Japan, for capital accumulation and technological progress.[2]

Why then was Japan not colonized in the mid-nineteenth century? Baran's answer is that Japan was simply lucky. It was not only poor in resources, but unattractive as a market, so that the Western Powers were not interested in it. Moreover, Britain, the major imperial power at that time, was busy elsewhere, and could not devote much attention to Japan. Although other Western Powers, France in particular, were looking for opportunities to establish colonies in Asia, rivalry among them worked in Japan's favour. In short, according to Baran, the fact that Japan was not colonized was an accident of history.

As will be argued shortly, Japan was not as vulnerable to Western Powers as Baran claims, but it would also not be true to say that there was no element of luck involved in Japan's transition to a modern nation. In the 1850s, when Commodore Matthew C. Perry forced open Japan's doors, there was no clear indication that Japan would emerge as a modern state a few decades later. Various negative scenarios can be conceived for this period. For example, if the last shogun had not come from Mito, the home of a pro-imperial school of history, he might have accepted the offer of help from the French and decided to fight the military challenge of the Royalists to the end. Moreover, there were groups who were opposed to the new government. Some pro-Tokugawa daimyos fought against the new Meiji government, despite the shogunate's decision to surrender. Secondly, many conservative samurai became disillusioned with the new government's modernization measures. If these two opposition groups had been better organized, large-scale civil war might have ensued, and Japan's modernization could have been considerably delayed. Clearly, the future course of events was uncertain and there were elements of 'luck' in Japan's success in its transition to a modern state, but for reasons different from those Baran suggests.

Baran emphasizes external factors while paying too little attention to internal factors. It is true that if Britain or France, without interference from other Western Powers, had been able to pursue a policy of colonizing Japan, Japan might have found it difficult to fend them off, but given the course of events in the following few decades, it is unlikely that Japan would ever have become a colony. What made the Japanese experience unique was its cultural, social, political, and economic preparedness for modernization as well as its ability to create a new system required by modernization. Another Asian country, Thailand, remained independent, and it is often suggested that Britain and France's desire to create a buffer zone between their spheres of influence in the region allowed Thailand to remain so. Such an external factor was possibly important in the Thai case, but much less so in the Japanese case.

Many observers have blamed colonial policy for the underdevelopment of South and South-East Asia but, before one accepts this view, it is necessary to question the extent to which political independence is a guarantee of economic development. A comparison between Thailand and Burma (now Myanmar) is both useful and appropriate in this regard. These countries share the same religion, racial characteristics, and climate, and they are similar in many other respects. According to the view that political independence promotes economic development while colonialism suppresses it, the level of economic development should be higher in Thailand than in Burma, since Thailand was spared the colonial experience, while Burma was a British colony from the 1870s to the 1940s. Indeed, the Thai economy is more developed today than the Burmese economy. In 1991, per capita GNP was about $1,600 for Thailand while it was only $600 for Burma. (Since the Burmese currency seems to be overvalued, Burma's per capita GNP in dollars may be overestimated.) Undoubtedly, the course of events after independence in Burma was affected by the fact that British colonialism changed Burma's institutions to suit its purposes and unleashed negative nationalist reactions. But Thailand today is far from being a developed country. About a quarter of its population are still suffering from poverty, and there is a long way to go before people are able to enjoy the average standard of living prevailing in industrial countries. This shows that political independence is far from being a sufficient condition for economic development; other factors must be involved.

## Contrast with Thailand

Since neither Japan nor Thailand has been colonized, political independence cannot be a factor in their differing economic performance. A comparison of these two countries will clarify the internal factors which differentiated them and influenced the course of economic development in each. First, the difference in their development was not due to belated attempts at modernization in Thailand. King Chulalongkorn (Rama V) who ruled Thailand during the same time as the Meiji era was also convinced of the need to modernize. He undertook a number of institutional reforms, including the emancipation of 'slaves', the establishment of a secular educational system, the construction of railways, the institution of a postal service, the reform of the laws and the court system, and the creation of a public health service, and his reign is widely regarded as one of the greatest and most enlightened in Thai dynastic history.

Thai attempts at modernization did not stop with his death. Two of Chulalongkorn's sons who became king (Rama VI and Rama VII) continued their father's modernization policy. And after the period of absolute monarchy came to an end in 1932, the commoner prime ministers, who were drawn mostly from the military, carried on a policy of modernization. For example, Field Marshal Phibul Songkram, who became prime minister twice during the period 1938–57, undertook a number of measures to inspire nationalism among the Thai people and to push economic development under state initiative. General Sarit Thanarat, who succeeded Phibul, reversed his predecessor's policy to develop the country with state capital, relying instead on the private sector, including Chinese and foreign capital, for economic development. This policy has been basically followed by every prime minister since.

That Thailand has not yet succeeded in achieving full economic development does not mean that no major economic changes have occurred within the country. Modern physical structures such as office buildings, condominiums, airports, telephone and television networks, and highways have been built, and although the capital city Bangkok benefits from them out of proportion to the rest of the country, they are not confined there; they are also found in regional cities. Communications and transportation connections between regional cities and other cities, for example, Bangkok, have also improved considerably.

Furthermore, the economic structure of the country has not remained traditional. Before the Pacific War, in most other South-East Asian countries, the indigenous people continued to be largely involved with subsistence agriculture, leaving the cultivation of export crops to foreign capital. The Thai peasants, however, began the commercial production of rice and made it the country's main export. After the war, the market economy spread further with the improvement of infrastructure, especially the communications and highway systems, and distant places in north and north-eastern Thailand were brought into the commercial network centring on Bangkok. Furthermore, Thai entrepreneurs set up a number of factories and began producing many manufactured goods which were previously imported. Today, the country's major export is not agricultural products, nor is it such labour-intensive products as textiles; it is electronic and electrical products.

These changes, however, did not lead to the elimination of poverty or to any substantive improvement in the life of most of the Thai population. Only a small percentage of the population can today enjoy the standard of living of the average Japanese: the majority are poorly educated and eke out a living by earning wages not much higher than subsistence level.

The difference in economic performance between the two countries in the last few decades was not due to a difference in income at the initial stage of development, either, for as shown in Table 2, Japan's level of income in the mid-nineteenth century was close to subsistence, and in this regard, Japan was just as backward as Thailand. However, Japan had a greater capacity for internal change, perhaps as the result of institutional developments during the Tokugawa period. These developments included the strengthening of social control, the growth of education, an improvement in administration, and commercialization.

## Social Control

The American anthropologist John Embree, in a comparative study of Japan and Thailand, concludes that Thailand is a loosely structured society.[3] To support this contention, he gives a number of examples showing the individualistic nature of Thai behaviour and the lack of group discipline. Since it is not clear, however, how representative such examples are, and most of them are subject to different interpretations, Embree's thesis is not fully acceptable.[4] In contrast with Thai society, however, Japanese society appears to be more tightly structured, a recurrent theme in a number of studies.[5] This characteristic of Japanese society originated in the Tokugawa period.

In Tokugawa Japan, there was a complicated code of behaviour structured according to sex, age, generation, and status. In order to be accepted in society, an individual had to know which parts of the code applied to him and had to carefully observe them. The code of behaviour included a proper use of words of respect, a knowledge of how low one should bow, and even of when and how to smile or laugh. Tokugawa society imposed many obligations on people. The obligations of a son to his father, a wife to her husband, a retainer to his lord, an employee to his master, a patriarch to his household (*ie*), and a household to a village were all clearly defined and highly binding. In order to fulfil these obligations, personal interests were often sacrificed. For example, children accepted the marriage partner chosen by their father (marriage was a matter between households, not a matter of love); children who left home for employment sent remittances to their family over a long period; in cases of dire economic need, a daughter was sold by her father for the sake of the household; and retainers sacrificed themselves and their families in avenging their lord's death. If obligations were not observed, sanctions were often swift and severe. A recalcitrant son was disowned (*kando*); a selfish villager was ostracized (*mura hachibu*); and a commoner who behaved improperly towards the samurai could be cut down (*kirisute gomen*).

In a Tokugawa village, much work was co-operative, such as *mura shigoto* (work for the village). In this type of work, villagers worked together for the maintenance of public property, such as irrigation channels, roads, bridges, and common land, and also for the protection of the village from fire and theft. People shared in the preparation for village festivals. Another category of co-operative work was *tetsudai* (mutual help), which was extended to neighbours at such times as a funeral or marriage. Also, when a house was built or a roof renewed, neighbours helped each other. In the cycle of agricultural work, transplanting and harvesting were the busiest times: neighbours also helped each other on these occasions. This co-operation was called *yui*.

Co-operative work in a Tokugawa village was made easier by the existence of a well-defined and stable social hierarchy. In a typical village, the number of households remained much the same for generations, as did their relative social positions, because the wealth of a household was not subject to much change. The rule of primogeniture prevented the division of the wealth of a household, and feudal restrictions on land transfer minimized the fluctuation of family fortunes. The stable social stratification which resulted from these institutional factors meant that villagers knew from childhood where they belonged and what was expected of them. The landlord was born as a landlord, and from his childhood was expected to be the leader of the village. The tenant was born to be a tenant, and was expected to be subservient to the landlord. The owner-cultivator was more independent than the tenant, but, commanding less wealth than the landlord and needing his help from time to time, occupied the second stratum of the hierarchy.

In contrast with the Thai people, the Japanese people were thus more constrained by obligations, better disciplined, more accustomed to vertical relations, and less individualistic or more group-oriented. This social tradition has obviously been of benefit to Japan in its path towards modernization. For example, business organizations were able to utilize the ability of Japanese to work in a group although it is also true that some new values were required, such as meritocracy as a criterion for the hiring and promotion of staff. At the same time, modernization required what are often regarded as pre-modern values: submission to authority, discipline, *esprit de corps*, and mutual co-operation. The Japanese management method, which has demonstrated its strength to the world, is a peculiar blend of tradition and modernity. Without the social tradition of the Tokugawa period, the Japanese management method would be substantially different from what it is today. In contrast, the individualistic nature of Thai society has deprived Thai business organizations of the opportunity to make up for their deficiencies, in capital, for example, with a tribal sort of group cohesion which characterizes many Japanese business organizations.

## *Education*

Late Tokugawa Japan was a fairly literate society, as may be noted from the following description of the literary culture in that period:

It [Japan in the late Tokugawa period] was a world in which books abounded. Their production gave employment to several thousands in the official school presses and in the free enterprise publishing houses which sold their wares to the public. Works of scholarship now accounted for only a small part of the total output. There were story books, pornographic books, travel guides, novels, poems, collections of sermons; and they were bought, or borrowed at so much a day from book peddlers, not simply by the samurai, but also, or even chiefly, by members of the other classes.[6]

In spreading education to the masses, temples played an important role in both Thailand and Japan.[7] In Thailand, many children went to temples where their training included tuition in reading and writing. Later, in setting up a school system, King Chulalongkorn built upon this foundation. In Japan, also, education was once the monopoly of the priests: their importance in spreading education can be surmised from the fact that the private schools for children of the lower classes were called 'temple schools' (*terakoya*).

In Japan, however, most 'temple schools' had ceased to be religious institutions by the end of the Tokugawa period. Most became private schools run by unemployed samurai and other non-priests, and parents sent their children to these schools solely for secular education. Even where priests taught children in the temples, the purpose was primarily to provide basic education. In

Thailand, however, children went to temples primarily to learn the Buddhist way of life, and secular education was an informal and unsystematic part of their tuition.

The centre of education in Tokugawa Japan moved away from Buddhism with the rise of Confucianism in the early seventeenth century. This change brought about not only a decline in the importance of temples as teaching institutions, but also a diversity of scholarship. In the mid-nineteenth century, the educated élite in Thailand were mostly Buddhist priests, but in Japan it was the Confucian scholars who replaced the Buddhist priests as the intellectual leaders. The rise of Confucianism seems to have had positive effects on Japan's modernization, because Confucianism is more worldly and more logical in its teaching than Buddhism.

A large part of Confucianism is concerned with morality, offering guidelines for human conduct. Since this aspect of Confucianism was regarded as useful for maintaining social and political stability, it was given official patronage during the early Tokugawa period, which led to its spread. Confucianism is, however, more than a set of moral codes: it explains the structure and order of the world. The Chu-shi version of Confucianism (neo-Confucianism), which was the official doctrine of the Tokugawa shogunate and many *han* (provincial) governments, contained a number of logical philosophical constructs. Neo-Confucianism thus instilled a great deal of rationalism into Japanese scholarship.

Confucianism was not, however, the only teaching which spread in the Tokugawa period. *Jitsugaku* (practical learning), which included agronomy, surveying, mathematics, medicine, astronomy, and natural history, developed with utility or usefulness as the guiding principle. One of the most outstanding *jitsugaku* scholars around 1700 was Seki Kowa, whose mathematics is often compared to the calculus developed by Newton and Leibnitz. In general, however, Japan lagged greatly behind the West in technical fields. Thus, after the study of Western science—called *rangaku* (Dutch learning)—was officially approved in the early eighteenth century, *jitsugaku* progressed rapidly. In the first few decades, *rangaku* concentrated on medicine but, in the early nineteenth century, it branched out into other scientific fields, such as astronomy, surveying, physics, chemistry, metallurgy, navigation, tactics, and artillery. Western books were translated and expository books were written. In some fields, practical results were obtained. The most outstanding example of this is Ino Tadataka's map of Japan, completed in 1821.

Because of this earlier educational progress, Japanese intellectuals were equipped with some knowledge of Western science and technology in the mid-nineteenth century when Japan began to modernize. The fact that the decentralized political system of the Tokugawa shogunate created various regional cities—the headquarters of *han* governments—and that the educated class—mostly the samurai—were there, made it easier to spread compulsory education throughout Japan in the modern period. This, in turn, eased the task of the government in encouraging people to accept and work for modernization goals, for economic progress in the Meiji era greatly depended on the response of a large numberof people in various parts of the country to the new economic opportunities created by Meiji reforms. Such response would not have been forthcoming without the spread of education.

In mid-nineteenth century Thailand, however, scholarship concentrated on Buddhist teachings to the detriment of scientific studies. When, for example, cholera spread across the country, it was common practice to resort to magical rituals to propitiate the gods rather than to any scientific explanation or remedy.[8] Although Thai educational (and cultural) tradition was later to become an asset, especially in comparison with other developing countries which lack such a tradition, compared to Japanese tradition it was weak. For example, the literary tradition in the bureaucracy was largely confined to a small number of people who were directly assisting the king, and the small size of the educated class handicapped the modernization attempts of such progressive kings as Chulalongkorn. In the field of business, there was practically no educated class. The traders were almost exclusively immigrant Chinese with little formal education, who adhered to conservative business methods partly because of their limited intellectual horizon. Nor could they employ high school and university graduates to make up for their deficiencies as Japanese traders did, because secondary and tertiary education was slow in developing in Thailand. In the post-war period, there was substantial progress in education, but as the economy expanded even faster, the generally slow growth in education has continued to be a barrier to Thai economic progress.

## Administration

Western visitors to Japan in the mid-nineteenth century had difficulty, apparently, in understanding precisely who ruled the country; was it the emperor in Kyoto or the shogun in Edo? In

Tokugawa Japan, the emperor was, in theory, the ruler but, in practice, his was a nominal rule and he conferred the authority to govern the country on the shogun.

Similarly, the shogun did not rule the country directly. His fief extended through various parts of the country, comprising about a quarter of the land, with the rest divided into about 270 *han*, ruled by his vassals, the daimyos. The ultimate authority to rule the *han* resided in the shogun, though he rarely interfered in their internal affairs. In a sense, Tokugawa Japan consisted of some 270 autonomous states. However, in matters of security, coinage, foreign policy, and other national and inter-*han* affairs, the shogun exerted his authority. Also, in order to control the daimyos, a *sankin kotai* (hostage system) was instituted, which required the daimyos to live in Edo in alternate years.

In the *han*, as in the shogun's government, elaborate administrative systems were established. Marxist historians often quote the brutal remark attributed to the founder of the Tokugawa shogunate, Tokugawa Ieyasu, to the effect that peasants should be treated in such a way that they would 'neither live nor die', and thus tend to characterize the Tokugawa administrative system as highly exploitive. To what extent Ieyasu's dictum was put into practice is debatable, but without question the administrative machinery was pervasive and efficient enough to extract tribute from the peasants amounting to as much as 50 per cent of their crop. One strength of the system lay in the daimyos' ability to buy off wealthy peasants and to impose group responsibility on villagers; it was also important that the rulers formed the warrior class who could use physical force against anyone who questioned their authority. The submissive attitude of the Japanese in the modern period is closely linked with the supremacy of the warrior class which was established in the pre-modern period.

The effectiveness of the Tokugawa bureaucracy is demonstrated by the fact that it managed to govern a population of over 30 million for a period of approximately 250 years with little evidence of political breakdown. An important contributing factor for this was undoubtedly the strengthening of the civil bureaucracy. After peace was firmly established under the Tokugawa shogunate, the main role of the samurai changed from fighting to civil administration, which increased the importance of education for them. This was very different from the early seventeenth century when the samurai placed primary emphasis on martial arts at the expense of reading and writing. Their successors at the end of the

Tokugawa period, however, were literate and had a knowledge of history, philosophy, and politics. As the educational level of the samurai increased, government became more impersonal and legally defined.[9]

Yet, there were many problems inherent in the Tokugawa bureaucracy. For one, there were far too many samurai (the Meiji government reduced the number of officials to one-tenth of the number of samurai); for another, because of the importance attached to status, the application of meritocracy was limited. Thus, the Tokugawa bureaucracy could not be passed on *in toto* to the modern period. Nevertheless, the effectiveness of the Meiji bureaucracy owed a great deal to what it inherited from the Tokugawa period. The administrative expertise of the samurai constituted the backbone of the Meiji administration, and *han* administration provided a basis for the establishment of modern local administration. Without these legacies from the Tokugawa period, it would have been extremely difficult to carry out appropriate reforms and to maintain political discipline in the critical period of transition to a modern nation.

In contrast with Japan, Thailand in the mid-nineteenth century was a 'loosely governed' country. This is reflected, for example, in the low rate of taxation. In Japan, as explained earlier, the peasants paid about 50 per cent of their crop as taxes, and this was used to pay stipends to the samurai who constituted the military and civil administration. In Thailand, however, the government could not impose such high taxes, and, since it could not often pay salaries to officials, it was not uncommon for them to make a living out of their posts. Even during the modern period, when France and Britain were threatening its territory, the government had difficulties in raising the necessary revenue to create a professional army, buy modern weapons, or improve the means of communication and transportation for defence purposes.[10] Investment in infrastructure, education, and other developmental tasks, being less pressing issues, faced even greater financial problems. One problem for the Thai government was that since the man–land ratio was low, the government could not tax people too heavily. At the same time, the taxing ability of the government was greatly compromised by the poorly developed administration.

The main task Thailand had to tackle in the modern period was, therefore, the creation of a professional civil service. In the pre-modern period, there existed no hereditary administrative class like the samurai, nor was there an examination-based recruitment system as in China. Provincial administration was run by the governor with the help of his kin and allies. Many of these people were illiterate or incompetent and were thus unqualified to participate in modern administration. But to replace them with qualified people was not simple, because no educational institution existed to produce such people. Although King Chulalongkorn placed emphasis on education and improved the situation somewhat, the poor state of administration, especially local administration, which he inherited could not be changed overnight, and thus remained a handicap throughout his reign.

### Commercial Development

The Tokugawa economy was feudal, and shared several features with the early medieval economy of Europe. It is, therefore, tempting to generalize that it was basically a subsistence economy and that any trade was largely barter trade, rarely involving the use of money. A close look at the Tokugawa economy reveals, however, that exchanges involving money and credit were considerable. In the period, the main form of money was coins minted by the Tokugawa shogunate. The *han* governments also issued paper money for circulation within their domains, largely to raise additional revenue. How much money was in circulation in this period is not known exactly, but that it was not a negligible amount can be seen from the following data on coins. In 1869, the second year of the Meiji era, gold coins worth 87.9 million yen, silver coins worth about 52.7 million yen, and other coins worth 6.0 million yen were in circulation.[11]

The use of credit was also widespread, especially in the major cities. According to an Osaka merchant at the end of the Tokugawa period, almost 99 per cent of all transactions among Osaka merchants used credit instruments, with cash payments being rare. This is probably an exaggeration, but the use of credit instruments was undoubtedly common among Osaka merchants. In other major cities, the use of credit may have been more limited, but transactions on credit were undoubtedly a familiar practice.

The credit instrument most frequently used among Osaka merchants was probably *shiroto tegata*—a note used in commodity or loan transactions as a promise to pay in the future. The value of these notes varied, and those who accepted them ranged from grand restaurants to wholesale fish merchants. But they shared a common characteristic: the payer was the person who wrote the note. Other common credit instruments of the period, such as *otegata*, *furidashi tegata*, and *azukari tegata*, all had a financial institution, such as a *ryogaeya*, as payer.

A bill of exchange was an important credit instrument which was used to collect payment for goods sold to distant places. When a local merchant shipped a commodity to an Osaka merchant and was not paid in advance, he usually drew a draft on the Osaka merchant and sold it to a local *ryogaeya*. He then sent the draft to a *ryogaeya* in Osaka with whom he had regular transactions, in order to collect payment from the Osaka merchant. The Osaka *ryogaeya* collected the amount and credited it to the account of the local *ryogaeya*. Bills of exchange were frequently used during the Tokugawa period because, as explained below, the *sankin kotai* necessitated interregional trade.

At the centre of credit transactions were the *ryogaeya*. They were originally money-changers. The Tokugawa shogunate issued three denominations of gold coins (*koban*, *ichibuban*, and *isshukin*). The services of money-changers were needed to convert one denomination to another. In addition to gold coins, the shogunate issued silver and copper coins. In the case of gold coins, there was no serious complication in conversion since the relative values of the three denominations remained the same throughout the period (1 *ryo* was equal to 4 *bu* and to 16 *shu*), but the exchange rates between gold, silver, and copper coins fluctuated, and this fluctuation introduced the element of risk in money-changing and made it a sophisticated business.

Money-changing was not, however, the only function of the *ryogaeya*. Over time, they came to perform various banking functions: for example, they accepted deposits, lent money, and issued drafts. Some large *ryogaeya*, especially in Osaka, even 'created money'. In issuing deposit certificates and accepting demand deposits, they were initially cautious and held a reserve fund of approximately 100 per cent. But some certificates always remained in circulation and some demand deposits were left unused. Therefore, in order to make the best use of the reserve and obtain more interest income through more loans, *ryogaeya* began giving loans by issuing more certificates, which thus reduced the reserve ratio. As long as people's confidence in the *ryogaeya* continued, a reserve ratio of less than 100 per cent was safe, and the reduced ratio made it possible to increase money in the form of certificates and demand deposits.

The economic philosophy of the Tokugawa period placed emphasis on agriculture as the major source of wealth, and thus the peasants were given the highest theoretical status among commoners. In contrast, commerce was considered unproductive and merchants supposedly occupied the lowest position in society. Ironically, however, commerce increased in importance during the Tokugawa period and merchants became enormously influential. (A similar rise in commerce took place in Western Europe in the late Middle Ages.)

In Tokugawa Japan, the rise of a money economy was influenced by two factors in particular. First, all samurai were required to live in a castle town, the headquarters of the *han* administration. Removed from agriculture, they became *rentiers*, who needed the help of merchants to exchange part of their rice stipends for daily necessities. The other factor was the *sankin kotai* mentioned above. Because this system required the daimyos to travel between their domains and Edo, and to live in Edo in alternate years, it contributed to the development of interregional transactions. Rice and other commodities in demand outside the domains had to be produced and sold for hard currency, and this could be used to finance the necessities which arose from the system. The development of coastal shipping, post-station towns, and financial and commercial institutions owed a great deal to this system.

It is often remarked that commerce was not an important part of the Tokugawa heritage since established merchants neither played a leading role in the Meiji Restoration nor became the industrializing élite of the modern period. Undoubtedly, they were tied to feudal interests in various ways, and cannot be compared to the bourgeoisie in the West who were the vanguard of economic, social, and political changes. But the commercial institutions they created were a positive factor for business development after the Meiji Restoration. The widespread use of credit instruments, the development of *ryogaeya* as banking institutions, the Shingaku movement which encouraged frugality and diligence,[12] the separation of management from ownership, and the accumulation of capital in such large merchant houses as Mitsui, Sumitomo, and Konoike[13] were parts of the Tokugawa heritage which were indispensable for the development of modern business after the Meiji Restoration.

Thailand in the mid-nineteenth century was not entirely a subsistence economy; it had a trading sector in Bangkok, and minted its own silver coins. However, the money economy in Thailand was much less developed than in Japan. One reason was that the urban population, which depended on traders for the supply of daily necessities, was smaller in Thailand—it was between 8 and 10 per cent of the total population,[14] whereas in Japan, the proportion was about twice as large. Another reason was that, because of the decentralized political system, Japanese cities were more widely scattered, and so the geographic spread of the trading network was much more extensive.

One other difference from the Japanese experience was that practically all traders in Thailand were foreigners. Internal trade was dominated by the Chinese. In pre-modern societies, it was not unusual for foreign minorities to dominate the trading sector; therefore, Thailand was not an exception, but it should be remembered that the Chinese population was fairly large: according to one estimate, they accounted for about 25 per cent of the total population in the mid-nineteenth century.[15] They were concentrated in Bangkok, giving it the appearance of a Chinese city. These Chinese traders were also important in foreign trade, especially with China, importing Chinese ceramics, medicine, and metal wares in exchange for rice and other Thai products, but in this field, Western merchants were also active. As for the indigenous Thai population, most were peasants living in the countryside. A small number in Bangkok were members of the nobility and government officials. There were practically no Thai traders. This separation of economic roles by ethnic group was a handicap for Thai business development, as a significant amount of capital was sent abroad as remittances. Since foreign traders did not want to make long-term commitments, such as industrial investments, the capital which remained in the country was used mostly as working capital in the trading sector.

## Contrast with China

When Japan's readiness for modernization in the mid-nineteenth century is compared with that of China, the distinctions are not as clear cut as those with Thailand. In fact, if Western observers arriving in East Asia in the mid-nineteenth century had been asked which country had the better chance of catching up with the West, most would probably have said China. China had greater experience in dealing with Westerners and appeared to face fewer obstacles in introducing new ideas and institutions from the West. Compared with the urbane and self-confident mandarin, the samurai seemed insular and xenophobic. In terms of social structure, also, it appeared that the Chinese social system was more flexible. Chinese society was less stratified, the merchant class less constrained by government regulations, and the high civil bureaucracy recruited on a merit basis. In addition, China's natural resources and size served to give it an advantage. Japan, on the other hand, was a small, overpopulated country, with few natural resources.[16]

But it was Japan, not China, which modernized and developed its economy in the following decades. Today, while China's living standard is barely above subsistence level, Japan's is one of the highest in the world. This is reflected in national income figures. In 1990, while China's per capita GNP was $370, Japan's was about $25,000, which was higher than that of most Western countries; only Switzerland and Finland had higher incomes than Japan.[17] Moreover, in the human development index of the United Nations, which, in addition to per capita income, takes into account life expectancy at birth, the adult literacy rate, and educational attainment, Japan ranks first.[18] In the social and political arenas, also, Japan is enjoying greater freedom than China; the latter is often accused of violating human rights.

Why has Japan performed better than China? One might argue that it is because China stagnated under central planning in the post-war period while Japan became a dynamic economy under capitalism. While it is true that under the leadership of Deng Xiaoping, China has been rapidly transforming itself into a market economy since the late 1970s, before that time the country relied heavily on central economic planning which stifled private initiative. As in other Communist states, the result of this economic system was a disaster. In the meanwhile, under capitalism, Japan transformed itself into the most dynamic economy in the world. There are, of course, a number of capitalist states whose economic records have not been good, so the economic system itself is not the only determinant of economic performance. It has been demonstrated by the events in the past, however, that capitalism—or the market economy—is a necessary condition for a dynamic economy or that a dynamic economy cannot be created under central planning. Thus, the different economic systems of the two countries can be regarded as a major reason for China lagging behind Japan in the post-war period.

Even in the pre-war period, Japan had a better record than China of modernization and economic development. While China was forced to give territorial concessions and commercial privileges to the Western Powers, Japan first protected itself from Western intrusion, and then went on to renegotiate the unequal treaties it had been forced to accept at the end of the Tokugawa period. In the Sino-Japanese War, Japan demonstrated a clear military superiority over China. Then, in the Russo-Japanese War, Japan defeated Russia and joined the league of imperial powers. In the following years, China became the major victim of Japanese imperialism. In the economic field, Japan transformed the economy and raised the living standard of the masses faster than China. In industrialization, while China did not progress beyond textiles, Japan developed steel, shipbuilding, aircraft, general machinery, and other technologically sophisticated industries. One might even argue that China became a Communist state as the result of the failure of modernization in that period.

Why did Japan achieve more than China? This can be best answered by looking at the situations in the two countries in the mid-nineteenth century. Around this time, the West renewed its interest in East Asia as a market for its products and as a supply source of the raw materials needed for its economy which had been expanding rapidly with the Industrial Revolution. The arrival of the West stimulated social changes in both China and Japan, but the results were different: Japan modernized its country and developed its economy; China was not very successful at either. Instead, the political situation became anarchic over time. The factors which favoured Japan in generating the social changes which led to modernization and economic development can be found in its social organization and historical traditions, as discussed below.

## Cultural Borrower

One factor favouring Japan in meeting the Western challenge was that it was historically a 'cultural borrower'. From the early centuries of the Christian era, China had been a source of knowledge for Japan, particularly through Chinese Buddhism and Confucianism. It can be argued that because Japan had been a cultural borrower, it had few inhibitions about borrowing from the West, especially in the field of science and technology where the West was clearly superior. Through 'Dutch learning' (as discussed in the previous section), Western medicine was introduced into Japan and attracted bright students. In the field of military technology, Western superiority was demonstrated in the skirmishes the samurai and Western gunships (and soldiers) engaged in. Western guns were far more powerful and had a longer range than what the samurai used, and the spiritualism of the samurai could do little to overcome the technological gap. As Western superiority became demonstrably clear in many areas, the West was accepted as a new source of knowledge and 'Western learning' became a major intellectual trend.

On the other hand, China was the 'central kingdom', having always been the source of civilization. Even in the scientific field, until only a few centuries earlier, China had had much to offer to the world. Such a centre of civilization may have found it difficult to evaluate objectively the recent scientific progress in the West. Undoubtedly, having seen China's defeat in the Opium War and other skirmishes with Western Powers, some Chinese leaders recognized Western superiority in the area of technology, military technology in particular, but being locked into the glorious tradition of the past, the Chinese mandarins in general, particularly those close to the emperor, regarded them as tactical defeats, not a threat to the imperial system as a whole. They did not take seriously enough the fact that the world had changed and that the 'Western barbarians' might have surpassed China in its level of civilization.

It is important to remember, however, that Japan was not a habitual cultural borrower without any identity of its own. By the mid-nineteenth century, the assimilation process was so complete that Japan had a unique culture which acted as an inner source of pride, counterbalancing whatever feelings of inferiority that might have accompanied heavy borrowing from those who had hitherto been regarded as 'hairy barbarians'. The phrase 'Western Science and Oriental Morality', which meant that the West excelled in science but was inferior to the Orient (Japan in particular) in culture, instilled a sense of pride in the Japanese who might otherwise have lost their cultural identification in the swirling process of modernization.

'Western Science and Oriental Morality' was also a means of preventing 'Western learning' from becoming a source of social instability. Especially in the first couple of decades of the Meiji era, admiration for the West was diffused, not confined to the area of science and technology. Although Western science and technology could be imported without greatly disturbing the social system the Meiji government was trying to build, Western values and institutions had, from the viewpoint of the Meiji government, undesirable implications for social stability. While it is true that the Meiji government was trying to promote the market economy and establish a freer social and political system, as argued in the previous section, the system it tried to create was not an egalitarian, democratic society. Thus, even to more liberal Meiji leaders, many

Western values and institutions were not welcome, particularly after the traditional Japanese philosophy surrounding Confucianism was re-established as the guiding socio-political ideology of the government. The Japanese intellectuals who learnt about Western egalitarianism and democracy were not supposed to promote these ideologies too much among their contemporaries if they did not want to be marginalized. Once the transition period was over, the majority of them accepted the official line and worked within the established socio-political system, instead of challenging it from outside. It is tempting to think that conformity was obtained by force—which cannot be denied totally, especially after the Maintenance of the Public Order Act was passed in the mid-1920s—but the main reason why many liberal, let alone revolutionary, ideas were kept out was the strength of the intellectual tradition in Japan. It was rich enough—from its pre mid-nineteenth century borrowings from China, their adaptation, and indigenous development—to absorb Western ideas largely on its own terms and to gradually transform itself into the kind of socio-political order which it felt comfortable with. This distinguishes Japan from many developing countries today which have been buffeted by various newfangled Western ideas and have undertaken social experiments which have not worked.

One might say that as an intellectual counterbalance to things Western, *kokutai*, the socio-political structure of the nation, was more important than 'Oriental morality' in the modern period. The word *kokutai* stood for the fundamental characteristics of the Japanese nation, which were derived from the central position the emperor occupied in society. This ideological counterbalance worked well because there was no irrational religious zeal driving it. In fact, there was a great deal of pragmatism in it; it was not, for instance, a barrier to the introduction of science and technology and new economic institutions which had to accompany it. But after Japan became moderately successful in modernization, the high nationalistic content in it brought about conflicts with Western Powers, and eventually led to the disastrous Pacific War.

## Family and Community

The family was a basic social unit in both China and Japan, but its relative importance differed in the two countries. In China, when family interests came into conflict with those of the community or other non-kinship organizations, family interests usually took precedence over non-family interests. In Japan, however, family interests were often sacrificed in the interests of a 'higher' organization.

The conflict of interests between loyalty and filial piety may be illustrated through the following questions: If a retainer could save his lord's son by sacrificing his own son, should he do so? If a father broke a law, should his son report it to the authorities? If a lord died through the deceit of his enemy, should his retainers avenge his death even if this meant that they would sacrifice themselves and their families?

In Japan, there are traditional stories which give an affirmative answer to the first and third questions (for example, the story of 'Sugawara Denju Tenarai Kagami' on the first question and 'The Tale of the Forty-Seven Ronin'[19] on the third). To the second question, a negative answer was more typical, especially in cases where the father's offence was not serious. If the father committed treason, the son faced a serious dilemma: in this case, the Japanese value system contained no definite guide to the son's behaviour. In China, however, in answer to the second question, filial piety took precedence over loyalty, possibly more than in Japan. For example, Confucius disapproved of the behaviour of a son who reported to the authorities that his father had stolen a sheep.[20] There seem to be fewer stories in China which favour the affirmative answer to the first and third questions. This is probably because the family was a more important foundation of society and filial piety was a more important moral principle in China than in Japan.[21]

The question of family interest as opposed to community interest is not entirely a matter of the precedence of filial piety over loyalty, or vice versa. Another dimension of the problem is to what extent the upper stratum of a community is devoted to its cause. A village can be taken as an example. In Japan, a village head took a number of actions which benefited the village but not his family directly. In some cases, he sacrificed his family for the sake of the village. In a year of poor harvest, for example, he represented the village in negotiations with the government on tax reduction, and when he was not successful by the usual means, he sometimes bypassed normal channels and appealed to the lord directly, for instance, by breaking into his procession, or, in extreme cases, by raising a rebellion. In taking such actions, he might succeed in obtaining a tax reduction, but he, and perhaps his family, were sometimes executed. This type of sacrificial act was rare in a Chinese village (see the next section on village structure).

The paramount importance of filial piety was a negative factor in

China's attempts to build a modern organization. The American scholar William Lockwood shows in the following example how nepotism handicapped the building of a modern nation in China:

[In the naval battle of the Yalu in 1894] the Japanese fleet was already a businesslike affair under Admiral Ito. The Chinese fleet was fairly well matched in ships. But its creator, the great viceroy Li Huang-chang, had characteristically staffed it with 'needy relatives and greedy henchmen'. Its commander was Li's fellow Anhui-ite, Admiral Ting Ju-chang. Its Ordnance Department was headed by the viceroy's son-in-law, Chang P'ei-lun. Now Admiral Ting happened to be an ex-cavalry general, gallant but incompetent. Worse than that, Chang was a champion swindler. His Ordnance Department even loaded shells with sand. When the shooting began, the Chinese fleet found that its total supply ammunition amounted to fourteen shells per gun. Two 7,000-ton ironclads had only three shells in all for their 10-inch guns. The outcome was predictable. The Chinese navy was put to rout, and soon the army too. That was even more of a paper dragon. Japan handily won the war, with all the inestimable advantages that followed in its wake.[22]

A second example of conflict between family and community interests is reflected in the question of business organization. One important reason for Japan's success in business is that merit was already an important criterion for recruitment and promotion in the early Meiji period. The rapid growth of the typical *zaibatsu* in Japan before the Pacific War, for example, Mitsui, Mitsubishi, and Sumitomo, illustrates this feature. Although these *zaibatsu* were family concerns, they recruited talented people, mostly non-kin, and gave them management responsibilities. The Mitsui and Sumitomo families, in fact, left management completely to their employees. Mitsubishi was established more recently, but the owners, the Iwasaki family, have also depended heavily on professional managers. Many established merchant houses in Tokugawa Japan trusted competent employees who had served them for many years and gave them management responsibilities. However, the merit system was not widely adopted by business enterprises from the very beginning of the modern period, and when it was adopted, there was an element of regionalism in it. For example, many merchant houses in Osaka recruited people from neighbouring areas. But over time, this regionalism weakened, and merit became an increasingly important criterion for hiring and promotion. But even in the beginning, compared with China, the merit system was much more accepted in Japanese business establishments. In China, to recruit non-kin as future managers was a rarity; business was more obviously a family affair.

*Village Structure*

The Chinese political leader, Sun Yat-sen, believed that the loose structure of Chinese society, which he called a heap of sand, was China's basic weakness.[23] The lack of co-operation in a village, which was divided into kinship groups, was indicative of this weakness. In Japan, during transplanting and harvesting—the busiest times in the cycle of rice production—villagers helped each other. If one offered more labour than he received, or received more labour than he offered, payment in kind redressed the balance. In China, however, if family labour was insufficient for a particular task and extra help was necessary, it was sought first from kin, and if this was not enough, workers were hired.

The weakness of Chinese village society, reflected in the lack of co-operation between villagers, occurred partly because landlords themselves were not actively involved in agriculture and, therefore, their ties with ordinary peasants were fragile. Undoubtedly, landlords could have integrated the villagers if their ties with them had been closer. However, many landlords were government officials who bought agricultural land with their savings— much of it derived from the bribes they received—in order to retire to the village. Others were wealthy merchants who bought agricultural land as an investment, and were therefore more interested in rent than in agricultural work. Yet other village landlords took up classical studies, perhaps in order to prepare for the examination for government service, and did not engage in any agricultural work.

Another reason for the weak social integration in Chinese villages was the division of wealth over several generations. In a Chinese family, daughters were not entitled to an inheritance apart from the dowries they took with them when they married. Sons, however, received roughly equal rights of inheritance, so that when a father died, the family fortune was split between them. Naturally, even large fortunes tended to fragment over a few generations. Because land was transferable in China, families with money could reverse the process of the division of wealth by buying lands from poor peasants or from those who wanted to leave the village. Land transferability and the inheritance system were thus instrumental in injecting an element of fluidity into the social stratification of Chinese villagers.

In contrast, a typical Japanese village in the Tokugawa period enjoyed better integration because there were no absentee landlords. The landlords themselves were actively involved in village affairs, and often took the initiative in introducing new agricultural crops and techniques. Being agricultural practitioners, they shared many interests with the ordinary peasants. There was also less fluidity in the social stratification of Japanese villages because of the right of primogeniture and the feudal restrictions on land sales. Because landlords were normally born into the families which had headed the village for generations, it was easier for them to assume a leadership role and to integrate the village.

Certain features of a typical Tokugawa village appear to have become a model for modern organizations in Japan. Although it may appear a little unusual to trace the origin of Japanese personnel management to the Tokugawa village, the tendency of a Japanese company to make it a community, from which the main features of Japanese management seem to be derived, cannot be easily explained without looking for a prototype of social organization in the pre-modern period. Of course, if one looks for differences between a traditional village and a successful Japanese business organization, there are many. In particular, the greater importance of economic rationality in the latter necessitates a method of organization different from a traditional village. But the similarities between them are also striking. When people join a company, many of them intend to stay with the company for a long time; they readily accept the hierarchical structure of the company and even let it spill over into their social life; their non-kin social relations tend to be confined to co-workers in the company; managers or supervisors pay a great deal of attention to the welfare of their subordinates; and all workers co-operate and accept the company as a common destiny. Although Marxist scholars regard these features of a modern business organization as feudal remnants, when they were combined with modern management practices, they became a positive factor.

The influence of the Tokugawa village structure seems more pervasive than on business enterprises alone. It can also be observed in the government bureaucracy, in cultural and social organizations, and in national federations which involve the government and business enterprises; and it is an implicit model for teaching in schools when group behaviour has to be taught to children. The general ability to organize, which explains the smooth functioning of economic organizations in Japan, seems to owe a great deal to the heritage of the Tokugawa village organization.

### The Quality of Leadership

One weakness of Chinese leadership was the cultural orientation of the mandarins. They were recruited by an examination system which emphasized Chinese classics but not military skills. Because of their ignorance of military matters, the mandarins did not feel any urgency to undertake reforms to meet the threat posed by the Western Powers. Any who did were reluctant to strengthen the military because it would threaten their élite position in the government. In Japan, however, since the samurai were both administrators and warriors, they had a better understanding of the nature of the Western threat, and there was no rivalry between the civil and military bureaucracies.

It has also been argued that the modernization of China was delayed because it was ruled by 'foreigners'—the Manchu Ch'ing dynasty. The Manchus had their own language and, initially, stood apart culturally from the Chinese, although the Manchu leaders were soon assimilated into Chinese society. Those who blame the Ch'ing dynasty for China's delay in modernization question whether its leaders were really dedicated to China's national interest, quoting the remark attributed to Prince Ch'ung, the representative of the Empress Dowager, that 'it were better to hand over the Empire to the Foreign Devils, than to surrender it to the dictation of these Chinese rebels'.[24] It is unlikely that the Ch'ing dynasty leaders completely disregarded China's interests but, in view of the way in which they dealt with the Western Powers, they can be rightly accused of being interested primarily in maintaining their own rule at the expense of national integrity.

Their attitude can be contrasted with the intense nationalism of the samurai which prevailed in mid-nineteenth century Japan. The political ideology which had rapidly been gaining influence among them at that time held that Japan was a divine country which must not be contaminated by 'hairy barbarians' from other countries at any cost; to rule the country well and protect it from those barbarians were the primary obligations of the ruling class. The education and martial arts of the samurai were considered important, not in themselves, but for the purpose of fulfilling such obligations. This nationalistic ideology underlined the political changes from the 1850s when the Western Powers arrived in Japan.

After witnessing the defeat of China in the Opium War of 1840, and observing at first hand the superiority of Western weapons in Japan, the Tokugawa shogunate assented to the demands of the Western Powers to open the country. This was unavoidable in view of the gap in military strength between the West and the shogunate. Those who subscribed to the chauvinistic political ideology, however, regarded it as an indication of the shogunate's failure to govern the country properly. It therefore gave legitimacy to the movement to overthrow the shogunate, and led eventually to the Meiji Restoration of 1868. As the movement's leaders came into closer contact with some Western Powers, and became aware of their military superiority, they too gave up thoughts of expelling the 'Western barbarians' and began to feel it was necessary to open up the country and to learn Western technology.[25] Although there was a great deal of chauvinism in their nationalism, it was the reformist element in it which became the source of national progress. Even after the Meiji Restoration, this chauvinistic nationalism did not completely disappear. It remained in the form of dedication to national honour and glory, and became the spiritual foundation of the new generation of leaders, bureaucratic leaders in particular, who steered the course of modernization in Japan. As discussed a little earlier, however, it eventually led Japan into the disastrous conflict with the West, but the fact remains that it was a propelling force of pre-war modernization.

### Feudalism

Karl Marx argued that capitalism grew out of feudalism. Although he did not explain how this was so, one wonders whether or not the fact that Tokugawa Japan was a feudal state, divided into 270 *han* headed by daimyos and administered by their samurai retainers—in contrast to China which was a centralized state run by mandarins—influenced the course of modernization. One can think of at least two favourable effects of feudalism: one on law and order, and the other on capital accumulation.[26]

As pointed out earlier, the mandarins, the élite of the Chinese bureaucracy, were recruited by a system of rigorous examinations. Each local administration post was headed by a mandarin sent from Peking who stayed at his post for about three years and then moved on to another post. In contrast, each local administration post in Japan was headed by a hereditary lord (daimyo) whose family had ruled the area for generations, and he was assisted by his hereditary retainers. In short, the élite in Chinese local administration were recruited on merit and stayed at one place for only a short time, whereas the local administrators in Japan inherited their positions and were 'locked into' the area they ruled.

The daimyo had virtual autonomy in internal matters but was constrained by the possibility that, if his province was not well governed, law and order might break down. If, for example, a rebellion occurred, he would lose tax revenues and it would be expensive to restore peace. At the worst, the shogunate might step in and use the daimyo's misrule as an excuse to replace him. This was not a remote possibility: in the first hundred years of the Tokugawa period, a number of daimyos were removed.

In China, there was a system for checking on the mandarin at his post, but it was usually ineffective, and when the central government became corrupt and incompetent, it was totally useless. Consequently, a typical mandarin was mainly interested in accumulating wealth at his post. It was difficult for him to develop affection for the place of his appointment and to initiate long-term projects since he did not stay in one place for more than a few years. In Japan, however, the daimyo shared the fortunes and misfortunes of his domain with the people, and came to develop a sense of *noblesse oblige*. In addition, he was under pressure to rule effectively since misrule might worsen the position of his domain *vis-à-vis* other domains and cause the shogunate to intervene.

That the daimyos were constrained by the shogunate put pressure on local administration. It might be supposed that, since there was no higher authority over the shogun, he might have been more subject to corruption than the daimyos, especially as he controlled an area which included key posts like Osaka and Nagasaki and fiefs which yielded a quarter of Japan's total rice output. However, the shogun was constrained by the rivalry of the daimyos, who were ready to challenge him whenever his power weakened. This system of checks and balances made both the shogun and the daimyos strive for reasonable government.

Feudalism also seems to have created a favourable environment for capital accumulation. In order that wealth may accumulate not only in one generation but also over generations, it is, in general, necessary to contain the power of the government, and to prevent it from confiscating private wealth at will. The shogun and the daimyos did not completely refrain from the arbitrary exercise of power, but they were greatly circumscribed in their dealings with merchant houses whose co-operation was indispensable for the commercial development of their fiefs. Otherwise, a merchant house like Mitsui could not accumulate wealth over several generations. In China, however, there were no such large merchant houses with a long business history.

In China, there were few gaps in the political organization which merchants could exploit for their own benefit. The centralized bureaucracy covered the entire country, constituting a solid block which the merchants could not penetrate. Through bribes and kinship connections, they could sometimes obtain concessions from the government and thereby increase their power, but there were no structural fissures of which they could take advantage over generations. In Japan, however, competition between the daimyos, or between the daimyos and the shogun, required the co-operation of the merchants and enabled them to acquire greater freedom. Furthermore, Osaka, where there were many wealthy merchants, was under the shogunate. The power of the shogunate protected the Osaka merchants from the daimyos and forced the latter to honour their debts to the merchants.

## Conclusion

The fact that Japan has never been colonized had an important bearing on the course of its development. Therefore, it would not be reasonable to compare Japan with a former colony, such as Indonesia, and speculate why the former has developed and why the latter has not. However, to argue that Japan's independence was an accident of history and that this was the major factor for its development is erroneous. There may have been elements of luck involved in Japan's continuing independence, but one must also take into account the fact that Japan was better prepared to fend off the Western thrust in Asia. This preparedness seems also to have contributed to its success in economic development. That in-dependence alone was not a sufficient condition for development is simply demonstrated by the cases of Thailand and China, which remained politically independent, but which have not developed to the same level as Japan.

A number of explanations have been offered for the disparity in development between Japan and China or Thailand. The only hypothesis which may link these explanations is that Japan de-veloped because feudalism preceded its modern period. This hypothesis appears to resemble the Marxist paradigm, 'from feudalism to capitalism', although Marx did not explain the process of transition. However, it seems that feudalism produced competition between different power centres—the shogunate and the *han* governments in the Japanese case—forcing them to improve the administration, education, and economy of the country. Feudalism protected merchants and made it possible for them to accumulate wealth: in Japan, the shogun offered protection to the merchants under him when their security was threatened in their dealings with the daimyos, whereas in Western Europe the king, emperor, or Pope played a similar role. In Japan, however, unlike Western Europe, it was not the merchants who engineered the transition from feudalism to capitalism. The protagonists in this transition are discussed in the following chapter.

1. P. Baran, *The Political Economy of Growth*, New York, Monthly Review Press, 1957, pp. 151–61.

2. C. Geertz, *Agricultural Involution*, Berkeley, University of California Press, 1963, pp. 130–54.

3. J. Embree, 'Thailand—A Loosely Structured Social System', *American Anthropologist*, April–June 1950, Vol. 52, pp. 181–93.

4. See, for example, H. Evers (ed.), *Loosely Structured Social Systems: Thailand in Comparative Perspective*, New Haven, Yale University Press, 1969.

5. Among a large number of writings on Japanese society which gives this impression, a few representative ones are: T. Fukutake, *Japanese Rural Society*, translated by R. Dore, Ithaca, Cornell University Press, 1972; C. Nakane, *Japanese Society*, Harmondsworth, Penguin Books, 1973; R. Benedict, *The Chrysanthemum and the Sword*, Boston, Houghton Mifflin, 1946; and J. Embree, *Suye Mura: A Japanese Village*, Chicago, University of Chicago Press, 1939. Although Thai sociologists who studied Japan may not accept Embree's characterization of Thailand, most agree that Japan is a more tightly knit society than Thailand. See, for example, Prasert Yamklinfung, 'The Problem of Modernization of Thai Society', Paper presented at the Department of Sociology, Kyoto University, 2 June 1984.

6. R. Dore, *Tokugawa Education*, Berkeley, University of California Press, 1965, p. 2.

7. Unless otherwise specified, the following discussion on Thai education is based on D. Wyatt, *The Politics of Reform in Thailand: Education in the Reign of King Chulalongkorn*, New Haven, Yale University Press, 1969.

8. Prasert Chittiwatanapong, 'The Modernization Base in Japan and Thailand: Education and Science', Paper presented at a conference on 'The Emergence of Modern States: Thailand and Japan', Thailand–Japan Studies Program, Bangkok, 1976, p. 18.

Undoubtedly, magic played a large part in the popular imagination of Tokugawa Japan, but there was a relatively large intellectual class with a far more rational view of the world.

9. For a more detailed discussion on the Tokugawa bureaucracy, see J. Hall,

'The Nature of Traditional Society: Japan', in R. Ward and D. Rustow (eds.), *Political Modernization in Japan and Turkey*, Princeton, Princeton University Press, 1964.

10. Tej Bunnag, *The Provincial Administration of Siam, 1892–1915*, Kuala Lumpur, Oxford University Press, 1977, p. 16.

11. Sakudo Yotaro, 'The Reform of the Monetary System in the Early Years of Meiji', *Osaka Economic Papers*, September 1957, pp. 33–4. One yen was roughly equivalent to 1 dollar at that time.

12. For the Shingaku movement, see R. Bellah, *Tokugawa Religion*, Glencoe, Illinois, Free Press, 1957, Chapter 6.

13. The House of Mitsui employed about 1,000 people in its Edo stores alone, and a great deal of responsibility was given to *banto* (head clerks), who were recruited at childhood and promoted internally on the basis of merit. For a more detailed discussion on merchant houses in the Tokugawa period, see J. Hirschmeier and T. Yui, *The Development of Japanese Business, 1600–1980*, 2nd edn., London, George Allen & Unwin, 1975, Chapter 1.

14. J. Ingram, *Economic Change in Thailand, 1850–1970*, Stanford, Stanford University Press, 1971, p. 21.

15. Ibid., p. 7.

16. For China's advantage over Japan, see W. Lockwood, 'Japan's Response to the West: The Contrast with China', *World Politics*, October 1956, pp. 41–2.

17. World Bank, *Development Report 1992*, New York, Oxford University Press, 1992, pp. 218–9.

18. United Nations Development Programme, *Human Development Report 1991*, New York, United Nations, 1991, p. 119.

19. J. Allyn, *The Forty-Seven Ronin Story*, Tokyo, Charles E. Tuttle Co., 1970.

20. Confucius, *The Analects*, translated by D. C. Lau, Harmondsworth, Penguin Books, 1979, p. 121.

21. M. Levy, 'Contrasting Factors in the Modernization of China and Japan', *Economic Development and Cultural Change*, 1953–4, p. 183, and Bellah, *Tokugawa Religion*, p. 189.

22. Lockwood, 'Japan's Response to the West', p. 48.

23. The following discussion on the Chinese village structure is based on B. Moore, *Social Origins of Dictatorship and Democracy: Lord and Peasant in the Making of the Modern World*, Boston, Beacon Press, 1966, p. 199.

24. Quoted in J. Dower (ed.), *Origins of the Modern Japanese State: Selected Writings of E. H. Norman*, New York, Pantheon Books, 1975, p. 231.

25. How the content of the ideology which gave legitimacy to the Restoration Movement changed over time is discussed in Sakata Yoshio, 'Nihon Kindaika no Shuppatsu to Tenkai' [The 'Take-off' and Expansion of Japan's Modernization], *Jinbun Gakuho*, March 1970.

26. The following discussion on feudalism is based on F. Braudel's interpretation of Norman Jacobs's work on the origin of capitalism in East Asia. See Braudel, *Civilization and Capitalism, 15th–18th Century*, Vol. 2, *The Wheels of Commerce*, translated by Sian Reynolds, New York, Harper & Row, 1979, pp. 585–99, and Norman Jacobs, *The Origin of Modern Capitalism and Eastern Asia*, New York, Octagon Books, 1981.

# 5
# Institutional Reforms

THE two most important events in the political history of modern Japan were the Meiji Restoration of 1868 and the defeat in the Pacific War. They differed from other historical events in the modern period in that they brought about both a break in leadership and major institutional restructuring. When such momentous political changes take place, institutions are altered to suit the purposes of a new regime. This was certainly the case after the Meiji Restoration and after the Pacific War. In the first period, various feudal institutions were abolished and new ones created; in the second, the military and its supporting institutions were abolished and in their place a pacifist democratic system was set up. This chapter discusses these institutional changes and their impact on economic development.

Economists, whether neo-classical or Marxist, look upon themselves as economic determinists. This attitude is not entirely wrong since economic changes affect non-economic as well as economic institutions. For example, the emancipation of serfs in Western Europe can not be fully explained without considering the economic changes which had been occurring, especially the rise of real wages. At the same time, however, non-economic institutions—political, kinship, and cultural (such as schools and religious organizations)—can evolve independently of economic change, and can affect the economy. If the changes of non-economic institutions induce economic developments, the latter can not be understood by looking at economic variables and institutions alone.

To say that economic and non-economic changes interact to produce social changes may not add new insight, but to explain all social changes solely in terms of economic changes is too dogmatic. For example (as will be explained below), though the Meiji Restoration and the Pacific War are related to the economic conditions which preceded them, they cannot be entirely explained by these economic situations alone. In order to understand them, one has to examine a complex interplay of economic and socio-political factors. To complicate matters further, contrary to the claims of many social scientists, there is some undeterminedness in the pattern of interactions (or in the evolution of history in general). This is partly because external factors sometimes play an unexpected role at certain points in history. For example, though the role of the United States was crucial in reforms after the Pacific War, American influence might have been much smaller and Russian influence greater—and reforms might have been more socialist-oriented—if Japan had decided to prolong the war for a few more months and in so doing given time to the Soviet Union to control part of Japan proper. There was no economic predeterminedness in the timing of the Japanese surrender or in the content of subsequent reforms.

Development economists discussing Japan may give the impression that Meiji and Allied occupation reforms were the direct result of preceding economic changes and they would have come about anyway, sooner rather than later, and there is thus no reason to discuss them explicitly. Or they may argue that in the case of occupation reforms, their impact was almost nil because the economic variables which influenced post-war growth were not directly related to these reforms. But this is a fallacy. In the case of occupation reforms, even if they did not directly affect economic variables, they may have affected the parameters of the national economy. It is best to view the two sets of reforms as historical events which were brought about largely independently of economic changes, but which greatly influenced the course of Japanese economic development.

## Meiji Reforms

In theory, the collapse of a feudal system is preceded by social and economic changes which undermine the basis of its institutions; and Japan was no exception to this rule. Despite rules and regulations aimed at perpetuating the feudal structure of society, the money economy spread inexorably in the late Tokugawa period, shaking the very foundations of the feudal system. As the samurai became urban dwellers and discarded their traditional habits of frugality, government expenditure increased and, consequently, government budgets were constantly in deficit. At first, the deficit was met by borrowing money from merchants, but the interest incurred exacerbated the situation in later years. To solve the problem, the shogunate and many provincial governments modified the policy of economic self-sufficiency, and encouraged the production of commercial crops and handicrafts which could be sold in the major cities. When these measures were not successful, as was most often the case, the stipends of the samurai were cut, to such an extent that low-ranking samurai were forced to do piece-work at home in order to make ends meet. Conversely, many wealthy merchants were given permission to use surnames and to wear swords—privileges of the samurai class—and were allowed to participate in government administration. Although merchants supposedly occupied the lowest social status in Tokugawa society, their influence increased greatly in the late Tokugawa period as the samurai class became increasingly absorbed with economic problems.

Feudal foundations were also being shaken at the village level. Constant government attempts to increase rice taxes in order to reduce deficits made the lives of most peasants intolerable: some rebelled or left the villages for the cities, in defiance of regulations designed to keep them on the land. The spread of commercial crops increased the importance of money in the village economy and began to erode the basis of the natural economy—the basis of feudalism. Commercialization had a greater impact on the village economy towards the end of the Tokugawa period (1860–7) when prices began to fluctuate more widely as a result of the opening of trade with Western countries.

The spread of the money economy encouraged the development of institutions alien to the feudal system and created a gap between the ideal of feudalism and its reality. Yet, the leading role in institutional change was not played by the merchant class. The Meiji Restoration, which swept away feudal institutions and regulations, was not a bourgeois revolution, although a large part of the money required to finance the Restoration Movement was obtained from merchants. By initiating institutional reforms early in the era, the Meiji Restoration was beneficial for the bourgeois class. But these points are not sufficient grounds for the argument, propounded by some Japanese Marxist historians, that the Meiji Restoration was a bourgeois revolution. Although money was borrowed from merchants, they were by no means organized as a class in support of the movement; some merchants still supported the shogunate and contributed funds to its military campaigns.

Furthermore, Meiji leaders believed that the creation of a militarily strong nation was equally as important as economic development. In fact, they often placed a higher priority on the military aspects of modernization and considered economic development as a means to that end: the goal of achieving a strong military was never subordinated to economic development. Even if it is accepted that a strong military was necessary for economic development, the hypothesis that the Meiji Restoration was brought about by the bourgeoisie is untenable. It can not adequately explain the absence of leadership among the merchant class in the Restoration Movement and the subordinate position of the bourgeoisie in the Meiji government. It can not also explain why the leadership of the movement came from the economically much less advanced western *han*, such as Choshu and Satsuma, and not from the areas around Edo and Osaka where a higher state of commercial and financial development had been reached.

*Political Reforms*

The protagonists in the Meiji Restoration were the lower samurai of Choshu and Satsuma and a few other western *han*, and the various institutional reforms in the early Meiji era were undertaken by the progressively minded among these lower samurai. Capitalist development, which began in the Meiji era, was a consequence of these reforms. In contrast to the Marxist view of the pattern of historical development, that the economic substructure changes first and is followed by social and political changes, in Meiji Japan social and political changes triggered economic changes. The dictum normally attributed to the former president of Ghana, Dr Kwame Nkrumah, 'Seek ye first the political kingdom and all other things will be added unto you', is apt for understanding the process of historical change in Japan at that time.[1] The protagonists were the lower samurai in a few western *han* who wanted to create a new Japan, first by vesting political power in the emperor.

To achieve political reforms, the daimyos had first to be removed from power. This was accomplished through *hanseki hokan* (the return of the land registers) in 1869 and *haihan chiken* (the abolition of fiefs and the establishment of prefectures) in 1871— reforms which stripped them of their land and thus their power base. Such major political reforms would normally invite strong opposition, but in the case of the daimyos, most meekly accepted them. Why was this so?

First, the daimyos did not have the same psychological attachment to the land as did the princes and lords in other feudal or semi-feudal societies. Although the daimyos had been given land in return for loyalty to the shogun, they—and their retainers—mostly lived in castle towns as administrators. The rice and other agricultural produce they collected, which was cultivated by hired labourers or tenants, increasingly became taxes rather than rent,[2] and they lost their emotional attachment to the land.

There was economic interest in the land, certainly, and loss of land meant loss of income from it. But resistance on the basis of this consideration was weak, partly because of the financial difficulties most *han* experienced towards the end of the Tokugawa period. Many *han* did not expect to be able to pay their debts or to balance their budgets in the foreseeable future. The fact that the new government guaranteed the daimyos economic security, while removing administrative headaches, was a successful strategy.

The daimyos were also psychologically disarmed by the manipulation of imperial symbols and the appeal to their patriotism by Meiji leaders. By arguing that the threat of Western imperialism had to be met by establishing a new, unified political system with the emperor as the head of state, the new leaders created an atmosphere of immediacy which suggested that to resist the political reform was tantamount to treason. Also, the timing of the reform was advantageous to the new government's leaders; during the first few years after the Meiji Restoration, the nation was in a state of flux, and the daimyos were better prepared for political change. In a way, the daimyos were defeated by the 'psychological warfare' launched by the new leaders.

This does not mean, however, that the new government underestimated the importance of a strong military in carrying out political reforms. In fact, a major objective of the government in the early Meiji period was to create a modern military recruited from all social classes and equipped with the newest weapons; indeed, the government was willing to demonstrate its strength if the daimyos resisted the reforms. The government had under its command the most powerful army in the country at that time, which was strong enough to crush the resistance of any daimyo. Some daimyos did, in fact, have to be subjugated by force, but they were few in number, and their rebellions poorly co-ordinated. But if many daimyos had refused to accept the reforms, the country would have been dragged into a prolonged civil war and the subsequent course of modernization would have been adversely affected. It is significant that the new government accomplished this major political reform with a minimum use of force—a rare historical event indeed.

## Social and Economic Reforms

Social and economic reforms constituted the second part of the institutional reforms in the early Meiji era. The feudal Tokugawa society had been a class society. One major social reform was the abolition of the class system and the establishment of a more open society which would allow people with talent to advance irrespective of their social background. In line with this goal, the government opened the bureaucracy and armed forces to people of all classes by introducing a merit system. As a result, the samurai lost their monopoly of arms and government positions, and became the social equals of peasants and merchants. This ended the monopoly of political power by the samurai class which had ruled Japan from the late twelfth century.

Along with the abolition of the class system, the feudal rules and regulations restricting economic freedom were removed. The samurai class not only became free to engage in productive occupations, but was also strongly encouraged to do so. The regulations prohibiting peasants from leaving the countryside and from selling their lands or choosing which crops to raise were abolished. Peasants were released from bondage to undertake any activities which would increase their incomes. The feudal regulations which required merchants to join guilds and which restricted competition were also abolished. It now became possible for any person to start an enterprise in any field. In particular, because the capital of a single merchant was usually limited, the government encouraged the formation of joint-stock companies.

Restrictions on domestic travel and transportation were also lifted. *Han* governments had often imposed tariffs or restrictions on the movement of goods in order to preserve economic order. The Tokugawa shogunate, for reasons of internal security, prohibited the construction of bridges over certain rivers and intentionally preserved natural barriers to domestic travel and the transportation of goods. It also established check-points and required travellers and transportation agents to show permits. The Meiji government abolished these check-points and internal tariffs, and took measures to develop the national transportation and communications network for the purpose of economic, political, and social integration of the country. This new policy led to the construction of railways, the granting of subsidies to the Iwasaki family to establish a modern shipping line, and the establishment of postal and telegraphic services.

Trade with Western countries had resumed in 1859 but, under the Tokugawa system, various barriers inhibited its expansion. For one, the shogunate and the *han* governments took various measures to restrict the activities of foreign merchants in the event that foreign trade might threaten their political stability by causing a severe shortage or an excess of certain commodities. Also, the extreme nationalists, who were determined to expel the 'Western barbarians', interfered with foreign trade by carrying out terrorist attacks. The new Meiji government, conversely, made it clear that the country needed to increase its contacts with the West in order to gain new ideas and technical knowledge for modernizing the country. For this purpose, it removed the ban on foreign travel and sent students abroad. Foreign trade was promoted as one aspect of international relations and also as a means of increasing the wealth of the country. The feudal regulations which had impeded the growth of trade at the end of the Tokugawa period were thus removed.

Under the former feudal system, economic freedom had to be greatly restricted for two basic reasons. First, the competition accompanying economic freedom would undermine the ascriptive social order of the feudal society. Secondly, to allow a great deal of freedom to peasants, for example, the right to leave their villages, was inconsistent with the basic tenet of the feudal system in which agriculture is the main economic base. Were such freedom allowed, it would spell the end of agriculture as the dominant industry, and thus physiocracy, which provided the feudal system with a theoretical justification of its 'agriculture first' principle, would have to be replaced by a new economic philosophy. This, in turn, would entail a new political philosophy which would necessitate a new form of government.

Although there was a certain consensus among the lower-ranking samurai in the Restoration Movement that the Tokugawa political system had to be replaced by one centred upon the emperor as the head of state, there was considerable difference of opinion as to the extent to which feudal institutions should be reformed. The relatively radical social and economic reforms carried out in the early Meiji era reflected the view of the so-called 'new intellectuals' who had either studied 'Western Learning' or had visited Western countries near the end of the Tokugawa period. They believed it was essential to reform Japan's social and economic systems along Western lines. A small group of these people was formed at the Ministry of Finance in mid-1869 under Okuma Shigenobu. They drew up a programme of institutional reforms which they felt were necessary for the creation of a new socio-economic order.[3]

These modernizing intellectuals attributed the economic strength of Western countries to their free economic and social systems. They felt it was necessary to emulate this free society if Japan were to become a dynamic country. The economic freedom of the West was based on the economic doctrine of *laissez-faire*, which had become dominant by the mid-nineteenth century. The theory of *laissez-faire* capitalism is usually attributed to Adam Smith, who was, if not the founder of the doctrine, at least its most prominent advocate in the late eighteenth century when government interference in the economy was rampant. Smith argued in *The Wealth of Nations* that a nation's wealth resulted from the diligence and ingenuity of its citizens and that these attributes were best guaranteed under free competition. The 'new intellectuals' did not particularly take to his notion of non-interference by the government,[4] but they agreed that a greater degree of competition was necessary to stimulate economic progress in Japan.

*Opposition to Reform*

Some of the new government's reforms were, naturally, opposed by certain sections of the population. The loss of social privileges, for example, had been hard on the samurai. Even worse was the policy of the new government to reduce financial support for them. After the fiefs were abolished, the Meiji government took over the responsibility of paying rice stipends to the samurai, but these soon came to occupy too large a share of the budget and seemed certain to interfere with the modernization programme. The government, which was determined to carry out the modernization programme, decided to lessen the dead weight of the past. It first reduced the amount of the rice stipends, and then, a few years later, carried out a compulsory commutation of the stipends to government bonds. Although the consequent interest burden incurred by the government was not light, the interest received by the samurai households ranged from 30 to 40 yen per annum on the average, far below the amount needed to support a family.[5] Many lower samurai had difficulty in understanding why they had to lose the social privileges they had enjoyed, particularly in view of the success of a movement to which they had contributed greatly. A number of these samurai were inspired to further revolution once the full scope of the reforms was disclosed, and an opposition bent on violence soon appeared.

At first, the opposition group tried to change government policy by assassinating supporters of the reforms, but this tactic did not alter the government's resolve to press ahead with modernization. From 1874 to 1877, the opposition raised rebellions in western Japan, hoping to overwhelm the central government. The last of the rebellions, the Satsuma Rebellion, headed by Saigo Takamori, himself one of the major architects of the Restoration Movement, presented the most serious threat to the prestige and financial resources of the new government. The rebellions were suppressed, however, in a relatively short time, and armed resistance to the new government ceased. These rebellions were clearly unable to challenge the modern army of the new government or to win popular support, but given the scope of the radical reforms being carried out, they seem to have been an unavoidable ordeal the country had to go through to create a new Japan.

By Western standards, the 'new intellectuals' of the early Meiji era appear conservative and traditional, especially in view of the authoritarian state they later helped to establish. They were but a small minority who had received ideological impulses from the West. There was a wide gap in outlook between them and the masses, probably as wide as that which exists in the developing countries of the present day, but unlike the intellectuals in those countries, who belong to or have numerous ties to privileged groups with vested interests in the institutional *status quo*, the 'new intellectuals' of the early Meiji era were former lower samurai who were extremely discontented with the ascriptive feudal society which often negated their talents. They translated their discontent into action and spearheaded a movement to establish a more just society.

The Western Powers, who, by renewing their interest in East Asia in the mid-nineteenth century, triggered chain reactions leading to the Meiji Restoration, were not only a model for institutional reforms, but also a great pressure on Meiji leaders to carry out those reforms. In view of what had happened to China and other Asian countries after their arrival, it was quite reasonable to assume that, if no precautionary measures were taken, Japan would become a colony. This Western threat created a sense of urgency and enabled early Meiji leaders to carry out rather drastic reforms in a short time.

The Meiji reforms were 'revolutionary' in the sense that they destroyed the feudal system and prepared the way for a new economic and political system, but it is important to note that the new government made efforts to help the samurai adjust to the new society. Most upper samurai were assured of economic security and given government bonds with which they could support their families rather comfortably. Some of them, the shogun and daimyos in particular, became members of the nobility and continued to enjoy social prestige. For the lower samurai, the government bonds did not provide full support, which forced many of them to use the skills they had acquired through education and experience in the old bureaucracy to become professional soldiers, officials in the central and local governments, policemen, or teachers. If they wanted to start a business or to undertake land reclamation and settle down as farmers, they were often given subsidies and other forms of government assistance. Furthermore, though they became commoners and the equals of former merchants and peasants in all practical ways, society continued to pay lip-service to the old class distinctions by calling them *shizoku* (descendants of samurai), to satisfy their need to feel socially different from others. Of course, these measures did not satisfy all the samurai, but they ameliorated the difficult situation faced by them in the transition.

The government policy to help former samurai to adjust to the new society had some bearing on the nature of the Meiji Restoration. Since the Restoration destroyed the feudal system and launched Japan into a modern era, it may be compared to the French and Russian Revolutions. There was, however, too much continuity between the new period and the old for it to be considered a true revolution. The old ruling class was not exterminated, nor did the new ruling class come from the ruled class of the former period, as was the case in the French and Russian Revolutions. The Meiji Restoration was also incomplete as a social revolution, for there were many feudal remnants in the social structure of the new period. In particular, the social structure of the villages, where the bulk of the population lived, was deliberately left intact.

The Meiji Restoration was incomplete as a revolution mainly because it was not instigated by the ruled; rather, it was a revolution within the samurai class and was, in a way, a power struggle within the ruling class.[6] There was, however, a great difference between those discontented samurai who participated in the rebellions and the early Meiji leaders who steered the course of modernization. The latter wanted to abolish feudal privileges and restrictions and to introduce Western ideas and institutions. In this, they were far more 'revolutionary' than the former, but they were not concerned with sweeping away all pre-modern institutions and values and creating a society based on egalitarian principles. Such a course was not possible, in view of the vested interest of their fellow samurai participants in the Restoration Movement. As a consequence, the measures they undertook are a peculiar mix of modernization and conservatism.

## Occupation Reforms

As far back as the beginning of the seventeenth century, some Western countries had begun establishing colonies and seeking special privileges in Asia. In the mid-nineteenth century, when they renewed their interest in the region with greater intensity as a result of the Industrial Revolution, and enlarged their colonial territories, Japan was still a backward country and a likely victim of their imperial ambition rather than a challenger to it. But, as has been discussed so far, spurred on by this imperial Western ambition, Japan modernized the country and developed its economy.

By the end of the Meiji era, Japan had become an imperial power in its own right, and in subsequent years, began challenging the Western Powers in Asia. The socio-economic order these powers established was undoubtedly designed to protect and expand the markets for their products and the sources of the raw materials needed for their industries. By the 1930s, however, it had become much more than that. Various non-economic interests—political, military, bureaucratic, religious, and ideological—were involved. From the Japanese point of view, the Western Powers were a major obstacle to the expansion of its own interests in Asia, and this was more acutely felt as Japan increased its national strength and nationalistic feeling escalated with it. In retrospect, the Pacific War was the inevitable consequence of Japan's increasingly shrill challenge to the Western order in Asia.

The military leaders who plunged Japan into the Pacific War undoubtedly overestimated its ability to fight a war with the West. However, the first few months of the war went well for Japan: the attack on Pearl Harbor was a severe blow to the Pacific Fleet of the United States, and all of South-East Asia came rapidly under

Japanese control. The course of events began to change, however, with the Battle of Midway in mid-1942, and turned definitely against Japan after the Battle of Guadalcanal. By mid-1944, Japan had lost its naval supremacy and was cut off from its overseas territories which had supplied the raw materials necessary for its strategic industries. From then on, Japan's defeat became inevitable, although the war continued for another year. Finally, in August 1945, Japan surrendered unconditionally to the Allies. A few weeks later, occupation forces arrived, and for the first time in history, Japan came under foreign control.

The first and foremost task of the Supreme Commander for the Allied Powers (SCAP), who directed the occupation policy, was to destroy the military superstructure that had devastated Asia in general and had caused considerable losses to the Allies before their victory. In accordance with this policy, the SCAP abolished all military forces, returned all soldiers to the civilian sector, and stopped armament production. It was also necessary to carry out reforms in the political, economic, and social spheres, either as punitive measures or to prevent the re-emergence of the military.

In the political realm, 'Tennoism'—the political system which holds the emperor to be divine and vests him with absolute power—was overthrown; the Maintenance of Public Order Act and its watch-dog, the special political police who had terrorized persons or groups who objected to the war, were abolished; and the state was separated from the religion of Shintoism, which provided an ideological foundation for xenophobic nationalists and was used to glorify death for the cause of the state. Furthermore, a large number of Japanese leaders who were judged to have actively supported the war were purged from public office. In the economic sector, the *zaibatsu*, which had collaborated with the military and greatly benefited from it, were dissolved. Land reforms were also carried out, first to destroy the economic base of the landlords who had supported the army, and secondly to improve the living conditions of the peasants, lest they support rightist causes again. In the social area, educational reforms were carried out, to prohibit teachings which glorified the military and encouraged worship of the emperor. Labour reforms were also enacted, to develop labour unions into a force capable of preventing the rise of fascism in industry.

*Economic Reforms*

Although the destruction of the military backbone of Japan was the top priority of the SCAP, it was clear from the beginning of the occupation that a new political system had to be established. The Meiji constitution, which had defined the emperor as the sovereign ruler of the country and had made it possible for the military to dominate national politics, was replaced by a new democratic constitution which incorporated popular sovereignty, woman's suffrage, and the guarantee of fundamental human rights. The economic and social reforms needed to destroy the military were also useful in creating institutions to sustain the democratic political system and to help it to take root in Japanese society. The dissolution of the *zaibatsu* and the land reforms spread economic power more evenly over the population, making it more difficult for a small group of people to dominate national politics. Labour reforms made it possible for workers to bargain for better pay and working conditions, and to use their organizations for voicing political demands. Educational reforms also served the purpose of democracy by teaching democratic values, developing powers of rational thought, and creating greater opportunities for education.

Of particular interest here are the three economic reforms implemented at this time: land reforms, the reduction of economic concentration, and labour reforms. The essential feature of the land reforms was the transfer of ownership of leased land to the tenants who were cultivating it. First, the government bought all the leased land held by absentee landlords and, in the case of resident landlords, leased land in excess of 1 *cho* (4 *cho* in Hokkaido).[7] The government then sold the land to the tenants who were cultivating it. Consequently, the proportion of land under tenant cultivation decreased dramatically. From 1941 to 1950, the proportion of leased paddy land decreased from 53 to 11 per cent, and leased upland from 37 to 9 per cent. As for the land which remained in the hands of landlords, the reforms made it difficult for landlords to terminate leases without the consent of tenants, and rents were commuted into money terms and were set in terms of the 1945 official price of rice, well below the market price. At the time of the reforms, rents constituted only 10 per cent of the total yield.

The major step to reduce economic concentration was the dissolution of the *zaibatsu*; this was carried out by the Holding Company Liquidation Commission set up in 1946. Mitsubishi, Mitsui, Sumitomo, and Yasuda were the largest *zaibatsu* at the time. In addition, there were lesser national and local *zaibatsu*. The commission ordered 83 holding companies and 57 *zaibatsu* families to surrender their holdings, which amounted to 233 million shares. It then disposed of them in such a way that they could be bought by a large number of individuals and associations. In the process, the holding companies were dissolved, companies which had been under their control became independent, and *zaibatsu* families lost their economic power. Further legislation in 1947 provided that any *zaibatsu* family member holding an official position in a former *zaibatsu* company had to retire and could not return to his former position for 10 years.

The second measure to reduce economic concentration was the dissolution of all cartels and other control associations which had been formed since 1931, when the Major Industries Control Law was passed. The third was to purge business leaders who had collaborated closely with the military. By mid-1947, about 2,000 persons who had been key officials in major companies during the war had been purged. In December 1947, the Elimination of Excessive Concentration of Economic Power Law was passed, and the Holding Company Liquidation Commission was empowered to break up companies which held excessive economic power. The commission designated 325 companies but, since there was considerable objection to the law both within and outside Japan, only 11 companies were broken up.[8] Finally, in March 1948, the Board of Small Enterprises was set up, to promote the growth of small, efficient, and independent companies.

The labour reforms started with the passage of the Trade Union Law of 1945, which guaranteed workers the right to organize, to bargain collectively, and to strike. Two and a half years later, there were about 34,000 unions with a total membership of 6.6 million. Since at no time before the Pacific War had union membership exceeded half a million, the increase in union membership was quite astonishing. In 1946, another law was passed, to provide a mechanism for settling labour disputes. In 1947, three more laws were passed, to establish protective labour standards, to provide a free employment service, and to eliminate feudalistic labour practices.

The economic chaos and hyper-inflation of the early post-war years provided tremendous opportunities for enterprising people to make money but they dealt a severe blow to the *rentier* class. Their savings were frozen as a means of maintaining the solvency of financial institutions and so, as inflation progressed, the real value of their savings declined. They also bore the brunt of the capital tax, which was levied on the property of individuals that was valued at over 100,000 yen. The tax increased from 10 per cent in the lowest bracket to a maximum of 90 per cent. Landlords lost heavily not only because of the land reforms but also as a result of the hyper-inflation, which caused the value of fixed incomes from land sales or rent to plummet. Around 1950, when the major reforms were completed and economic stabilization was restored, a large number of peasants were better off, but at the expense of their former landlords; the dead weight of the *rentier* class was lighter; and the *nouveaux riches* who emerged during these chaotic years showed that there were new opportunities for enterprise.

## Impact on Post-war Growth

One might argue that the rapid growth which followed the occupation can be regarded as sufficient evidence of the contribution which the reforms made to Japan's post-war economic growth. But the causal relationships need to be examined more specifically for, while there is a consensus that the reforms in the Meiji period were an essential step for future economic development, in the case of those of the occupation period, there is no such consensus. It is sometimes argued that the post-war growth was not related to the reforms, since the purposes of the reforms were often not achieved; and where they were, their impact on economic growth was ambiguous.

The negative view on this question may be summarized as follows. In spite of far-reaching effects on the structure of the rural economy, the land reforms were not related to agricultural growth. Agricultural production increased mainly because of the development of new varieties of rice at government experimental stations and the increased production of fertilizers—neither of which had anything to do with land reforms. The measures designed to reduce economic concentration were ineffective in various ways. The Elimination of Excessive Concentration of Economic Power Law was not enforced after the late 1940s, and was finally repealed in the mid-1950s. As a consequence, large companies dominate the economy today. The *zaibatsu* dissolution was also ineffective, as can be seen from the pre-eminence of Mitsubishi, Mitsui, and Sumitomo, virtually as before. In the field of labour reform, the effects of trade unionism are more likely to have been negative, as might be inferred from the British experience. Furthermore, the paternalistic employment practices, which the labour reforms attempted to eliminate, remained intact in many companies, operating in some ways as positive factors for productivity increase.

Although these arguments have a certain validity, they do not wholly negate the contribution of occupation reforms to post-war economic growth. In the case of land reforms, it is true that they have no place within the framework of growth accounting, which measures productivity increase in terms of input increase, but such an approach completely ignores the question of motivation—why peasants decided to increase the use of fertilizer and other inputs, why they readily adopted new varieties, and why they decided to increase investment in agricultural infrastructure which would pay off handsomely only in the long run. The land reforms increased the returns to the cultivating tenants and eliminated the uncertainty concerning land tenure which had discouraged long-term investment. The contribution of land reforms was especially large where the lands were held by absentee landlords who lived in cities and siphoned off agricultural income for conspicuous consumption.

The effects of the measures to reduce economic concentration were not as far-reaching as those of the land reforms; nevertheless, they did contribute to the reduction of economic concentration. The business groups which emerged in the 1950s, such as Mitsubishi, Mitsui, and Sumitomo, and which have played an important role in the economy since then, have quite a different structure from when they were *zaibatsu*. The holding companies which controlled and co-ordinated the *zaibatsu* companies were made illegal, and have not been reinstated. Also, the influence of a former *zaibatsu* family on the companies carrying the *zaibatsu* name is completely gone. Companies in the same group consult each other and co-ordinate their activities to a certain extent, but the co-operation is loose in comparison with that among the former *zaibatsu* companies, when they functioned as if they were different departments of the same organization. It is, in fact, more important to note the independence that companies now possess in regard to personnel, finance, investment, and technology than to emphasize the co-ordination of their activities.[9] Finally, these three groups—Mitsubishi, Mitsui, and Sumitomo—are much less important in the overall national economy than the *zaibatsu* were in the 1930s, as a result of the growth of many other companies in the post-war period, for example, Sony, Matsushita, Toyota, and Honda.

It may appear that competition is highly restricted and economic efficiency low today because many industries are oligopolies, but this view is not entirely correct. First, since competition with foreign companies in both domestic and export markets puts the pressure on oligopolies to strive for greater efficiency, the concentration of production cannot be equated with low efficiency. Secondly, the Anti-Monopoly Law, passed during the occupation, makes various practices which restrict competition illegal, and its supervisory body, the Fair Trade Commission, keeps a close watch. It is more difficult today than in the period when the *zaibatsu* were pre-eminent, for a company to control competition by merger, stockholding, or take-over.

Even the trade unions which were created under the labour reforms have been a positive factor in economic growth. Trade unions are normally regarded as having a negative influence on productivity, because of their strong demands for wage increases and their objections to the introduction of new technology, but these problems are minimized in Japan because unions are enterprise unions, that is, there is one union for one enterprise, and accept lifetime employment, the seniority-based wage system, internal promotion, and other peculiarly Japanese management practices. They do not, of course, always co-operate with management; in the immediate post-war period, when wages were extremely low, there were a number of radical demands. But these negative aspects of the union movement have not generally been a serious problem to Japanese management. In one area, however, the unions fought fairly effectively—to reduce distinctions in status and differences in security and material privileges between manual workers and salaried staff. This victory seems to have promoted corporate solidarity and to have raised the morale of ordinary workers. If, as is often argued, QC circles and other small-group activities have been effective in raising productivity, the unions should be given some credit for this since they have raised the status of manual workers and given them corporate identity.

When other non-economic reforms are considered, the contribution of post-war institutional reforms to economic growth becomes even more apparent. One indisputable contribution comes from disarmament. From the Meiji era until Japan's defeat in 1945, military expenditure formed an important part of government expenditure. Even in peacetime, the proportion was close to 20 per cent, and in wartime, which was by no means infrequent, the proportion exceeded 50 per cent.[10] Since the defeat, Japan's security has been maintained—under the American nuclear 'umbrella'—by a small national defence force, and the burden of military expenditure has been light. It has declined to several per cent of government expenditure, rarely exceeding 1 per cent of GNP.[11] Not only did wasteful expenditure sharply decline, thus making capital available for constructive purposes, but technology and manpower were also released from war industries. After the Pacific War, the technology of heavy industry, which had produced such war machines as the Zero fighter plane, was made available for the production of non-military goods.[12] In addition, the absorption of talented individuals into the military halted, and such people were able to apply their abilities to building up the post-war economy.

The changes which the reforms of the occupation period brought about have been emphasized, but it must also be remembered that there was a great deal of continuity between the Japan of 1935 and the Japan of 1950. Nevertheless, the changes were too dramatic to have been brought about by internal forces alone. It would be unfair to say that, before the war, no Japanese wanted democracy or disarmament, or that no Japanese saw the excesses of the *zaibatsu* or the injustice of land distribution. The fact remains, however, that the Japanese were not able to change the system on their own. The pre-war system was still relatively new and, despite some problems, was not close to crumbling under domestic pressure as had Tokugawa feudalism. Nor was there an immediate need to change the system to meet external threats, since it had been established to create a 'strong military and a rich nation' to counter Western threats and had been performing fairly well, as seen from the fact that Japan won the wars with China and Russia.

The pre-war situation implies that once a moderately rational system is established, even if there are some problems, it is very difficult for substantive change to take place internally. If strong external pressure is applied, however, such change can take place rapidly, triggering a spurt of economic activity, as shown in post-war Japan. Unfortunately, this process is bound to involve violence, for institutions which need to be changed are built into the power structure of a society and can not be changed without substantially weakening it. If external pressure is weak, there is no violence, but there are also no major changes. Herein lies the basic dilemma of people who advocate institutional reforms as a major catalyst for economic development in the Third World.

1. The question of whether historical materialism is applicable to the Meiji Restoration is not the same as whether it was bourgeois revolution, although the two are often confused. The former is a question of whether or not economic forces explain the Meiji Restoration. Historical materialism is rejected here because it is more natural to consider that the Restoration was brought about by the lower-ranking samurai as a political response to the decay of feudalism and Western challenge. For this view, see, for example, Horie Yasuzo, *Nihon Shihonshugi no Seiritsu* [The Establishment of Japanese Capitalism], Tokyo, Yuhikaku, 1948, Chapter 2, and Sakata Yoshio, *Meiji Ishin-shi* [History of the Meiji Restoration, Tokyo, Mirai-sha, 1960. Those who argue that the Meiji Restoration was a bourgeois revolution, as the *Rono* school of Marxist historians do, are on much more shaky ground, for Japanese capitalism was at an incipient stage of development in the mid-nineteenth century.

2. Horie, *Nihon Shihonshugi no Seiritsu*, pp. 1–6.

3. Sakata Yoshio, *Shikon Shosai* [Samurai's Soul and Merchant's Acumen], Tokyo, Mirai-sha, 1964, p. 6.

4. Smith believed that when there was no competition, people tended to become indolent and reluctant to submit themselves to the trouble and inconvenience of altering their habits by adopting new and promising inventions. Thus, he contended that, since free competition—a condition indispensable to human progress—was best assured when people were free to pursue their own interests, the government should avoid interfering, as much as possible, with the free interplay of individual pursuits.

5. Noro Eitaro, *Nihon Shihonshugi Hattatsu-shi* [History of the Development of Japanese Capitalism], Tokyo, Iwanami Shoten, 1954, p. 141.

6. It can be argued that, in this respect, the Meiji Restoration was similar to the American Revolution.

7. One *cho* is equivalent to 2.451 acres, or approximately 1 hectare.

8. For opposition in the United States, see Holding Company Liquidation Commission, *Nihon Zaibatsu to sono Kaitai* [Japanese *Zaibatsu* and Their Liquidation], Tokyo, Hara Shobo, 1951, Vol. I, pp. 316–17.

9. For a discussion on whether or not such groups can be considered *zaibatsu*, see E. Hadley, *Anti-Trust in Japan*, Princeton, Princeton University Press, 1969, Chapter 11. R. Caves and M. Uekusa discuss the nature of group activities in *Industrial Organization in Japan*, Washington, Brookings Institution, 1976, Chapter 4.

10. Emi Koichi and Shionoya Yuichi, *Government Expenditure: Estimates of Long-Term Economic Statistics of Japan Since 1868, Vol. 7*, Tokyo, Toyo Keizai Shinpo-sha, 1976, Chapter 3.

11. The proportion of military expenditure to GNP was about 2 per cent in 1954, the highest in the post-war period. Since then, it has declined to around 1 per cent (below 1 per cent in most years).

12. The Zero was fully comparable to any fighter the Allies had in the years 1940–2.

# 6
# People and Organization

THE economic development of a country is greatly influenced by the quality of its people. Needless to say, a country develops faster if its people are frugal, hard-working, and well-educated. This chapter, then, looks into the work ethic, attitude towards consumption, and level of education of the Japanese people, and then into the family and cultural institutions, the school in particular, as the organizations which produce such human qualities.

Economic development is often regarded as a result of the economic institution alone but, in fact, it depends equally on such non-economic institutions as the family and the cultural institution since the economic institution in itself is not the major determinant of the quality of people who work in it. To give an example of this interplay, the decline of family values prevalent in the United States today may be regarded as primarily a social issue, but it is equally an economic problem because it affects the quality of children who join the economic institution when they reach working age.

The structure of the economic institution is, of course, vitally important in an industrial economy, because corporate productivity is the major determinant of overall national productivity. Although corporate productivity is inevitably affected by the quality of people who join corporations, it is not the only determinant. Even good-quality people may produce poor results if personnel management does not motivate them, or if management faces an unfavourable business environment which, for example, discourages investment. Among the factors affecting the environment, one unique to Japan is the corporate alliance (*keiretsu*). The second part of this chapter will consider the system of business organization prevailing in Japan as the second determinant of corporate productivity.

There is a saying that 'it takes two to tango'. If 'tango' means to develop the economy, it takes four to do it well. In addition to the economic, kinship, and cultural institutions in a country, economic development also depends on the political institution. Corporate productivity, or the performance of the market economy, depends first on the government's supply of public goods (infrastructure, law and order, etc.). The government is in the best position to supply these because the principle of price discrimination does not work because of the nature of joint consumption in the case of public goods, but if the government does poorly in supplying them for some reasons, for example, it can not collect enough revenue because people are not properly taxed, the market economy is seriously affected. Furthermore, the government intervenes in the market economy in various ways and affects its performance. The last section of this chapter argues that the Japanese government has done a reasonable job of supplying public goods at a level appropriate to different stages of economic development, for example, by maintaining law and order and investing in infrastructure, and that government intervention, which has become a major stumbling-block to economic development in many countries, has promoted the transformation of industrial structure in the Japanese case.

## The Quality of People

An individual's set of values affects the economic performance of a country if it is shared by many others. For example, an individual may hold values which attach great importance to fun and pleasure, in which case he is unlikely to set high targets and make an effort to achieve them. On the other hand, if he possesses self-discipline and translates this into economic action, he is more likely to work hard and save a large part of his income. A nation may also be said to possess a strong work ethic and frugality if a large majority of its people share these values.

Knowledge is not necessarily related to self-discipline, since a person may be well informed but lack discipline. Yet, the two are not unrelated since a person may rationalize his behaviour to attain a higher standard of living if his intellectual horizon broadens with education. From the viewpoint of economic growth, it is best if a worker is well educated, hard-working, and frugal.

An appropriate level of education is important for various types of workers. Education enables the peasant to understand what is going on outside his village and to make more rational economic decisions. It enables the factory worker to absorb new information and adjust to ever-changing economic and technological circumstances.

This section examines the qualities that constitute the calibre of the Japanese work-force.

## The Work Ethic

When considering attitudes towards work, one must examine attitudes towards such aspects as working hours and the length of holidays, as well as towards the quality of work performed.

In Japan before the Pacific War, it was normal for workers to work for 12 hours or more every day, with no more than one or two holidays a month. It was not until the early 1960s that the average Japanese worker received a half-day off on Saturday and a full day off on Sunday and the daily working hours of the other five days were reduced to eight. In the early 1970s, large companies began making Saturday a holiday, but about 20 years later, in the late 1980s, in a number of large companies, including banks, Saturday was still a half working day. In many developing countries today, however, every Saturday and Sunday is a holiday and there are, in addition, a number of statutory holidays. When all of these are added up, about a third of the year is spent on holiday, and working hours are normally only eight hours per day.

People in Western countries seem to work even fewer hours than in developing countries. In addition to every Saturday and Sunday, they take a long annual holiday. (The French, in particular, are known for this.) The Japanese are entitled to about 16 days of paid annual leave, but the tendency is to use only half of this amount, despite the fact that in the past few years trade unions have been working with the government to encourage workers to take advantage of paid holidays. In Western industrial countries, workers are typically entitled to about 20 days paid leave and invariably use all of them. To Westerners, the Japanese appear to be addicted to work.

In the mid-1980s, Japanese workers in the manufacturing sector worked a little less than 2,200 hours per annum. The Americans worked about 10 per cent less, and most West Europeans about 15 per cent less than the Japanese. The working hours of the West Germans were among the shortest (about 1,770 hours).[1] Although labour contracts in Germany specified a 40-hour week, national holidays and paid annual leave reduced the number of hours actually worked to about 35. Yet, German workers were not satisfied, and went on strike for even shorter working hours.

In the second half of the 1980s, Japanese working hours declined somewhat, but in 1990, they were still a little above 2,100 hours. This was considerably higher than the 1,950 hours put in by British and Americans, the 1,700 hours of the French, and the 1,600 hours of the Germans.[2]

Attitude towards work is not just a matter of working hours. It also determines how well one performs in one's job. Although it is difficult to empirically compare attitudes towards work performance, on average the Japanese seem to be more committed to quality work performance than Westerners. Many Japanese feel *kiga sumanai* (not satisfied) unless they do their work well.[3] Some, having a compulsion for perfection, feel *kiga sumanai* with even a moderate level of workmanship. One might say that Western craftsmen also strive to produce work of a high quality, but what is striking in Japan is that many ordinary or even menial workers feel responsibility for their work and are *kiga sumanai* unless they do their work well. A noted American scholar of Japan was impressed with the care a janitor exercises in mopping a floor or a refuse collector in manning his truck.[4]

To have *gaman* (patience) is also related to *kiga sumanai*. If an individual does not have *gaman*, he is forced to admit his failure in whatever assignment he is given, and to do so makes him feel *kiga sumanai*. So, even if an assignment is extraordinarily difficult— even in the sense that he does not like it at all—it is praiseworthy for him to have *gaman* and to do it well.

The saying *ishi no uenimo sannen*, which literally means that even a cold rock warms up if one sits on it for three years, is often used to exhort the Japanese to overcome whatever problems they may have with *gaman*. One might say that every nation possesses a certain amount of *gaman* and that it is not the monopoly of the Japanese. But the Japanese people appear to have *gaman* in larger quantities, for longer periods, and under more trying circumstances. To this stoic characteristic, one may be able to attribute the learning ability and the commitment to work of the Japanese.

*Frugality*

The Japanese people tend to be frugal. In about 1960, when Japan's per capita income was still low, they saved about 18 per cent of their household income. At this time, the savings ratio was about 6 per cent for the United States, 8 per cent for France, 13 per cent for West Germany, and 5 per cent for Britain. As Japanese income increased in subsequent years, there was a parallel increase in the savings ratio. In the mid-1970s, about a quarter of all household income was saved. In the 1980s, however, the savings ratio declined, and was down to about 15 per cent in the early 1990s. But it was still one of the highest among the industrial countries; only Italy had a higher savings ratio. In the United States, the ratio once came close to 10 per cent in 1973, after which it declined and was down to about 5 per cent in 1987. Since then, it has gone up by a few percentage points.

The difference in the savings ratio between Japan and the United States is due partly to economic and partly to institutional factors. Japanese growth has been faster, and there may have been a time-lag between income and consumption growth. Another factor that may have made savings easier is that Japanese workers are given lump-sum bonuses, the amount of which is not known in advance. The frequency and size of such bonuses depend on the profits of the company. On the other hand, such institutional factors as the adequacy of old-age insurance and availability of low-cost public tertiary education in the United States may explain its low savings ratio.

These arguments, nevertheless, do not adequately explain Japan's higher savings ratio. Many Americans seem to have fallen victim to a severe case of what Richard Darman, Budget Director under President Bush, called 'now-now-ism', a reluctance to defer gratification for the sake of future gains. In contrast, many Japanese, especially those above 40 years old, feel a greater inhibition regarding consumption. They say that it is *mottai nai* (wasteful) to throw items away simply because they have become old, or to use them carelessly and make them unusable in a short time, or to use them unnecessarily or unproductively, as, for example, leaving a light on when no one is in the room. To spend more money than necessary is *mottai nai* not only because it is wasteful but also because it is disrespectful to the gods and the ancestors. This *mottai nai* syndrome inhibits many Japanese from buying big cars and big houses, or taking expensive vacations even if they can afford them.

*Asceticism and Religion*

The importance of asceticism in economic development was brought to the attention of economists for the first time by the German socio-economist Max Weber in his book, *The Protestant Ethic and the Rise of Capitalism.*[5] According to him, Protestantism—unlike

Catholicism which was hostile to profit-oriented activities but tolerant of human weaknesses—required its adherents to practise diligence and frugality every day as proof that they were the chosen people of God. It also approved of the accumulation of capital if it resulted from such diligence and frugality. Weber argued that the insistence of Protestantism on diligence and frugality made it possible for wealth to accumulate and, as a result, brought about capitalism in Western Europe. He supported this thesis by pointing out that Protestant countries, or areas, in Western Europe were industrialized while Catholic countries, or areas, remained economically backward.

Was there a religion in Japan which played a similar role to Protestantism in producing asceticism? Certainly, there was no parallel religious upheaval in Japan to the Reformation in Western Europe which produced Protestantism. One can not, however, state categorically that there was no relation between religion and asceticism in the Japanese case. This is partly because of the definition of religion. If such ethical movements as Shingaku and Hotoku[6] and also 'the ways' like bushido[7] are to be included as religions, then one cannot deny the impact of religion on Japanese asceticism.

But here one must ask, as the British economic historian R. Tawney did, whether religion was really the cause of asceticism.[8] Just as Tawney argued that Protestantism grew in more economically advanced areas whose people required a religious rationalization of what they were doing, one can argue that, for Japan, asceticism was needed for non-religious reasons, and that the Shingaku and Hotoku movements developed in the Tokugawa period as its rationalization. Shingaku, for example, grew out of the need of merchants to prevent such human weaknesses as laziness, gambling, or dissolute habits from bankrupting their businesses. Shingaku teachings were incorporated into the 'house rules' of some merchant houses. This may have prevented the adherents of Shingaku from going astray, or it may have spread the need of asceticism to new areas where business traditions had not been well established. But it is difficult to argue that the diligence and frugality of the Tokugawa merchants grew out of Shingaku. Shingaku or another religion was needed to preserve, spread, and rationalize diligence and frugality among the merchants.

Recently, it has become fashionable to give credit to Confucianism for the tremendous growth seen in East Asia. The four Newly Industrializing Economies (NIEs) of Asia—Korea, Taiwan, Hong Kong, and Singapore—are 'Confucian' states, and so is Japan in the sense that Confucianism has been an important cultural influence. It appears, therefore, that since 'Confucian' countries alone are showing economic dynamism, Confucianism may have played a comparable role to Protestantism in economic development.[9] One problem with this hypothesis is that the homeland of Confucianism, China, is still at a low level of economic development; its per capita GNP in 1990 was only $370. Another problem is that Confucianism was born more than 2,000 years ago, and so one must ask why it took so long for its beneficial economic effects to appear.

Confucianism was introduced into Japan more than 1,000 years ago, but it was only during the Tokugawa period that it became standard learning for anyone who sought education, especially for the samurai class. This tradition remained as an important influence in the modern period, especially in the area of moral education, and it strengthened, if not created, the value system of loyalty, benevolence, etc. which helped capitalistic development in a direct or indirect way. Thus, although the economic success of Japan—and the Asian NIEs—may not be unrelated to Confucian tradition, it is difficult to argue, as Weber did about Protestantism, that Confucianism brought about Japanese capitalism. For one, its economic philosophy was anti-commercial, regarding agriculture as the basis of the economy, and placing merchants below samurai, peasants, and artisans in the social hierarchy. One might counter that Protestantism was not pro-commercial, but neither was it (especially Calvinism) anti-commercial, and it even justified the pursuit of profits. One can not find such justification in Confucianism.

A further problem with assessing the impact of Confucianism is that its influences were felt not alone but together with other teachings. For example, Confucian teachings were incorporated into Shingaku, but so also were Buddhism, Shintoism, and the business ideologies which prevailed at the time Shingaku was founded. Similarly, Confucian teachings were incorporated, with others, into bushido and the Hotoku movement. Thus, even if it is not possible to link Confucianism directly to the rise of capitalism in Japan, its indirect effects, through its influences on bushido and such ethical movements as Shingaku and Hotoku, can not be totally denied.

No single factor explains how Japanese asceticism arose. Probably, a number of factors were involved, and over a long period of time these combined to make it the prevalent value in the country. One factor is climate. In a hot, humid, tropical climate, it is not easy to work diligently for many hours every day. One should not, however, be a climatic determinist. There are countries or areas with a temperate climate where asceticism is not prevalent. Climate can be best understood as a necessary, but not a sufficient, condition. Another factor which needs to be considered is that economic life was harsh for most Japanese in the mid-nineteenth century when Japan started to modernize. The supply of good agricultural land was low, and there were no readily available foods to support the population. Hard work was the only way to survive. This harsh reality was hammered into the minds of children by parents at home and by teachers at school.

Asceticism was helped by a stable social order. It was widely accepted in society since it was a rewarding ethic. By accepting diligence and frugality as the values guiding their lives, people could make a living and possibly add something to what they had inherited from their parents, to pass on to the next generation. If diligence and frugality are not rewarded, for example, because what they produce is destroyed or taken away by the breakdown of law and order, it becomes more difficult to save and invest or more tempting to resort to speculative or predatory practices. Social stability characterizes the past few centuries of Japanese history. It is true that the years of the Pacific War were a chaotic period, but even then there was a great deal of peace and order in the rural areas where the mass of the population lived. Social stability enabled the values which pay off over the long run to take root in Japanese society. Asceticism thus became an important value in the process of historical evolution, as the result of the interaction of natural, social, and political factors.

As the living standard of Japan has improved, there has been some decline in asceticism, but many people still continue to work hard and save a large part of their income. The older generation, who grew up when life was difficult, believed until relatively recently that economic prosperity was unreal and that difficult times were just around the corner. They felt they had to be ready for such times and did not abandon hard work and frugality. But after Japan became prosperous, the younger generation, who grew up in the 1970s and later, did not experience life as an economic struggle. Employment opportunities were plentiful, and money came easy. As a result, they have become less work-oriented and less frugal than their elders. In view of the longer working hours and the higher household savings ratio, however, one can say that the level of asceticism in Japan is still higher than that in the West, but this seems largely due to the traditional values of the older generation.

As the number of people who do not know poverty increases,

Japanese asceticism will be further eroded. It is difficult to believe that the Japanese nation alone will continue to practise strong asceticism while enjoying a high standard of living;[10] only the question of the speed of decline remains. The decline of asceticism in the United States, for example, was not caused by affluence alone; it was caused also by the fraying of the fabric of society. In Japan, although such institutions as the family and the school, which teach moral values, have become weaker, they have not declined to the extent of those in the United States, and may remain effective for some time to come.

*Education*

Meiji leaders, following Confucian tradition, viewed the purpose of education as not only to impart knowledge but also to teach moral values. This educational philosophy was clearly manifested in the Imperial Rescript of Education of 1890, which exhorted people to fulfil their obligations as the subjects of the country. In the Confucian ethical system, fulfilment of one's duty, either to the family (filial piety) or to the state (loyalty), is at the very heart of society. Because it is a duty-oriented moral system, it was banished from the school curriculum in the post-war period as being unsuitable for the newly created democratic Japan. But Confucian ethics had taken deep roots in pre-war Japanese society, and they remained alive outside the school system even in the post-war period.

Though Confucian morals have not been specially taught in the post-war period, duties were given due emphasis at school. Social obligations are discussed in class in connection with subject-matter in textbooks. In addition, students are given work assignments to train them in collective responsibility. For example, divided into small groups, students take turns in carrying out work assignments such as cleaning their own rooms after class and serving *kyushokoku* (school lunch meals) in class.

In most people's minds, there is an urge to be free from constraints. The Western egalitarian system tries to satisfy this by advancing an individual's rights. Although it tries to balance this with one's obligations, the rights of an individual tend to predominate with the result that people lose sight of obligations, and society starts to malfunction. This is precisely what Confucianists warned people against. In the case of Japan, the demand for greater individual rights was inevitable as a result of the spread of Western culture to the country, but this was modified by the duty-oriented nature of the society.

In contrast to the West, Japanese women are still constrained socially. To be a devoted housewife is regarded as the ideal role in life, a role Confucianists commend to girls as they grow up. Although this situation is anathema to the women's liberation movement, it undoubtedly contributes to the stability of the family. In Japan, the incidence of illegitimate births is still minimal (about 1 per cent of total births), and divorce is less common, although it is recognized that wives often put up with their husbands for the sake of the children. Most children grow up in a family with both parents, who are able to do a better job of disciplining and educating them than single-parent families.

Clearly, freedom is an important goal of human life; if, despite a good record of economic growth, which liberates a person from economic constraints, freedom is restricted (or aspirations denied) in other areas of life, individual welfare can not be said to have achieved a high standard. But individual welfare depends on how well a group—such as the nation and the family—functions, and that in turn depends on how well individual obligations are fulfilled. If these obligations are not fulfilled, law and order breaks down, and families disintegrate. Thus, social obligations must be taught and enforced. One could say that the pre-war Japanese school placed too much emphasis on Confucian ethics, but from the viewpoint of social stability, it was better than not teaching them at all or doing so half-heartedly.

The older generation of Japanese today—those above 40 years old—went to school when Japan was poor and backward, and learned that Japan was a small, overcrowded, resourceless country. They were taught that diligence, discipline, and co-operation with others were necessary moral values in such a country. Despite high economic growth in the 1960s, this poor country mentality continued well into the 1970s because many people were uncertain that the rising standard of living was not a temporary phenomenon. These same values of diligence, discipline, and co-operation were also useful in inculcating a serious attitude towards education. People were taught that they were the only asset the country had and that only through education could they improve their living conditions.

From the very beginning of the modern period, another important goal of education was to impart knowledge. In Confucian education as well, seeking knowledge was important, but, in contrast, it sought knowledge in the past. For example, government leaders were encouraged to read books to find models of government and personal conduct in history. In the modern period, a broader education was necessary. The new intellectuals thus concentrated their study on the West, unlike the traditional Confucian scholars who concentrated on Japan and China. To introduce such new knowledge to Japan, the school curriculum was changed, and the role of Confucianism became largely confined to moral education.

In the post-war period, as a consequence of occupation reform and the vigilance of Nikkyoso (the Japan Teachers Union) in protecting it from attempts at counter-reform by traditionalists, moral education declined in importance in the school curriculum. The major accomplishment of post-war education was in raising the overall level of education. As a result, only 0.7 per cent of the Japanese population is illiterate today, compared with 20 per cent in the United States.[11] Japanese students do consistently well in science and math tests; the lowest math and science test scores in fifth grade classes in Japan are higher than the highest test scores in comparable American schools.[12] High school graduates in Japan and university graduates in the United States match each other in terms of basic knowledge and math and science skills.[13]

While Japanese schools have created few Nobel Prize winners— or even creative minds—they have done an excellent job in raising the *average* level of education. They have also done a good job of keeping down the variation of achievement, so that Japan today does not have a population with a large number of illiterates coexisting with an educated élite. Even after leaving school, people are encouraged to continue educating themselves for self-improvement. Japan publishes large numbers of newspapers and books every year, and several hours a day are devoted to educational and news programmes on television.

Newspaper circulation (of Japanese dailies) per capita is twice as high in Japan as in the United States. The largest bookshop in the world is not in an American city, but in Tokyo near the Tokyo Station (Yaesu Book Center). The Japanese mass media disseminates information clearly in language suited to people who have finished 9 years of compulsory education. The depth of knowledge one gains may not satisfy a sophisticated public, but it serves the purpose of information dissemination and knowledge enhancement for the general public. In a functional sense, Japan is the most literate country in the world.

One factor which has contributed to the dissemination of education in Japan is that it is a monolingual country. Children speak

Japanese at home and study it at school, a situation very different from the United States where many first-grade children do not speak English well because they come from minority groups whose mother tongue is not English. In Japan, since every Japanese child speaks the language, it is assumed that he will become literate in it in the course of 9 years of compulsory education. To meet this objective, language instruction is programmed at different levels (for example, which Chinese characters are to be taught at what grade). Literacy is such a basic requirement that no exceptions are made. If children are seen to be falling behind, teachers make an extra effort to bring them back into the mainstream by exhorting them to work harder and giving them extra tuition after class. This is quite a different situation to a multiethnic country like the United States where uniform language instruction is difficult and children are allowed to study English at different speeds. Many minorities and slow learners never catch up and therefore never develop basic literary skills. In the United States, about 13 per cent of 17-year-olds are functionally illiterate, and among minority youths, the rate of illiteracy is as high as 40 per cent.[14]

The Japanese school is much like a factory producing a specified product based on a mass-production method. Specifications are laid down by the Ministry of Education. As a bureaucracy situated in Tokyo, the Ministry is insulated from populist pressure to lower standards, which is what happens in the decentralized school system of the United States. It is relatively free to set national standards, and gives detailed instructions about what is to be taught at each grade. A school is free to select its own textbooks but only from a limited range since these have to be screened by the Ministry. As there are about 40 students in one class and the aim of education is primarily to impart basic knowledge, students are required to be disciplined listeners and to memorize what the teacher teaches. Frequent tests check on progress. In this preferred teaching method, initiative is discouraged and creative thinking penalized.

It is easy to criticize this teaching method, but it is the most economical way of raising the average level of education in Japan. If the country is willing to spend more money—and Japan spends only about 5 per cent of GNP on education, which is less than the percentage spent in the United States—the school could make instruction more individualized, but if the budget allocation for education is only 5 per cent, the present method is the only one able to meet national objectives. The alternative is to sacrifice standards, but in the long term this is no solution.

It would seem that under the Japanese method, students can not develop analytical minds, but this is not necessarily so. While the American method certainly relieves bright students of the necessity to memorize the facts which can be easily looked up in a reference book, and lets them concentrate on problem solving, to the Japanese, memorization is an important part of intellectual development. Memorization of a pattern or a line of causation can implant a framework in the mind, and help many students develop an analytical mind over time.

Another reason for the comparatively high level of education in Japan is that students study more. They go to school 240 days a year, 60 days more than their American counterparts, and thus at the end of the 12 years of elementary and secondary education, have received 4 more years of schooling.[15] They also spend more time studying outside the classroom. They spend more time on homework, go to *juku* (private tuition centres) a few days a week, do not watch television too often, and spend little time in socializing. Although there are students at high school who join sports clubs, and those at vocational high schools who are not required to study much, for the 40 per cent who aim to go to college (from the 96 per cent of 18-year-olds who graduate from high school), the 12 years of schooling before they enter college is a period of intense study. Even for those who do not go on to college, it is necessary to graduate with decent records from a high school in order to find employment.

Japan has a hierarchy of colleges based on the test scores of entering freshmen. Job prospects after college depend on which tier of colleges one goes to. Since college admission is solely determined by the scores of entrance examinations, students make an enormous effort to develop their test-taking ability. As this requires a long period of intensive study, students aiming to enter college just concentrate on studying. Though family connections and personality count, at the time of finding a job, the college one has attended is an important—often crucial—determinant. This makes studying in the first 12 years a very serious undertaking indeed.

Educating children is a joint effort of the family and the school. In recent years, neither has succeeded particularly well in teaching morals to children, but they have co-operated remarkably well in the other primary task of education—imparting knowledge. Since fewer and fewer children will be able to earn a living in the same occupations as their fathers, the only way to help them find good employment is to educate them. Many families therefore push their children to study hard and invest a great deal in their education. The *kyoiku mama* (educational mother)—by no means an uncommon phenomenon in Japan—prods her child to study; she tutors him when he is in elementary school, while she can still understand what he is studying, and acts as his servant so that he can concentrate solely on studying.

A high literacy rate in Japan can also be attributed to a more equitable distribution of income; the bottom 20 per cent of households receive 8.7 per cent of total household income, which is higher than in any industrial country.[16] Japanese marginal tax rates for high incomes are high, and since foreign workers are not allowed to enter the country, real wages for unskilled people are relatively high. These and other economic factors seem to account largely for the more equal income distribution of Japan. This has, in turn, contributed to the stability of Japanese families, a positive factor for the education of children in low-income households.

Another reason for the family's greater contribution to education is non-economic. As pointed out earlier, the rate of illegitimate births is low—about 1 per cent in Japan compared to 10 per cent in West Germany, 25–28 per cent in the United States, Britain, France, and Canada, and 52 per cent in Sweden.[17] The divorce rate is also low, largely because many parents exert greater efforts to make their marriage work for the sake of their children. Single parenthood may be the choice of a few, but single-parent families tend to be poor and do a less than satisfactory job of educating children. Parents' willingness to sacrifice for the sake of their children is also reflected in investment in children's education. One might say that the Japanese can not get away from old-fashioned values about the family, but their attachment to the family has been an important contribution to children's education. Without the family's support, the school would have been much less effective in educating children.

## Business Organization

In the past few decades, Japanese companies have grown rapidly and have demonstrated their strength in the world market. This growth was founded on a strong work ethic and the relatively high level of education of general workers. But for these qualities to be relevant in a corporate setting, people have had to be motivated and capital has had to be invested in their training, in plant and equipment, and R&D. How these were done is a matter of business organization. If people had been poorly motivated, or if there had been no strong commitment to investment, even well-educated and potentially hard-working people would have achieved low productivity.

Japanese personnel management has attracted international attention as a key factor in the strength of Japanese companies. It certainly differs in many respects from the management of Western companies. For example, such practices as lifetime employment, seniority-graded wages, internal promotion, and Quality Control (QC) circles are either unique to, or more extensively practised in Japan. These practices are believed to have contributed to productivity increase and quality control.

Another strength of Japanese companies, manufacturing companies in particular, is their willingness to invest in the future. This is believed to be related to the ownership structure of Japanese companies. They often form a group (*keiretsu*) and hold the shares of other companies in the group. This makes it difficult for outsiders to take over a company in the group and thus gives management stability. When there is a bank within the group, which is usually the case, the debt–equity ratio is high, which further reduces the importance of outside shareholders. Its share prices are important, but intercorporate holdings and reliance on banks for a large part of capital reduce the impact of share price fluctuations on management. This makes long-term planning easier and sometimes compels management to increase output, and consequently obtain a larger market share, at the expense of profits.

A vertical *keiretsu* promotes investment, and thus technological progress, but at the same time, it is important as an organizational set-up for promoting efficiency. In a typical case, it consists of an assembler and its suppliers; a supplier may have its own subcontractors. There may be some intercorporate holdings between the assembler and its suppliers, but they are separate companies. Their business relations, therefore, are part of market transactions, although they are held together by long-term ties, unlike those in the market-place which are freely formed and terminated. The vertical *keiretsu* is believed to have contributed to high productivity in such industries as motor cars and electronics, since it avoids the inefficiency arising from making the assembler produce what its suppliers are producing—this is likely to result in organizational overreach—and since it co-ordinates the assembler and its suppliers in product development, quality control, and investment better than the market. This section of the chapter examines the *keiretsu* and personnel management as the two unique features of Japanese business organization which contribute to its strength.

## Incentives

Workers will not continue working hard indefinitely if they are given no incentives. Incentives usually take the form of money and promotions, which must be distributed fairly if workers are to be motivated. If all are piece-workers and are paid according to the amount of work accomplished, the problem of incentives is relatively simple. In a normal corporate setting, however, a number of people must co-operate, and the question of wage distribution, that is, who gets paid how much, arises. Equal pay is not appropriate, since the people who co-operate differ in skill, experience, education, motivation, and other aspects of labour quality.

Most Japanese workers today are paid by the day, week, or month. One important task of management is to determine how much each should be paid. For some categories of workers, there are market rates, or opportunity costs, but for many others, there are no such guidelines, so that there is some arbitrariness in wage determination. If the level of wages is too low, many workers will leave the company, thus increasing the turnover rate, or competent workers will not be attracted to the company. In either case, productivity will decline. Conversely, if the level of wages is too high, the turnover rate will become low and many competent workers will join and stay. The company will lose money, and even if it does not go out of business immediately, because profits are small, it will become difficult to raise capital. Even if the level of wages is right, there is no guarantee that workers will continue to make the same contribution to the company in the future. If wages can not be reduced, as is often the case, and workers can not be fired, the only way to minimize the imbalance between workers' contribution and their pay is to continue to motivate them to do their best.

One technique which Japanese management uses to motivate workers is the seniority-graded wage system. On average, older workers are paid more than younger workers, even if they perform the same work. Through this system, all workers may receive the same wages for a while after they join the company, but to proceed up the wage scale, they must not only satisfy seniority requirements, but must also receive a satisfactory rating from their superiors. This rating is called job evaluation (*jinji koka*).[18]

Japanese job evaluation is not the same as the seniority rule applied in the United States. The latter is automatic, and the range of wage increase possible under it much smaller; such increase may be due more to remunerative work assignments. Although Japanese job evaluation allows workers to advance on the scale only a step at a time, and the difference in pay at each point is not great, this system produces a substantial difference in wages over a long period. Furthermore, job evaluation in Japan is the prerogative of management, whereas the seniority rule used in the United States is the prerogative of trade unions.

Job evaluation allows fast learners and energetic workers to go up the scale more quickly but, since seniority is the other factor in promotion, they can not move up as quickly as their counterparts in Western companies, which do not give much weight to seniority and base promotion primarily on merit. However, this system does not discourage Japanese 'high-flyers' from working hard. In Japan, people do not, in general, move from one company to another for better pay or work, and so the only place where they can advance their careers is with their present company. Furthermore, their whole life is spent with the company. They spend numerous hours working in the company's premises. When not working, they are often eating, drinking, or playing golf with their colleagues in the company or with their customers. They rarely have any other social life. As a result, their evaluation in the company becomes the evaluation of not only their work but also their whole personality. This gives them added incentives for working hard for the company. Because of this, there is no strong need for big bonuses or salary increases to motivate bright, energetic people, which is so necessary in the Western system. One might say that the Japanese system can keep such people rather inexpensively.

Job evaluation is a very important incentive to ordinary workers, as a favourable evaluation enables them to move up the wage scale, even if they continue to do the same work. 'Step-wise' increase in wages can also lead, eventually, to higher positions within the company. In the Western system, however, the range of wage increase, without promotion, is limited. As a result, ordinary workers, most of whom continue to do the same work until retirement, generally have low morale and become antagonistic towards management. Corporate performance is also highly dependent on ordinary workers, not only on managers, and it suffers if they are poorly motivated.[19]

In the late 1960s at Hitachi, a large Japanese manufacturer of electrical machinery, manual workers' wages increased by between 2.5 and 4.0 times during their careers. For example, the wages of the average primary school leaver stood at the index level of 71 when he was in the age-group 15–19, increased to 85 by the age of 24; to 100 by the age of 29; to 115 by the age of 34; to 132 by the age of 39; to 158 by the age of 44; to 173 by the age of 49; and to 179 by the age of 54. The increase tapered off when he was over 50 years, but the increase had continued throughout his career. In contrast, in a British factory, for example, English Electric, the wages of manual workers hardly increased after they passed the age of about 25.[20] Though this difference in the time profile of wages in Japan differed by company and changed somewhat over time, it remains valid today.[21] One should, however, add that the difference of pay by age is not as pronounced among office workers as among factory workers. It was not particularly pronounced, either, in the early 1960s.

Another important aspect of the Japanese wage structure is that, although the size of wage increases during one's career differs according to the level of education—being largest for university graduates—the wage scale is structured in such a way that a university degree is no guarantee of higher wages. For example, among Hitachi workers aged 30 years, some hard-working middle school graduates, that is, those who had completed only compulsory education, received higher pay than some slow-learning university graduates; and the average high school graduate received almost as much pay as the average university graduate.[22] Among workers of the same age, the highest pay went to university graduates and, over time, the average university graduate received more pay than the average non-university graduate. Thus, education was of value, but its effects on wages were felt gradually and could easily be neutralized by poor job performance.

Another method of motivation is to respect workers' initiative. They are not, however, encouraged to work on an individual basis. Each worker is expected to work as a member of a team and to participate in setting the team's work target, determining the working procedure, and the role he plays in the team. There is an officially appointed head of the team, whose primary function is not to issue orders to his subordinates but to act as a co-ordinator. He occupies his position not necessarily because of his technical expertise but by virtue of his seniority and his skill as a co-ordinator. He often does not possess enough professional or technical expertise to make decisions. To make up for this, he needs to depend on his subordinates: hence their active participation in the decision-making process.

Typical Western management neither trusts workers nor assumes that they are capable of making right decisions. For example, a section chief is expected to possess enough technical or professional knowledge to make decisions for his subordinates. So, unlike the Japanese system, his subordinates do not participate in setting work targets or deciding on the work procedure. They are expected to follow the chief's instructions. In such an organization, at all levels up to top management, decisions are made from above, and people below are not active participants in the decision-making process. They may not be consulted at all; even if they are consulted, the substance of decision-making power rests with the people above them. This management is called top-down or authoritarian, as against the bottom-up or participatory management in Japan.[23]

The most publicized small-group activity in Japan is the QC circle. It consists of a group of up to a dozen people who are responsible for one aspect of the work process, and is headed by the foreman; there are also QC circles among office workers, but they are not typical. They choose a certain problem of quality or process control, and work on it for a number of months. During this time, each member has to study the problem by himself, but all members also meet periodically, usually once a week, and try to solve it as a group. The group approach is emphasized because collective wisdom is believed to produce better results.[24]

For a QC circle or any small group to produce good results, the members must have a basic knowledge of their work. The members of a QC circle, in order to be able to find a solution to the problem they want to tackle, must have some engineering and technical knowledge. If they do not have such knowledge, they must be willing and able to acquire it. A QC circle serves also as a device to help workers be interested in the work they are doing and encourage them to take the initiative in work improvement. Better results are often achieved if the workers' initiative is respected than if they are required to work according to a procedure determined for them by someone else. For one, they know the problems better since they do the actual work. For another, people work best when they are given a degree of autonomy.[25]

As an overall method of inducing its employees to contribute to the company, efforts are made to convince them that their welfare and the company's prosperity go hand in hand. In a Western company, many workers have a weak sense of identification with their company. To them, the company is a place where they earn a living. The interests between the two are often in conflict; the workers want to be paid more for working fewer hours, but the company wants to make them work longer for less pay. A Japanese company puts in a great deal of effort to convince its employees that there is no such conflict. Despite group-oriented education at school, when workers join a company, they often possess ego-centred values which do not harmonize with corporate life. A Japanese company tries to change this by 'educating' them about its corporate philosophy. By listening to pep talks given by executives, going through various training sessions, and seeing the importance of spiritual commitment to the company in corporate life, workers, especially office workers, begin to develop a sense of identification with the company.

## Labour–Management Relations

Management success in inculcating a sense of worker identification with the company is made possible partly by co-operative trade unions. Unlike those in the West, Japanese unions are willing to work together with management. They rarely hold long strikes for wage increase. Nor do they readily strike because of attempts by management to introduce new technology. In contrast, it is not unusual for Western companies to be unable to introduce new technology which is needed to raise productivity because of ob-jections by unions. Because of the co-operative attitude of Japanese trade unions, the total man-days lost due to strikes in 1990 was only a little over 100,000. Strikes were more frequent in earlier years, for example, the early 1970s, but even then, industrial disputes were much less of a problem in Japan than in the West; 5 million man-days were lost in Japan compared with 27 million in the United States in 1972.

The major reason for better co-operation between labour and management in Japan is that the labour market is vertically structured and wages depend on seniority. A person who joins a relatively large company after leaving school usually wants to stay with that company until retirement, because it is very difficult to find equally attractive employment elsewhere. A worker, therefore, develops a lifetime commitment to his company and, as a result, the vertical labour market is perpetuated.

The trade unions representing workers in Japan are enterprise unions. This means that members of each union are all workers in the same company. In Britain, on the other hand, a typical union is a craft union, which covers workers of the same craft who work in many companies. Different crafts are needed for factory work, so more than one union represents the workers of the same factory.[26] This British system is inherently problematic for company management. If any one union strikes, for instance, it can paralyse the whole factory. There are also complicated demarcation problems. For example, if a machine stops because of an electrical fault, only an electrician can repair it, and if he is not around, nothing can be done until he returns. If another worker tries to repair the fault, he is usurping the prerogative of the electricians' union. Moreover, if management wants to introduce new labour-saving technology, affected unions will make a strong protest, since it means a reduction in their membership and thus a smaller representation in the company.

These problems do not arise in a Japanese factory because there is only one union. In particular, the introduction of new technology does not pose such a serious problem as in a British factory, since workers identify with the company, not with something which transcends it, such as the craft union in Britain. The company may assign a worker to a certain job at one time, but if the situation changes, it may move him to other work. When a worker joins a large company where lifetime employment is the norm, there is an implicit agreement that the company is buying his lifetime work, not his particular skill. During a worker's career with the company, he is often moved from one job to another (in job rotation), and is expected to be able to handle different jobs so that, when he occupies a position of responsibility, he will be able to understand the different jobs his subordinates are performing and act as a good co-ordinator.

In theory, a single union per enterprise could be militant and cause problems to management, but the seniority-graded wage system makes the Japanese enterprise union relatively weak. As explained above, since job evaluation is carried out by management, and not by the trade union, workers tend to be loyal to management, and this weakens the power of the union.[27] Another factor which militates against the union is the importance of length of service in the determination of wages. Workers who have stayed with a company for many years are receiving higher wages than they could have obtained by moving to another company, and they expect this difference to widen as their length of service increases. The union obtains little support for strong demands because workers fear that, if the union's demands should affect the company adversely, many workers, or, in the case of bankruptcy, all of them, could be dismissed.

## Lifetime Employment

The unique features of Japanese management, as mentioned earlier, are lifetime employment, seniority-graded wages, seniority-based promotion, job rotation, emphasis on management philosophy and objectives, flexible management (characterized by little dependence on the job manual), group decision-making, group responsibility, emphasis on smooth human relations, *ringi*,[28] and the minimization of status differences between workers and managers. Among these, the most crucial is lifetime employment, for the others are either dependent on this, or, by themselves, not so crucial a factor in determining Japanese corporate productivity. For example, job rotation is dependent on lifetime employment, as explained earlier. Seniority-based wages and promotion also can not be separated from lifetime employment, for, if a person can not be dismissed or demoted, wage increase and promotion have to be gradual. Even in the West, in government service, where dismissal and demotion are difficult, seniority-graded wages and promotion can be observed.

Why did lifetime employment become established in Japan? Before answering this question, a few points must be clarified. Lifetime employment and all the other features of so-called Japanese management are prevalent among large companies and apply largely to male employees. Although women are employed in such companies, most of them leave at the time of marriage or, at the latest, when they become pregnant. Lifetime employment is not practised in most small companies. It would appear, therefore, that a cultural factor, by itself, does not provide a sufficient explanation for this practice.

Another question to be resolved is whether lifetime employment is really a unique feature of Japanese management. It is also observed in some large Western companies. For example, Hewlett-Packard emphasizes employment stability and have many long-serving workers. On the other hand, some male workers in Japan leave their employers in the middle of their careers, and some companies have to dismiss workers in times of financial difficulties. Therefore, this question is a matter of degree. When one says that lifetime employment is practised in Japan, it means that most school leavers who join a large or expanding company stay with the same company until retirement. There must be such people also in the West, but the proportion is much smaller. It is much more common for workers in the West to 'job-hop', especially when they are young.

Why is lifetime employment, as defined above, prevalent among large companies and not among small ones? Large companies have become large because they have enjoyed monopolistic advantages in marketing, finance, or technology. Some of these advantages may have accrued in the process or as a result of growth but, to become large, they must have possessed some initial advantages. They developed these advantages at least partly because they employed people of better quality—with more drive, better skills, and more professional knowledge—than the companies which did not grow. Lifetime employment can be seen as a means of keeping such people.

One might counter this explanation by arguing that, although large Western companies faced the same problem in the process of their growth, they did not develop the practice of lifetime employment. In this context, one must remember that Japan was a latecomer on the scene of industrialization and grew much faster than Western countries.[29] Rapid industrialization meant a scarcity of skilled and professional people. In order to meet their requirements, Japanese companies had to recruit people with good potential and train them. If they lost such people after training, it meant they would lose money, so they had to devise measures to induce them to stay. A guarantee of employment in the future was such a measure. This became an established practice among the *zaibatsu* and other large companies, especially those involved in heavy industry, in the early 1920s.

If rapid industrialization had been the only reason for lifetime employment, Korean companies, which have grown more rapidly in the past few decades than Japanese companies did in the early decades of this century when lifetime employment was being adopted, would have had very good reasons for adopting lifetime employment. But 'job-hopping' is common in Korea, and lifetime employment is not an established practice. Although it is still too early to tell, it seems likely that factors other than rapid industrialization were involved in establishing lifetime employment in Japan. Important among them are business tradition and the psychological make-up of Japanese workers.

The personnel management of large merchant houses in the Tokugawa period, such as Mitsui and Sumitomo, became a model for newly established companies in the modern era. The personnel management adopted by those merchant houses was a result of trial and error in the preceding few centuries, embodying a great deal of wisdom, and thus could not be easily ignored if one wanted to make a company a success. Those houses recruited their employees when they were children, trained them, and promoted them as they gained experience and proved to be trustworthy. This was the best way since education was poorly developed and there were plenty of dishonest people. The situation improved in the modern period, but very slowly initially, and it was safer to copy the management model of established merchant houses, especially when people were hired for promotion to responsible positions in the future. Even among factory workers, the problem of stealing tools, raw materials, and products existed, and lifetime employment, which enabled workers to reap benefits over years, was an important means of making them committed to the prosperity of their workplace.

The psychological make-up of Japanese workers may also have had something to do with the establishment of lifetime employment. As was pointed out in Chapter 2, there was practically no transition period in Japan from feudalism to capitalism. Thus, although various institutional reforms were carried out in the early Meiji years, the feudal tradition could not be eliminated overnight and Japanese capitalism had to start with a number of feudal values. Important among these, for the present discussion, are those derived from the low degree of horizontal mobility and the subsistence nature of the economy. In the rural areas from which the mass of workers came during the Meiji period, monetary relations were not strong; there was not much choice in establishing or dissolving social relations, for people were born into certain relationships and maintained them until they died; there was a well-defined and stable social hierarchy; and there was a great deal of co-operation in economic and social fields.[30] These aspects of rural society were important influences on the character of people who moved into the modern sector.

Because of these influences, compared with their Western counterparts in a comparable stage of industrialization, Japanese workers put more emphasis on social needs, stable relations, and long-term interests. They did not want to consider relations with their employers purely in monetary terms, and they also wanted their social needs to be met. They did not wish, as long as their economic needs were reasonably satisfied, to move from one social setting to another. They appear to have taken a long-term view in assessing benefits from work, and to have been willing to accept low pay initially with the prospect of higher pay in the future. These psychological traits seem to have contributed to the establishment of lifetime employment.[31]

## Corporate Alliance

A large Japanese manufacturing company enjoys high productivity because its workers are committed to their work and because they co-operate with management, but that is not the whole story. Its high productivity is also linked to the fact that it is helped by its business allies in reducing the risk involved in inter-firm co-ordination, in having access to capital, and in being shielded from financial Vikings who push management to pursue speculative profits. If its business allies are subcontractors, the large manufacturing company depends on them for the supply of good-quality parts at reasonable prices at a particular time. These business relations are made possible by a system called the *keiretsu*.

A horizontal *keiretsu* consists of a number of large, independent companies in different industries. Being a business group of independent companies, it differs from the pre-war *zaibatsu* in that it is not headed by a holding company. Although *zaibatsu* names are attached to some horizontal *keiretsu*, such as Mitsubishi, pre-war *zaibatsu* companies were owned by a family holding company. In the case of the Mitsubishi *zaibatsu*, the insurance, mining, trading, shipbuilding, real estate, steel manufacturing, and warehousing companies, including a bank, prefixed with 'Mitsubishi', were owned by Mitsubishi Goshi, the holding company of the Iwasaki family. The *zaibatsu* was thus a family-owned conglomerate.

On the other hand, the Mitsubishi group of today consists of about 30 independent companies engaged in a diverse range of activities. There is no holding company which makes them operate like separate branches of the same company, as was the case of the pre-war *zaibatsu*. Nevertheless, to say that the Mitsubishi companies today are completely independent is misleading. For instance, they hold the shares of other companies in the group to the extent that it gives them management stability and makes it difficult for outsiders to take control of them. As pointed out earlier, although there is no holding company which directs the activities of the group, the bank, with the assistance of the trading company, acts as the linchpin of the group. When companies in the group undertake a business jointly, it is usually done by mutual consultation, but although the bank may have more influence, it is not in a position to dictate to member companies what to do.

There are a large number of business groups in Japan today. Some, like Mitsubishi and Sumitomo, are rather cohesive, but others, like the Fuyo group, are loosely structured.[32] What is significant is that companies in the same group tend to do business together so that it is difficult for outsiders to break in, especially if they have to compete with companies in the group. The more cohesive the group is, the more difficult it is for outsiders to penetrate intragroup transactions.

A business group is formed because there are advantages to be derived from it. From the viewpoint of management, one clear advantage is the intercorporate holdings which give it stability. Unlike in the United States, financial institutions in Japan, including banks, can own the shares of another company—in the case of a bank, up to 10 per cent—and sit on its board of directors. When their shares are combined with those of other companies in the same group, the intragroup holdings form a core of stability. Furthermore, when the holdings of companies which are outside the group, but have business relations with it, are added, the holdings often exceed two-thirds of total outstanding shares. This insulates management from the pressure of shareholders who are interested in short-term gains from the fluctuation of stock prices. Without such stability, as has happened in the United States, management, even of manufacturing companies, can come under the control of lawyers, MBAs (those who have MAs in business administration), and accountants who know nothing about technical problems but are consumed by monetary gain. This is guaranteed to destroy the technology base.

The central role played by a bank in the group also contributes to management stability. The debt–equity ratio is high in large Japanese companies; it was over 10 in the 1970s in the case of large trading companies. In the case of a *keiretsu* company in a business group, this is made possible largely by the co-operation of the bank in the group. The bank does not lend all the money the company requires, but provides the largest amount and acts as a sort of guarantor for the other banks which lend money to the company. The stock market is poorly developed compared with the financial institutions, possibly because people generally think that to buy a stock is speculative, and thus bank loans are important for a company in general. Because of this, the bank's voice is felt on the board of directors out of proportion to its shareholding.

A business group is also useful in co-ordinating a deal involving companies in different fields. For example, a plant export, which constitutes an important pillar of Japanese machinery export, normally involves a trading company, various manufacturers, a bank (as financier), an insurance company, and a shipping company. The plant export is greatly facilitated if uncertainty is reduced as to whether the companies involved carry out their part in good faith. Otherwise, transaction costs become so high that the export may not be viable. Although it is not always true that non-member companies are not involved in such endeavours, a business group tends to nurture the trust necessary among its member companies through a network of business and personal relations to facilitate such joint undertakings as a plant export.

A vertical *keiretsu* usually involves a large assembler and its suppliers. In the case of motor car manufacturing, a few tiers of suppliers are involved: the first tier of companies supplies directly to the car assembler, the second tier works for the first tier, the third tier for the second, and so on. The vertical *keiretsu*, in this case, constitutes a pyramid of about 50,000 companies, with the assembler at the top and the number of companies increasing as the tier descends. Unlike a horizontal *keiretsu*, power relations are unequal. The assembler wields much more power than its suppliers, and this can easily result in exploitive relations.

A vertical *keiretsu* is an intermediate arrangement between the market and a corporate hierarchy. Unlike a company which has various departments producing parts internally, a vertical *keiretsu* consists essentially of independent companies, though there may be some intercorporate holding. The assembler retains an option of terminating relations, while its suppliers can always leave the *keiretsu* and join a new *keiretsu* or become completely independent suppliers. Basically, the relations between the assembler and its suppliers in a vertical *keiretsu* are voluntary. On the other hand, their relations are more stable and long-term than those formed specifically for a transaction and terminated when it is completed.

An extreme example of the vertical *keiretsu* system is that of an assembler who depends completely on outside suppliers for parts. At the other extreme, the assembler produces every part internally. In Japan, however, a typical assembler produces some parts but subcontracts many more; for example, in car manufacturing, an assembler usually produces engines. An American car assembler, in contrast, produces more parts than its Japanese counterpart, but also gets many parts produced by outside suppliers. In the 1980s, General Motors produced half of the sales value of its cars inside the company, whereas Toyota produced a quarter of its sales values.[33] It is said that the system of relying more on outside suppliers has strengthened Japanese car companies *vis-à-vis* American companies.

The basic reason for subcontracting parts is that whatever benefits arise from internal production (for example, the economy of scale), these are outweighed by increased cost. In Japan, it is very likely that the cost of cars would be higher if more parts were produced by an assembler. A typical Japanese assembler instead uses more than one company to supply the same part and lets them compete. Since a 'divorce' can take place, this acts as pressure on suppliers to perform well, but if the assembler internalizes part of the production, such competitive pressure disappears, and this is likely to result in higher costs.

Another reason is that wages are lower and working hours longer in part supply companies than in an assembly company. In Japan, working conditions vary according to the size of the firm, and since an assembler is a large company and suppliers are small companies, the assembler pays higher wages than the suppliers.[34] From the viewpoint of an assembler then, as long as its suppliers can produce the quality of parts which it requires at acceptable prices, and can deliver them when needed, it is more profitable to get those parts produced outside. In the United States, it is probably because those conditions could not be met that car assemblers like General Motors have had to produce more parts than their Japanese counterparts and incur larger costs.

A vertical *keiretsu* system has, none the less, had to be nurtured in Japan because of the inadequacies of suppliers. Many suppliers initially depended on the assembler for capital, technology, management know-how, and manpower, though this dependence was probably less than that of American suppliers on their assembler. A Japanese assembler had therefore to invest resources in some of its suppliers but, at the same time, get a fair return on the investment. A *keiretsu* can be regarded as the system to ensure this.

What makes a vertical *keiretsu* work is goodwill on the part of both the assembler and its suppliers.[35] The assembler can easily exploit the arrangement if it tries to deny a fair return on investment to its suppliers by regarding their investment as sunk cost. Once the suppliers invest money in machinery, the best they can do under such an assembler is to cover variable costs, but over the long run, the assembler suffers, too, because its suppliers hesitate to undertake new investment.

A supplier can equally well exploit the assembler. If the latter helps the former by investing its resources, for example, by lending money and providing technical assistance, it expects the former to remain loyal to it for quite some time. But since the supplier can easily break business ties, which is possible because the assembler rarely has a shareholding large enough to control the supplier (assuming it holds a share), it can decide to become a completely independent supplier or join another *keiretsu*.

Another element necessary in the working of a vertical *keiretsu* is the dynamism of small supply companies. If they have to be always protected and nurtured by an assembler, a vertical *keiretsu* becomes too expensive to maintain. In this case, it is better to follow the American example and produce parts internally. What makes Japanese small companies strong generally is the availability of people who are willing to work hard under poorer conditions. A small factory may be poorly lighted, badly arranged, demand longer working hours, and pay lower wages, but the rate of absenteeism among its workers is very low. At the same time, because of the spread of education, especially vocational education, many workers are able to absorb any new knowledge needed to adapt to ever-changing economic and technological conditions. The companies are also usually headed by entrepreneurs who have a strong work ethic, are reasonably well-educated, and are serious about studying changing economic conditions. They are usually willing to invest a large part of their profits for future growth. Without the availability of workers and entrepreneurs with such qualities, a vertical *keiretsu* can not function efficiently.

The psychological traits of the Japanese may have also contributed to the working of the *keiretsu*. The Japanese tend to view society as vertically structured and believe that as long as authority is properly exercised, it is their duty to obey it. At the same time, they are trained to work in a group. Although individual effort is emphasized (otherwise a strong work ethic would not be born), strong individualism, such as a hero culture, is discouraged. Instead, the Japanese are taught to be good team players by fulfilling their obligations to the team faithfully and competently and by sacrificing individual interests for the sake of group interests. They are trained not to develop strong inner values as a guide to individual behaviour, but to seek social recognition through a group. Such an attitude is ideal for forming and sustaining a *keiretsu* arrangement.

## The Government

In order to understand the level of economic performance of a country at a particular time, it is important to consider the interaction of the market economy with the government, which intervenes in the economy and supplies the public goods the economy needs in order to perform. If government intervention is accompanied by a great deal of corruption, or if public goods are not adequately provided because the government cannot raise the necessary tax revenues, the environment for the market economy deteriorates. Many developing countries suffer from these problems.

The law may be badly enforced and corruption common; guerrilla and criminal groups may extort money from businessmen or demand ransoms by kidnapping their family members; ethnic wars may explode from time to time; or people may resort to large-scale violence for gaining political independence or overthrowing the existing government. These conditions make long-term planning and business modernization difficult. Furthermore, when government is oligarchical, economic policy is captured by a small group of influential people who have vested interests in government intervention and who promote the growth of inefficient industries.

In Japan's modern history, the government has provided a reasonably stable environment for business. Having become a nation of one culture and one language, the country has never faced a separatist movement nor an ethnic war, and because of its long history of self-government, it has developed a reasonably effective bureaucracy for administration. The legitimacy of the government has, therefore, not been the problem as it is in newly independent countries in the post-war period, except in the early years of the Meiji era. Being relatively free from political interference and having a tradition of its own, the government bureaucracy has often intervened in the market economy for the national good, but has not created a proliferation of inefficient industries. This section of the chapter examines the problem of public goods, in particular, law and order, and government intervention, especially the Ministry of International Trade and Industry's (MITI) industrial policy.

### Public Goods

It is fashionable today to talk of privatization, liberalization, and deregulation, and one is easily led into believing that if everything is left to the market, economic welfare will increase. This is far from the truth. One major reason is that there are goods called public goods which the market cannot supply efficiently.[36] These are the goods which are jointly consumed so that the principle of price discrimination does not apply. In other words, a person can enjoy their consumption without paying for them, so that there is a tremendous incentive not to pay; this produces a 'free rider' problem. Of course, if many people fail to pay, public goods can not be supplied. The best arrangement in this case is that the government takes over the responsibility of supplying public goods and taxes people to cover their costs.

In industrial countries, despite some efforts in the past to reduce the government sector, it has continued to expand, partly because the demand for public goods is increasing all the time. Typical public goods are national defence, law and order, public health, and infrastructure, such as roads. Some of these goods are needed by the public because they affect their personal welfare. Others may be opposed by the business sector, for example, a careful inspection of imported foods on the grounds that such inspection is too time-consuming. Yet other public goods, for example, law and order, affect not only the personal welfare of the public but also the performance of the market economy directly.

Education is a controversial public good. Strictly speaking, it is not a public good, as seen from the existence of private schools. But the government usually assumes the task of educating people because if this were left to the market economy, many people would remain illiterate, undisciplined, and uneducated. Because the social cost of these ills is believed to exceed the cost of running schools, the government usually steps in to provide it at low cost. Education is sometimes called a merit good since society wants to encourage people to consume more of it than they would if it were left to the market.

The reason why education is considered a private rather than a public good is that people who receive it benefit from it economically in the long term. This is clearly the case for people who go to professional or technical schools. At higher levels, it is not clear whether or not education should continue to be subsidized by the government, but there is almost universal consensus that children should be provided free basic education. Even at this level, of course, children can become literate and use this skill for further training and other types of self-improvement when they join the work-force. But literacy can not be separated from the other benefits of basic education, which are indispensable for social and political stability. First, children must be taught social rules: what to do and what not to do, and the consequences of their actions. Secondly, they should be taught about their country—its geography, society, culture, and history—so that they develop a sense of togetherness with people from other parts of the country.

Moral and civic education has important implications for law and order since the maintainence of the civil peace is both difficult and expensive if carried out by physical force alone. Law and order are best maintained if people respect the law. If they do not, the armed forces have to be large, which is obviously costly. Furthermore, business organizations which consider police protection to be inadequate may employ private security guards to protect their property and personnel. In some countries (for example, the Philippines), there exist private armies of a few hundred well-armed men. In Japan, however, the need for such security guards is minimal, and the size of the armed forces for internal reasons is relatively small.

Security guards—and private armies in extreme cases—and increased armed forces are not the only cost to the economy when people do not respect the law. Adverse effects are felt in many other ways, though they are not as serious as the destruction of property and the threat to personal safety. For example, if factory owners with financial problems arrange for their factories to be set on fire in order to claim insurance, the fire insurance scheme breaks down. Or if many people resort to fraud, business transactions—which are often based on mutual trust between the parties involved—are seriously curtailed. If a company feels that it cannot trust its employees because, for example, there are many instances of cheating, it may feel that it can not delegate power to those outside the family.

Some problems of law enforcement arise because government officials exercise their power arbitrarily—or to enrich themselves. The police may not charge traffic violators who bribe them; they may provide better protection to offices and factories which give them food and pocket money; or they may extort money from people. Customs officials may participate in smuggling. Tax assessors may accept bribes. Government officials in the agencies which issue licences and permits may also succumb to bribes. When such corrupt practices become rampant, people are less willing to obey the law, and the rule of law, on which the working of the capitalist economy system rests, becomes seriously impaired.

Japan has not escaped from problems of law and order. There have been terrorist attacks on business leaders, for example, the assassination of Dan Takuma of the Mitsui *zaibatsu* in the early 1930s, and instances of the destruction of private property, such as the rice riots of the late 1910s. In the first few years following the Pacific War, the political situation was chaotic: many people broke laws, and the law enforcement agencies were in disarray. The number of murders, thefts, robberies, and frauds has increased in the past few decades.

On the whole, however, Japan has been reasonably successful in maintaining law and order. Despite an increase in crime in recent years, the crime rate is still low in Japan compared with Western countries. In 1990, the number of crimes per 100,000 people was 1,324 in Japan, but was 6,169 in France, 7,108 in West Germany, 8,630 in Britain, and 5,820 in the United States. A similar difference is observed in the figures for violent crimes such as murder and manslaughter; the number per 100,000 people in 1990 was 1.0 for Japan, 4.5 for France, 3.9 for West Germany, 2.3 for Britain, and 9.4 for the United States.[37]

Several factors have contributed to this comparatively good record. By the mid-nineteenth century, when modernization started, Japan was culturally unified so that secessionist movements, which are not uncommon in newly independent countries, have never been a feature in Japan. Cultural unification also helped educational progress in the modern period. What was particularly important for maintaining law and order was the emphasis on civic and moral education in schools. Since religious influences were already weak in mid-nineteenth century Japan, in order to make children behave when they grew up, the government had to emphasize the teaching of morals, based largely on Confucian ethics, at school, and this was to have a positive influence on modern Japan. In Western countries, religious influences declined with economic and social changes, and with the spread of liberalism, moral education could not be emphasized at school to counterbalance the decline.

A cohesive community was another positive factor. Its prototype, as discussed earlier, was a Tokugawa village. One might imagine it was run by the samurai in a castle town or by the *daikan* who represented the shogunate, but it was, in fact, a self-governing community.[38] Although it had to pay taxes and fulfil other obligations to the daimyo or shogunate, as long as these duties were fulfilled, it was left to manage its internal affairs. Interference from outside, in the event it could not manage its own affairs (resulting in, for example, violent disputes), was a situation to be avoided, since a samurai contingent sent to run the village was very likely to abuse its power. A Tokugawa village, therefore, developed a social system to manage its own affairs, and since it was a small community, it could not afford to maintain a full-time police force. It was important for villagers to co-operate for the sake of smooth village administration by fulfilling the obligations assigned to their respective social positions. There was also need for mutual co-operation springing from the nature of rice cultivation, for irrigation, transplanting, harvesting, and other agricultural work could be carried out more efficiently if people helped each other. Such need for co-operation gave rise to the development of social norms for people to observe as well as sanctions (for example, *mura hachibu* or social ostracism) to punish them if they violated it.

In cities as well, people created a community, and were bound by its informal rules. The proliferation of such communities undoubtedly contributed to law and order.[39] An American observer, Lafcadio Hearn, impressed with the law and order he observed in Meiji Japan, wrote: 'I have lived in districts where no case of theft had occurred for hundreds of years,—where the newly-built prisons of Meiji remained empty and useless,— where the people left their doors unfastened by night as well as by day.'[40]

For the government to maintain law and order and to provide other public goods—and merit goods such as education—it must have the necessary revenue. However, it is not easy to obtain revenue since people do not, in general, want to pay taxes. In developing countries, direct taxes are especially difficult to collect, since those who have to pay the bulk of such taxes have political influence and block attempts to improve tax collection or to enlarge the tax base. Such governments are frequently short of funds, and can not undertake the necessary investments for modernization. This impairs the country's development potential. For example, Bangkok, the capital of Thailand, is often flooded, but the government has done practically nothing to alleviate the situation. The roads are also congested with private vehicles, but no adequate mass transit system has been developed, although it is presently being planned. Education is also given low priority in Thailand, because the effects of education are not immediately felt and because there are more pressing political demands. Despite these and other needs for government investment to promote development, no inheritance or property taxes have been introduced, and personal and corporate incomes have been poorly exploited. Indirect taxes still account for about 75 per cent of tax revenue.

The economist G. Myrdal termed the state which cannot coerce its people a 'soft' state.[41] This term generally applies to developing countries. In contrast—as can be judged from Japan's ability to maintain law and order—Japan was a strong state. This strength is reflected also in the field of taxation. In the feudal Tokugawa period, the peasants paid as much as 50 per cent of their rice output as taxes. In the modern period, although the peasants shared the major burden of taxation initially, the government taxed new sources as they arose in the course of development. The government's powers of taxation ensured the collection of revenues needed to finance the supply of public and merit goods commensurate with the level of development of the country at a particular point in time.

One has to consider the nature of government in trying to understand Japan's ability to provide public goods. It has always been largely an élitist institution, respected but sometimes feared by the people. It was not a government which received its power from the people, as in a Western democracy, but was a government which had 'sovereignty' vested in itself. It began extending freedom to people only reluctantly in recent years. Even if the government exercised power arbitrarily and people felt that they were wronged, the recourse available to them was limited. For quite some time, the best course of action for ordinary people was not to act in ways that might invite government intervention, and to avoid government authorities as far as this was possible. If they had some dispute, it was better to resolve it among themselves.[42] Since the government was not a populist institution where people could go to seek help, the public demand for social expenditure, such as livelihood assistance and other welfare measures, was limited. In contrast, in many Western democracies, social expenditure absorbs more than half their national budgets, and this seriously constrains the governments' ability to spend money on public goods, despite the fact that the government sector is bigger; in the past few decades, Japan's government spending has accounted for about 25 per cent of GNP in contrast to a little over 30 per cent for the United States and about 40 per cent for Britain.

The authoritarian nature of government was fostered by its capacity to attract competent people to the bureaucracy. A number of factors have contributed to this. One was the social prestige bestowed on bureaucrats since the feudal Tokugawa period. Another was the high salaries of career bureaucrats, especially in the earlier phase of modernization; in recent years, their more modest salaries have been offset by *amakudari* (descent from

heaven) to lucrative posts in private and semi-government corporations after retirement or by entry into politics, another
immensely lucrative career. The third attraction was the power
which bureaucrats could exercise. Before the Pacific War,
bureaucrats, as the representatives of the emperor in whom
sovereignty rested, exercised a great deal of authority in contrast
to the legislative branch which was relatively powerless. After the
war, sovereignty was transferred to the people, and the legislative
branch increased in strength, but since many former bureaucrats
became leading politicians in the ruling Liberal Democratic Party,
there emerged symbiotic relations between bureaucrats and
politicians. Even the politicians who were not drawn from the bureaucracy found it advantageous to co-operate with the bureaucracy
since they could benefit from its influence on business. Former
Prime Minister Ohira Masayoshi advised that a minister 'must
consider himself only a temporary visitor to his government office
and must try as hard as he can not to be disliked by his officials'.[43]
If politicians tried to blatantly interfere in policy affecting the
general welfare of the nation, bureaucrats could rely on an active
mass media to expose them. Thus, even under the post-war democracy, bureaucrats in Japan were relatively free of blatant political
interference, and throughout the modern period they have enjoyed
a large measure of autonomy. (In theory, the emperor was
supposed to control them in the pre-war period, but in practice, he
rarely interfered.)

Despite such autonomy, corruption did not become entrenched
in the bureaucracy, primarily because it did not enjoy absolute
power. In the post-war period, it shared power with politicians, the
mass media, and the business world. In the pre-war period, it was
more independent, though not completely free from the mass media
and politicians who influenced public opinion against it if it became
corrupt.

At the same time, one has to recognize the tradition of principled
governance in the bureaucracy, partly as a result of Confucianism
which acted as a moral constraint. Confucian ethics were developed
partly to guide bureaucratic leaders in the running of an authoritarian government. For example, Confucianism teaches that power is
entrusted to those in authority and that they must exercise it fairly
and have the ability to use it for the benefit of the public. It teaches
also that if they misuse power, they will lose the mandate of heaven
to run the country. As long as they are exercising their power
properly, Confucian ethics also demand that people fulfil their

obligations as members of the political community by obeying government authority. Although bureaucratic leaders tend to emphasize the behavioural obligations of the public, the concept of mutuality can not be overlooked in Confucian teaching.

Nationalism has also played a role. Career bureaucrats joined the government by passing rigorous examinations, and were promoted on the basis of merit. They came largely from élite national universities where they not only gained knowledge but also nationalistic biases, which fostered the belief that it was their mission to help the country progress. This was reinforced in the bureaucracy by their superordinates who had experienced a similar educational process and had been demonstrating national leadership in the country's modernization and development.

## Government Intervention

The Japanese government has been investing in various kinds of infrastructure, not all of them public goods since these can be supplied by the private sector, such as telephones, railways, and air transportation. But the government has undertaken such investment believing that an adequate infrastructure is essential for accelerating economic development, and that private capital is too slow in providing it. To what extent and in what way a government should be involved in building an infrastructure is debatable. The Japanese government, however, has been more involved in this than the average Western government, largely because it was able to copy from the West and because it did not want to waste time in experiment and commercial implementation.

The role of the government in providing infrastructure was not challenged during the developing stage, when the availability of such an infrastructure was essential, but more recently the public has begun to question the continued involvement of the government in services which can be provided by the private sector. After the country was industrialized and had caught up with the West, the efficiency of infrastructure services became an important issue. In the 1980s, NTT, which had a monopoly on telephone and telegraph services, was partially privatized; and the deficit-ridden Japan National Railway was split into six regional companies and one nation-wide freight service company, all of which are scheduled to be privatized in the near future. Clearly, the need for government involvement in the infrastructure services, which can be handled by the private sector, changes during the course of development.

In manufacturing industry, the government was not active in setting up factories. Although it set up a number of model factories in the early Meiji years—and later the Yahata Steel Mill and armaments factories were set up—most of these model factories were privatized in the first half of the 1880s. After this, the government avoided participation in civilian industries. In the post-war period, the armaments industries were dismantled or privatized for non-armaments purposes. It may appear, then, that the government's role in industrialization declined after the war. But the fact is that through its industrial policy, backed by various control measures introduced in the 1930s and during the war period, the government increased its influence on industry.

One might question the usefulness of industrial policy. Free market economists hold, as their central tenet, that the government should not get involved in areas where the market can. But under certain conditions, the government can perform co-ordination functions better than the market. The market system may be slow in inducing complementary activities or may give wrong signals and induce unnecessary activities, thus wasting productive resources. These problems can be avoided if the government uses its authority and acts as a co-ordinator. The Japanese government has taken an active role in this and, as a result, industrial transformation has been greatly facilitated. The government agency in charge of industrial policy was MITI.

As discussed in Chapter 1, the shift to heavy industry began in earnest in the early 1950s. Until then, Japanese industry depended heavily on light industry, textiles in particular, but this dependence meant that the Japanese economy would face slow growth in the future because the domestic and export demand for light industrial products was increasing only moderately. MITI felt that for Japan to grow rapidly, it was essential to change its industrial structure in favour of heavy industry, as the demand for heavy industrial products was growing more quickly. The fact that technical progress was taking place more rapidly in heavy than in light industry further justified the promotion of the former.[44]

In order to promote heavy industry, MITI performed two tasks. One was to encourage the private sector to invest in new, promising industries. At this time, MITI still possessed a number of control measures so that it was in a position to offer inducements. Specifically, it could ensure the provision of the foreign exchange necessary to import technology, machinery, and raw materials; conversely, it could refuse foreign exchange to competing imports;

it could make available low-interest loans from the Japan De-velopment Bank and other semi-government financial institutions (the major source of their capital was postal savings); it could give special tax incentives, such as accelerated depreciation and special allowances for losses; and it could ensure the provision of the necessary infrastructure, including industrial estates.

MITI's other task was co-ordination. Investment in heavy industry is usually large because of the capital-intensive nature of the industry, so it is important to regulate the flow of investment in a particular field at any one time. If this occurs, excess capacity is created and investment is unprofitable, which discourages future investment. MITI used its authority to prevent new investments when there was no adequate demand—at present or in the foreseeable future—which could justify them. If persuasion was not enough, MITI could suspend inducements or resort to other punitive measures. In some fields, it could even refuse a licence to operate. Although it was not always successful, MITI tried to create an oligopolistic structure by limiting the number of companies in one industry, and letting them invest on a rotation system if simultaneous investment could not be justified.

Another measure which MITI used to prevent excess capacity was the adjustment of related investment projects so that one investment would not become much larger than others. For example, if a steel company had an expansion project which would result in too large an increase in supply, it was told to scale down the project; alternatively, the users of steel were encouraged to step up their investments in order to use more steel. This type of co-ordination could be achieved more easily in an industrial complex. For example, if a company wanted to set up a refinery, MITI could persuade an electric power company to set up a plant, which would use heavy oil from the refinery as fuel, and a chemical company to set up an ethylene factory, which would use naphtha from the refinery, in the complex. The ethylene factory would, in turn, be assured of business from factories which would use ethylene to produce various chemical compounds. One major problem of large investments is that they may prove unprofitable because other complementary investments may not be forthcoming. MITI minimized this problem by promoting a parallel set of investments.

One might ask whether a private investor could have played the role of co-ordinator equally well or even better. In the United States, for example, investments have been co-ordinated primarily by the private sector. However, to leave co-ordination to the private sector is often time-consuming and expensive since the private sector can not use coercion. For example, the purchase of land from a number of individual owners for the building of an industrial complex can be a very time-consuming and expensive affair if the acquisition meets strong resistance. There may also be demands for compensation from adversely affected parties. For example, in the case of an industrial complex to be built in a coastal area, local fishermen may demand compensation for pollution which affects their livelihood. The government has powers to enforce the purchase of land or to negotiate compensation, and can thus handle more effectively the problems which private investors face in settling such matters.[45]

MITI was also able to influence the location of industrial estates. Japan's shortage of raw materials for heavy industry, such as oil, iron ore, and coal, dictated that industrial complexes be built along the coast, so that imported raw materials could be processed and exported directly from there without costly inland transportation. The success of the Japanese steel industry depended on production at such locations.

MITI played an important co-ordination role in areas besides investment. For example, when there was excess capacity, as is inevitable in the market economy, MITI allowed a temporary cartel to be formed and production to be regulated. Unlike a clandestine arrangement, this cartel made it mandatory for the members of the industry to come to an agreement on production quotas, and enabled them to earn a minimum rate of return on their investment even during times of recession. When prices returned to normal levels, the cartel was disbanded. Such cartels were formed in the textile industry, which is especially prone to fluctuations in demand, and in the steel industry. For such declining industries as textiles, MITI paid some compensation for scrapping machinery, and co-ordinated the reduction of capacity. MITI was also active in setting industrial product standards, which made parts interchangeable and enabled their mass production.[46]

MITI's success in promoting heavy industry does not necessarily favour the argument for industrial policy, since it was possible under certain conditions which may not in general prevail. Important among these conditions was that the private sector was willing to accept MITI's authority, which came partly from the tradition of the supremacy of the government over people. MITI was also entrusted with powers, so that if persuasion was not enough, it could use these powers to enforce its policy, especially in the 1950s and

1960s when wartime control measures remained. Moreover, it was relatively free from political interference, and comprised competent career officers, among whom morale was high. Finally, the private sector was dynamic enough to absorb new technology and become internationally competitive after a relatively short time of government protection.[47]

In recent years, MITI has lost much of its effectiveness because some of its above-mentioned powers have been weakened. For example, with the spread of democratic values, the private sector is now less submissive and MITI's power, after a series of liberalization measures in the past, has declined. Equally important is the fact that Japan has closed the economic gap with the West in those fields where it was possible to do so in a short time. In frontier areas, it appears that since trial and error is necessary in finding new processes or products, the private sector performs better. This is the basic reason for the failure of MITI's 'fifth-generation' computer project.

There are still some industries in which Japan has to catch up with the West, for example, pharmaceuticals. Although Japan is behind the United States and other Western countries in this area, MITI can not be effective in promoting it since it is a knowledge-intensive industry in which the only way to catch up is to increase the number of highly qualified scientists. Such an increase can not be 'produced' according to a programme, as was done for the steel and petrochemical industries in the 1950s and 1960s. The aircraft industry is another field in which Japan lags behind. In this area, MITI could be more effective, but is politically constrained. The aircraft is the only major industrial product the United States can export to Japan in order to redress the imbalance of bilateral trade in which Japan enjoys huge surpluses.

1. Tokai Bank's *Chosa Geppo* [Research Monthly], September 1984, p. 24. The original source is an article in the German newspaper *Handelsbaltt Zeitung*. Similar figures are reported for Japan, West Germany, and the United States in *Asahi Shinbun*, 26 January 1985 (2,136, 1,682, and 1,851 hours, respectively). These figures are for manufacturing workers in 1982. The source quoted is the Japanese Ministry of Labour.

2. Keizai Kikaku-cho [Economic Planning Agency], *Keizai Hakusho 1992* [White Paper on the Economy], Tokyo, Printing Office, Ministry of Finance, 1992, p. 272.

3. A noted Japanese psychiatrist relates this psychological disposition to *amae*. See T. Doi, *The Anatomy of Dependence*, Tokyo, Kodansha International, 1973, p. 111.

4. E. Seidensticker, 'Preface' to J. Taylor, *Shadows of the Rising Sun*, New York, William Morrow and Co., 1983, p. 13.

5. M. Weber, *The Protestant Ethic and the Rise of Capitalism*, translated by T. Parsons, New York, Charles Scribner's Sons, 1958.

6. These are included in religion and discussed by R. Bellah in *Tokugawa Religion*, Glencoe, Illinois, Free Press, 1957.

7. For discussion on bushido, see Bellah, *Tokugawa Religion*, Chapter 4, and I. Nitobe, *Bushido*, Tokyo, Charles E. Tuttle Co., 1969.

8. R. Tawney, *Religion and the Rise of Capitalism*, New York, Harcourt, Brace & World, 1926.

9. M. Morishima discusses Confucianism and Japanese development in *Why Has Japan 'Succeeded'?*, Cambridge, Cambridge University Press, 1982.

10. Some culturally oriented Japanese scholars seem to believe that the 'deep structure' of Japanese culture does not change, or only very slowly. Even if this view is accepted for the sake of argument, it is difficult to believe that the attitude towards work and consumption is part of it.

11. M. White, *The Japanese Educational Challenge: A Commitment to Children*, Tokyo, Kodansha International, 1987, p. 2.

12. Ibid., p. 73.

13. T. Rohlen, *Japan's High Schools*, Berkeley, University of California Press, 1983, p. 160.

14. B. Duke, *The Japanese School: Lessons for Industrial America*, New York, Praeger, 1986, p. 60. The original source is the report of the Commission on Excellence in Education, *The Nation at Risk*, 1983, p. 16.

15. Rohlen, *Japan's High Schools*, p. 160.

16. World Bank, *Development Report 1992*, New York, Oxford University Press, 1992, p. 277.

17. *National Review*, 5 October 1992, p. 19.

18. Discussion on job evaluation in this section is based on Urabe Kuniyoshi, *Nihon-teki Keiei o Kangaeru* [Thinking on Japanese Management], Tokyo, Chuo Keizai-sha, 1978.

19. 'The excellent companies require and demand extraordinary performance from the average man', T. Peters and R. Waterman, in *In Search of Excellence*, New York, Harper & Row, 1982, p. xxii.

20. R. Dore, *British Factory–Japanese Factory*, Berkeley, University of California Press, 1973, p. 109.

21. Keizai Kikaku-cho [Economic Planning Agency], *Keizai Hakusho 1992*, [White Paper on the Economy], Tokyo, Printing Office, Ministry of Finance, 1992, p. 268.

22. Dore, *British Factory*, p. 101

23. This is the average tendency. There are Western companies which emphasize bottom-up management.

24. There is a saying in Japan which reflects the belief of the people in collective wisdom: *sannin yoreba monju no chie* [three heads can equal the wisdom of Manjushiri]. *Monju* or Manjushiri is the god of wisdom and intellect in Buddhism.

25. W. Ouchi, *Theory Z*, New York, Avon, 1981, p. 72. For further discussion on QC circles, see this source, Appendix Two.

26. Dore, *British Factory*, Chapter 4.

27. For this reason, it is difficult for Japanese companies to use job evaluation in their subsidiaries in Western countries where unions are strong.

28. *Ringi* is the method of obtaining the approval of superiors to a proposal by circulating the draft prepared by a person in charge.

29. Dore, *British Factory*, Chapter 15.

30. These features of rural society are discussed in Chapter 4.

31. The psychological traits of the Japanese are given strong emphasis in J. Abbeglen, *Japanese Factory*, Glencoe, Illinois, Free Press, 1958, and Iwata Ryushi, *Nihon-teki Keiei no Hensei Genri* [The Organization Principle of Japanese Management], Tokyo, Bunshindo, 1977.

32. For further discussion on business groups, see M. Gerlach, *Alliance Capitalism: The Social Organization of Japanese Business*, Berkeley, University of California Press, 1992, pp. 79–91.

33. Reported in 'Survey: The Japanese Economy', *The Economist*, 6 March 1993, p. 14. Around 1992, General Motors was producing about 70 per cent of its parts. *International Herald Tribune*, 17 March 1993.

34. For wage differences by size of firm, see Keizai Kikaku-cho, *Keizai Hakusho 1992*, p. 285.

35. R. Dore, *Taking Japan Seriously: A Confucian Perspective on Leading Economic Issues*, London, Athlone Press, 1987, p. 170.

36. Another reason is the problem of externality, which often invites the government's intervention. The government's intervention in externality is not discussed here, but Chapter 7 discusses the government's mismanagement of a pollution problem.

37. Homu-sho Homu Sogo Kenkyu-sho [Research and Training Institute, Ministry of Justice], *Hanzai Hakusho 1992* [White Paper on Crimes], Tokyo, Printing Office, Ministry of Finance, 1992, pp. 23–5.

38. J. Haley, *Authority without Power: Law and the Japanese Paradox*, New York, Oxford University Press, 1991, p. 195.

39. In 1880, there were only 912 local government officials in the Tokyo Metropolitan area, whereas the police bureau had a force of 4,400 men. D. E. Westney, 'The Emulation of Western Organizations in Meiji Japan: The Case of the Paris Prefecture of Police and the Keishi-cho', *Journal of Japanese Studies*, Summer 1982, quoted in Karel van Wolferen, *The Enigma of Japanese Power*, London, Macmillan, 1989, p. 183. As a newly expanding city which served as the headquarters of national government, Tokyo may have been an exception. But the figure may include a large contingency force to be dispatched to other parts of the country when peace and order problems arose. Anyway, it is wrong to portray Meiji Japan as a police state. The government maintained law and order relatively well by depending on people's acceptance of its authority; otherwise, the size of the civil bureaucracy, including the police but not the military, had to be much larger.

40. L. Hearn, *Japan: An Interpretation*, Tokyo, Charles E. Tuttle Co., 1959, p. 13.

41. G. Myrdal, *Asian Drama*, New York, Pantheon Books, 1968, pp. 895–900.

42. The number of lawyers is small in Japan, and so is the number of public prosecutors and judges. In the late 1980s, Japan had one lawyer per 9,294 people, as compared with one for 360 in the United States, 872 for Britain, and 1,486 in West Germany. See Wolferen, *The Enigma of Japanese Power*, p. 214.

43. Ibid., p. 143.

44. M. Shinohara, *Industrial Growth, Trade, and Dynamic Patterns in the Japanese Economy*, Tokyo, University of Tokyo Press, 1982, p. 24. For further discussion on MITI's industrial policy, see this source, Chapters 2 and 3.

45. The Japanese government did not always succeed in this task. For example, the government made a bungle of land acquisition for the Narita Airport. In recent years, as the public has gained more power, the government's land acquisition has become slow and expensive. Also, in the case of compensation, the government has been paying large sums. However, one can not argue, as the free market economists do, that the private sector can co-ordinate better than the government even in the case of infrastructure building.

46. MITI was not, however, always successful in standardization. In the case of VTRs, Sony and Matsushita adopted different standards.

47. For the first four conditions, see C. Johnson, *MITI and the Japanese Miracle*, Stanford, Stanford University Press, 1982, Chapter 9.

# 7
# The Dark Side of Development

JAPANESE economic development is, in many ways, a remarkable achievement. In particular, the transformation of the country from a feudal agricultural economy into an industrial giant is a feat only Japan accomplished among the 'developing countries' in the mid-nineteenth century. It liberated the Japanese from poverty and other economic miseries, and in more recent years, allowed them to enjoy a living standard comparable to that in Western industrial countries. But in the process of development, the non-economic components of people's welfare were unduly sacrificed. It was an inextricable part of imperialism which brought great misery to the Japanese as well as to people in the countries Japan occupied during the Pacific War. These negative aspects of modernization were brought about partly by 're-feudalization' of the country in the Meiji era, which imposed greater constraints on society in order to create a rich and militarily strong nation. In the post-war period, as the result of reform during the Allied occupation, these constraints have become much weaker, but compared with other industrial countries, the degree of freedom the Japanese enjoy in social and political areas is still limited. If these are taken into consideration, unalloyed admiration for Japanese development must undergo considerable qualification. This chapter looks at the negative side of Japanese development in the historical context, and then considers the meaning of economic development in human life.

## The Cost of Capitalistic Development

*Winners and Losers*

Although economic development brings about a rise in the standard of living for the average person, some people are invariably left out or harmed in the process of development. For them, economic development is a misery rather than a blessing. Factory workers may be included in this category. In the early phase of Japanese industrial development, factories were dirty, and in summertime unbearably hot and humid places. Workers could take off only one or two days each month and during the remaining days, normally worked 12–15 hours. They were also often forced to work for a few extra hours each day. When they became sick, rest was not always assured because of various pressures applied by their employers. In the worst cases, gangsters were employed to 'discipline' workers. Nowadays, when workers are not satisfied with their conditions of employment, they have the option of leaving their jobs, but before the Pacific War, young workers were often indentured by their parents and did not have the right to leave until the term of indenture expired. Most workers endured horrible working conditions, and many died as a result of industrial accidents or diseases. They enjoyed none of the fruits of industrial progress. For these people, the factory was a living hell.[1]

The evils of Japanese economic development are not confined to working conditions. Critics point, as a second example, to the extreme poverty of many people in the midst of increased prosperity. Those who have done well in economic competition have been rewarded, but the losers have been severely punished. One group of 'losers' in the pre-war period were tenants in villages. They were the poorest among the rural population, and their economic hardship is well documented. It is important to note, however, that the problem of tenancy did not originate in the modern period; it existed also in the Tokugawa period. In villages where the money economy had penetrated, some small farmers lost their independence during times of poor harvest or other economic difficulties and became what was known as *mizunomi byakusho* (water-drinking farmers).

Although the problem of tenancy is not confined to the modern period, in at least two respects the problem became more pronounced at this time. First, in the Tokugawa period, the relationship between tenants and landlords was social as well as economic, and economic factors alone did not determine land tenure. After the Meiji Restoration, however, the new property law increased the power of landlords, and many tenants' hold over their land became uncertain. The increase in the proportion of tenants was the other serious problem. Towards the end of the Tokugawa period, the rate of tenancy was about 25 per cent, but by the mid-1930s, it had increased to roughly 50 per cent.[2] This increase caused some concern about land productivity, but it was also a serious social problem. A large number of peasants were tied down to a subsistence income and were not able to enjoy the benefits of agricultural development.

In cities, there was also a widening gap between rich and poor, because living conditions for many people did not improve despite overall economic progress. In major cities, there were large slum areas which did not diminish significantly for at least the first few decades of economic development. Most of the slums which originated in the Tokugawa period remained and some new ones were added in the early modern period. Some of the inhabitants enjoyed equal opportunities for education but, because of incompetence, misfortune, or lack of effort, many had drifted to the slums. The slum inhabitants who grew up without education suffered for their illiteracy. They participated in economic competition with little knowledge, and from the beginning, their chances were nil. Forming the marginal stratum of the population, they lived in crowded shacks and were tied to subsistence living. To exacerbate the situation, in order to escape temporarily from their miserable conditions, many resorted to drink or gambled on money borrowed at usurious rates of interest from moneylenders. This created a vicious circle of poverty. Ignored by the government, they languished in slums, while people outside were enjoying the fruits of economic progress.[3]

*Environmental Disruption*

Japanese economic development is also at the root of environmental disruption. While this is not a uniquely Japanese phenomenon, it became serious in Japan in the early 1970s. The mental as well as physical health of many Japanese people was affected by noise, air, and water pollution. Noise pollution became particularly problematic in the vicinity of airports (for example, the Osaka Airport) and along railways and highways. Air in major cities and near industrial complexes (for example, Amagasaki in Hyogo Prefecture and Yokkaichi in Mie Prefecture) became polluted with carbon monoxide, sulphuric acid gas, nitric oxide, or lead compounds, which caused people to suffer from asthma, bronchitis, and lung cancer. To a certain extent, the pollution problem originated from the high population density of the country, which made the relocation of houses and effective city planning difficult. However, a large part of the responsibility fell upon enterprises which pursued private profits and ignored the social costs of production, and upon the government which allowed business interests to dictate environmental policy.

The most publicized case of environmental disruption is the mercury poisoning at Minamata in Kyushu. Fish in the sea around Minamata were poisoned by the organic mercury discharged by a factory owned by the Chisso chemical company, whose head office is in Tokyo. Many people in the area became sick from eating contaminated fish over the years. About 100 later died, and the health of several hundred others was seriously affected. Many lost the ability to walk, hear, or see properly, while others were totally incapacitated; many of these people are still alive today. Although the chemical factory may not have intentionally caused the poisoning, it could have taken steps to halt the discharge of mercury much earlier, in the late 1950s, when its ill-effects on the human body were first brought to public attention by a medical team. It would thus have reduced the number of victims and the extent of their suffering. It was also unfortunate that the government, the Ministry of International Trade and Industry (MITI) in particular, objected to proposed precautionary measures for fear that approval of such measures might necessitate a re-evaluation of its overall development policy, thereby adversely affecting industrial production within the country as a whole. The government allowed the factory to continue discharging mercury for another 10 years after the causal relationship between the discharge and poisoning was made known. The poisoning at Minamata is a clear example of a crime committed by the establishment.

It is sometimes argued that these problems of Japanese economic development could have been avoided under socialism. The miserable working conditions in factories, the exploitation of workers, inequalities in the distribution of income, the presence of a fairly large marginal population, and serious pollution problems are, in many ways, the excesses of capitalistic development. Unlike capitalism, socialism espouses egalitarian principles and the welfare of workers; problems arising from external diseconomy, such as pollution, are to be avoided by central planning. To advocates of socialism, capitalism is immoral, inhumane, and exploitive.

Socialism had much appeal until a few years ago, but with the recent collapse of socialist states in East Europe, people have become disenchanted with it. Most people would argue today that, although some of the problems pointed out above would not have arisen or would have been less pronounced under socialism, capitalism has produced better overall results. Undoubtedly, the rate of economic growth in the past century would have been much slower under socialism. Japan is poor in natural resources and suffers from a high population density, with the result that it has to import primary products and food in order to increase the national standard of living. To pay its import bill, Japan has to export manufactured goods. As discussed in Chapter 3, Japan's standard of living depends on the terms and volume of trade. There is little Japan can do with regard to the former, but the latter depends on the country's competitiveness in the international market, which is, in turn, determined by industrial efficiency.

Industrial efficiency is higher in a competitive system in which success is rewarded and failure punished. Under capitalism, firms which increase output when demand expands or reduce the costs of production through inventiveness or the introduction of better technology are rewarded with profits; those which fail to be adaptive and innovative suffer losses, and eventually are phased out of the economic scene. The fear of failure in the competitive struggle and the expectation of reward for success arouse productiveness and inventiveness in firms.

The basic problem of socialism, as observed in East European countries, is that there is no such fear or expectation. The planned economy is essentially a bureaucratic system, in which economic decisions are made by government planners, who often ignore the law of supply and demand. Managers at production sites are often political appointees, who are better qualified as political entrepreneurs than as business managers. The morale among workers is low because there is no incentive for hard work. Even if they work hard, there are many barriers for that to translate into economic benefits since the whole system is not geared to that end. Technological progress is also slow, and production is wasteful.

The economic inefficiency of a centrally planned economy is well demonstrated in international trade. For example, in the trade between the Soviet Union and the United States, there were few manufactured goods which the former could sell to the latter. Exports from the Soviet Union consisted predominantly of primary products. On the other hand, a large quantity of industrial goods was sold by the United States. The situation was similar in the trade between any capitalist industrial and East European country. In the developing countries, also, a centrally planned economy can not compete with capitalist industrial countries in industrial exports. Latin America, Africa, and South Asia import the bulk of their industrial needs from capitalist industrial countries, excluding the industrial goods given by socialist countries as part of economic assistance.

The fact that economic efficiency is more likely under capitalism is still not sufficient justification for the great excesses of Japanese economic development. It is relevant to ask whether there is an economic system which ensures efficiency and, at the same time, avoids the excesses pointed out above. To some economists, avoiding such excesses and maintaining high efficiency at the same time are not compatible. To them, if the excesses are to be avoided, economic efficiency must be sacrificed. This is a fatalistic attitude. As pointed out already, one cannot offer socialism as an alternative model if it entails a centrally planned economy. The countries which have tried it, including China and Vietnam, found that it would not work. Another possibility is a welfare state, as practised in such countries as Sweden. This model, however, has been losing appeal because it tends to lead to bankruptcy. Since people try to take advantage of government assistance without contributing to the national economy, bankruptcy can only be avoided by greatly sacrificing economic efficiency.

The best path is to adopt capitalism as the basic economic system and try to reduce the problems it creates with government intervention. This is a simple formula, but implementation is not easy. Success depends on three factors: the first is the capability of the bureaucracy; the second, a modal consensus on a just economic system and the quality of life possible at a certain level of income; and the third, the political mechanism for translating consensus into government intervention. For avoiding the excesses of capitalistic development, Japan can not be a good model, in view of poor performance, particularly in the pre-war period, but in the past couple of decades, the situation has greatly improved. Income distribution is more equitable in Japan than in any other industrial country, working conditions have improved, and environmental disruption is better controlled. Thus, capitalism can be improved. What constitutes the 'excesses' and how they can be corrected by government intervention are the major political parameters determining the quality of capitalistic development.

## The Cost of Imperialism

### *The Human Toll*

The Japanese military expansion not only killed, maimed, or otherwise injured a large number of soldiers, but also inflicted severe hardship on the rest of the country. In its early phase—the period up to the end of the Sino-Japanese War of 1894–5—the human costs of warfare were smaller; since the war was short, the battles were fought in restricted areas, and the destructive capability of the weapons used was limited. For example, the number of soldiers killed in the Sino-Japanese War was about 17,000. In the next war, the Russo-Japanese War (1904–5), the human sacrifice escalated: about 100,000 Japanese soldiers died. Even this number, however, was small compared with the deaths of 2.3 million Japanese soldiers and 660,000 Japanese civilians during the Pacific War.[4]

There were other dimensions to the human cost of war. An unknown number of people were crippled and disabled. Many others suffered from diseases, such as radiation poisoning, contracted during the war. Considerable psychological damage was also inflicted upon parents who lost sons, wives who lost husbands, and children who lost fathers. Furthermore, there was the suffering of people who held views in opposition to government policy, particularly of military expansion. Many of these people were sent to jail by the special police and some died from torture or prolonged imprisonment.

Japanese military expansion also exacted sacrifice from the conquered. In the colonies of Taiwan and Korea, the indigenous people were objects of contempt to the Japanese, and were discriminated against in education, employment, promotion, salary, housing, and other matters. After the Pacific War began, many Taiwanese and Korean males were either drafted to fight for Japan or to work in mines and other places in Japan where hard work was required; girls were drafted as 'comfort women' for Japanese soldiers there and abroad.

In the countries occupied after 1937, the Japanese presence brought about economic and political dislocation. In some cases, this contributed to the eventual rise of nationalism and political independence, but the number of atrocities Japanese soldiers committed during their occupation more than offset the positive effects of Japanese occupation. Their underlying feeling of superiority over other Asians, coupled with the desire for revenge after a hard fight, seems to have caused some Japanese soldiers to momentarily take leave of their senses to plunder, murder, torture, and rape in the newly conquered countries. The most notorious were the atrocities committed at Nanking in central China near the coast. When Japanese soldiers moved into the city chasing defeated Chinese soldiers, they pillaged stores, raped women, set buildings on fire, and killed several hundred thousand Chinese.

Manila and Singapore suffered a similar fate, although the scale of the atrocities was smaller. There were also a number of incidents of atrocity in other parts of South-East Asia. Large numbers of youths were drafted in the region to work for the Japanese military. In Indonesia alone, about 300,000 men were uprooted from their communities and sent to work in other places in the country where labour was needed for the construction projects of the Japanese military. About 300,000 men were recruited in the region, not only in Indonesia, for the railway project on the border of Thailand and Burma, between October 1942 and November 1943. Appropriately called the 'railway of death', it exacted some 60,000 lives. The disease-ridden jungle in the area was deadly to the workers who suffered from overwork and malnutrition. As in Korea and Taiwan, many girls were forced to become 'comfort women' for Japanese soldiers.[5]

*The Origins of Japanese Imperialism*

When did this imperialism, which exacted such a high human toll and caused so much anguish, begin? Some scholars consider the Pacific War as the only imperialist war of which Japan can be rightly accused, and thus see it as an aberration from the normal course of Japan's modern history. This apologetic view is convenient if the negative aspects of Japanese modernization are to be minimized, but it is more reasonable to think that Japanese imperialism began under the Meiji government. There seems to be a common thread of imperialist intention in the wars from the Taiwan expedition of 1874 to the Pacific War. Certainly, when Japan undertook the Taiwan expedition, it was not historically predetermined that Japan would plunge into a series of wars in subsequent years. The actual course of historical events was determined by a complex interplay of domestic and international forces which evolved over time. Nevertheless, the Taiwan expedition started the imperialist trend which culminated in the Pacific War.

Imperialism as an ideology existed in the late Tokugawa period, and such scholars as Yoshida Shoin (1830–59) argued that Japan should enhance its national power by conquering Korea, Manchuria, and China. This expansionist ideology was adopted by Meiji leaders who, having emerged from the former warrior class, were naturally inclined towards the view that the weak were destined to be ruled by the strong. Accordingly, in 1874, the first overseas expedition was sent to Taiwan. But Taiwan was not the main target: it was Korea which occupied the minds of Meiji leaders and moved them to fight two subsequent wars. After Korea was reasonably secure, northern China became the target.

If the imperialism of the 1930s was significantly different from the earlier experience, this was because militarism was rampant in the 1930s. Militarism, however, was rooted in the Meiji era when the military command became independent of cabinet control, and when the requirement that the Minister of the Army be a general and the Minister of the Navy an admiral became firmly established. At first, military excesses were checked because both political and military leaders were united by personal bonds which had been created in the Restoration Movement. As time passed, however, these bonds loosened and it became exceedingly difficult for the civilian government to restrain the military. A large part of the responsibility for imperialist activities must, therefore, be attributed to the Meiji government, which placed too much emphasis on the military in creating a modern nation.

It might be argued, however, that Japan had no alternative in those years when the Western Powers were threatening the independence of Asian nations with their superior military forces. They had wrested territories and various concessions from China by the time of the Meiji Restoration. Then, in the 1880s, France colonized Indo-China, England expanded its colonial rule in Burma, and Russia decided to construct the trans-Siberian railway for the purpose of eastward expansion. Faced with the thrust of the Western Powers into Asia, Meiji leaders judged that the survival of the fittest was the law of international relations and acted accordingly.[6]

Nevertheless, other courses of action were open to Meiji leaders. It might have been excusable to have built up a military force for defence purposes but never to have used it for aggression. Furthermore, it was only asking for potential trouble when Meiji leaders imposed conditions on the vanquished that they themselves did not like, such as unequal treaties and territorial concessions, on neighbouring countries. They could have championed Asian nationalism and helped Asian nations to defend themselves from the threat of Western domination. It is clear, in retrospect, that a policy of pacifism would not necessarily have led to national ruin, as they believed. They should have paid closer attention to Switzerland and Sweden, two countries which had prospered without foreign conquest, but such was the samurai mentality that they looked to Prussia for a model. The course that Japan has followed since the Pacific War was by no means denied to Meiji Japan. In fact, some scholars and journalists at the time argued for such a course, but their views were brushed aside in favour of the expansionist ideology.

Who was responsible for Japan's imperialism? According to the materialistic interpretation of history, the bourgeoisie was the major architect of imperialism. There is no denying that, as economic development progressed after the Meiji Restoration, the bourgeoisie increased in power and came to participate in some political decisions. Also, the support of the bourgeoisie was important to both political and military leaders: the former needed contributions to finance campaigns, intrigue, and the expansion of their political influence, whereas the latter needed money to finance military escalation and overseas adventures. Leaders among the bourgeoisie were asked to co-operate, and they used the opportunity to increase their profits as well as their political influence, but they were never at the helm of major political and military decisions. Legislatures existed and elections were held, of course, in Japan before the Pacific War, but the political system was an absolute monarchy in which sovereignty rested with the emperor. The state was run for him essentially by the bureaucrats, who could in no way be considered the puppets of the bourgeoisie.[7]

The leading decision-makers were not bound by popular sentiment, although they could not completely ignore it. Military leaders, in particular, needed the support of the nation for their expansionist policies. Thus, they appealed to the bourgeoisie on the grounds that the expansion of Japan's political influence would bring them increased profits; to land-hungry peasants, they suggested that the conquest of foreign territories would provide more land for them to cultivate. They also undertook propaganda campaigns to intensify chauvinistic nationalism. Up to the beginning of the Pacific War, imperialism brought concrete benefits and won the approval of a large number of Japanese. Without their support, even though it may have been tacit support in a large measure, it would have been impossible for the military to have become a dominant force in pre-war Japan.

*Impact on the Economy*

Did imperialism benefit the Japanese economy? Imperialist activities did result in various concrete economic benefits. For example, territorial expansion eased the pressure on land which had built up because of the population increase. Reparations obtained after the Sino-Japanese War enabled Japan to adopt the gold standard and also to construct the Yahata Steel Mill, the first integrated steel mill in Japan. The various commercial concessions Japan obtained by the use or threat of force promoted the country's export industry. Primary products, such as sugar, pulp for paper-making, and iron ore, were brought back to Japan from its colonies, either at concessionary rates or without compensation. Furthermore, militarization required the domestic production of armaments and basic industrial materials, and thus became the driving force for the development of heavy industry.

At the same time, imperialism made certain demands on the economy. A significant portion of the nation's manpower was removed from the economy and wasted in the production of military weapons. Capital badly needed for economic development was diverted to the military build-up. The high proportion of military expenditure in the government budget retarded development of the infrastructure. Finally, the destruction of resources, physical as well as human, and the economic dislocation which occurred throughout the Pacific War were heavy blows to the economy.

An assessment of the overall effects of imperialism in 1945 would conclude that imperialism was more harmful than beneficial. Because of it, the economy was ruined and the country was threatened with the possibility of nation-wide famine. If the same type of analysis were made for the 1930s or earlier, however, it would be more difficult to reach a conclusion because the costs of imperialism were not as overwhelming as in 1945. The costs must be weighed against the benefits over time, and this involves complicated computation. People tend to take definite stands on this issue without taking into consideration both sides of the ledger; such positions are usually based on either subjective and emotional judgement or illogical reasoning. For example, we can not infer that Japan would not have deliberately pursued a policy harmful to itself and that therefore imperialism must have been beneficial economically, since this argument ignores possible non-economic objectives of imperialism, such as national glory.

It is also difficult to accept the inference that the course of development would have remained essentially the same even if the expansionist policy had not been pursued, for the militarism which gave rise to the expansionist policy was, in various ways, a dynamic force of modernization, inextricably interwoven with economic and other historical developments in the pre-war period. Thus, such exercises as an econometric model, which simulates an alternative path with zero or small military expenditure, must be regarded as an intellectual farce, since it changes the whole framework, and affects the whole set of parameters defining the pre-war economy.

## The Purpose of Development

### Economic Freedom

Economic development, defined as the long-term growth of income, is ignored or even disparaged by the so-called progressive intellectuals of industrial countries.[8] For some, democracy and human rights are all that matter, while for others, the environment must be protected at any cost. But for people in developing countries, economic development is an important social goal because it liberates them from poverty and gives them greater economic freedom. Poverty is not an admirable condition and people have a great desire to escape from it. Those who enjoy a high standard of living often fail to understand this strong desire among the poor and their willingness to put it above anything else. In the past, the Japanese have been no exception to this. Today, with a higher standard of living, the desire to improve economically is not as strong as previously, but many people still give it high priority.

Clearly, economic development is not the only human goal. Since people want to be free to pursue their beliefs and interests or to develop their full potential, an ideal society should allow them a maximum degree of freedom. No society, however, can give people all the freedom they desire, since it has to impose certain obligations and has to have an institution, the government, for implementing them. These obligations become constraints on individual freedom, but they are necessary in order to enhance it. For example, traffic rules are necessary so that people can drive more freely. In an ideal society, however, people should be free from the obligations which do not enhance the scope of individual freedom.

This conception of an ideal society may not be unique to the West, but it has developed most fully there and has come to embody the spirit of these modern times. Japanese nationalists, therefore, tend to regard it as a Western ideal, one which is not always pertinent to a non-Western country such as Japan. They believe that the Japanese are more group-oriented and find happiness in a group setting, not as isolated individuals. But given the rise of individualism among Japanese in recent years, one can easily question this assumption and argue that to be free is a basic human desire regardless of racial origin.

With this in mind, it is not enough to consider economic development alone since it is only one of many human goals. In judging the accomplishments of Japan, one must also ask whether it has succeeded in liberating people in non-economic as well as in economic areas. The answer is clearly no, for compared with Western countries, Japan imposes too many obligations on its people.

Even the level of real income in Japan is not outstanding, though people may think otherwise because of the country's industrial strength. Although per capita GDP is the third highest among the industrial countries, in real terms, as argued earlier, it is substantially—about 50 per cent—lower. This is keenly felt by many people in the Tokyo metropolitan area who can afford only a small living space (a 'rabbit hatch') and spend 2–3 hours commuting to and from work. The substantial rise of income is unquestionable, and Japan can be commended for having brought this about, but it has been accomplished at the expense of some social and political freedom.

Workers in Japan give up much of their freedom because their obligations to the company are diffused. Obligations are diffused because workers and the company share the same destiny due to the nature of the vertically structured labour market. As a result, workers put in long hours and make an effort to fit into a network of multidimensional personal relations, which is useful for good communications and teamwork, but is harmful for expanding the area of personal freedom. One might say that, since corporate productivity would be lower under a different corporate setting, Japanese workers are trading some of their social freedom for higher wages. Even then, what these sacrifices are and what needs to be done to rectify them should be spelt out, instead of just praising high corporate productivity in Japan.

It seems desirable to strike a balance between high corporate productivity and individual social freedom. If too much emphasis is put on the latter, corporate productivity may suffer, and unemployment may become a serious problem—with workers receiving less income and experiencing a decline in economic freedom. This will become a more serious concern in Japan, since given high wages (at least nominally), Japanese companies are now vulnerable to foreign competition. Especially worrisome for Japanese workers is the competition from Korea, Taiwan, and China. American and

European workers have gone too far in advocating individual social choice and this has contributed to the decline of their competitiveness. They did not realize early enough that Japanese and other foreign competition would pose a serious challenge. In the case of Japan today, what freedom workers can obtain is greatly influenced by the strength of its new Asian competitors. It is quite likely that the workers in these countries will be willing to sacrifice individual social freedom for higher wages and this will act as a constraint on the demands of Japanese workers.

Even so, economic development is an 'unfinished revolution' in Japan, for people have not yet been allowed to enjoy as much social freedom as people in the West. One step towards rectifying this situation is to make workers' relations with the company contractual. Since people work for a company for money, it is unfair to turn the company into a community by imposing unnecessary constraints on individual freedom. Both obligations and rewards need to be clearly specified and the structure reorganized so that workers are free to leave at any time. Under the present arrangement, workers work too long, sacrifice individuality for the sake of group harmony, and are discriminated against if they belong to a minority group. Women are not encouraged to develop a career in the company on the assumption that their proper place is in the home. Korean residents and *burakumin* (pariah) are not welcome because it is felt that they disturb group harmony. They also do not fit into the group of workers who have intimate relations even outside the workplace. To integrate these minorities into a company requires a different organizational set-up.

*Socio-Political Reform*

Equally important is reform of the socio-political organization of Japan. It is fashionable to make fun of lawyers as an unproductive, even harmful species, but the Japanese situation, which offers legal redress to a very few people, is too extreme for an industrial country. Since there are only a small number of lawyers, their fees are high, and therefore beyond the reach of most people. The whole judicial system, in fact, militates against 'small' individuals, and it is especially difficult for them to sue large corporations or the government. There is no product liability law in Japan, either; this discriminates against the ordinary man. Certainly, the litigiousness of American society should not be imitated, but the fact that it takes a long time for a court to decide on a civil case is far from an ideal or just situation. For instance, it took about 30 years for a local court to decide on the case brought by coal-miners and their families in Kyushu against their company, Mitsui Coal Mines. Some of the cases of the Minamata victims against the chemical company Chisso also took about 20 years and some are still pending.

Japanese government leaders have not been anxious to change the present situation, for it allows them to enjoy unfettered power. The whole political system is run on the philosophy that sovereignty rests in the élite of the country, not in the ordinary man. This is not, of course, what the law says, but what happens in practice. The system gives too much discretionary power to government leaders—political leaders and high bureaucrats—who use it in consultation with business leaders. The bond of the triad is cemented by common interests, school ties, and intermarriage.[9]

At the end of every fiscal year in February or March, when many bureaucrats retire, newspapers announce the many hundreds of *amakudari*. A large percentage of these retirees end up in the companies and semi-government corporations which come under the supervision of the ministries they formerly belonged to. The companies which take them in do so not so much because of their general merit but because of their influence on the ministries they are leaving. Unless the discretionary power of bureaucrats is reduced, Japan will not change. They are the linchpin of the triad which lays roadblocks to the socio-political liberation of Japan.

The discretionary power of government makes people overly submissive because they do not know what their rights are. What is needed is a push towards liberalization, deregulation, and privatization. That liberalization is an effective weapon is de-monstrated in the decline of MITI's power, except in the area of energy, in the early 1960s. Other ministries did not 'suffer' from the liberalization programme as much as MITI. The Ministry of Finance, for example, retains a hold on banks, securities firms, and insurance companies, and has not even started privatizing semi-government financial institutions, such as the Japan Development Bank, which are no longer needed. The Ministry of Posts and Telecommunications performs a number of regulatory functions, and at the same time, collects a huge sum of money through postal savings, which account for about a third of total household savings. The private sector has to obtain licences or permits from the central government in over 10,000 areas. Undoubtedly, the government needs to perform a number of functions, but there is a great deal of room for liberalization, deregulation, and privatization in Japan.

The second step is to clarify 'the rules of the game'. As shown in the political scandal of former Deputy Prime Minister Kanemaru Shin, construction companies have contributed heavily to secret funds because they believe that this is 'insurance' for getting a fair share of government contracts. Kanemaru and high officials in the Ministry of Construction schemed to let the companies of their choice win contracts; construction projects are not open to any bidders, but only to the companies the government judges to be worthy contractors. Which companies are worthy for which projects is a matter of bureaucratic decision, whose criteria are ambiguous.

The best way of overcoming the problem is for people to become more politically conscious. Otherwise, the system will continue as it is. They must learn to choose politicians who will run the government cleanly and fairly and who will work for the expansion of personal freedom. Unfortunately, the public does not always behave rationally. For example, former Prime Minister Tanaka's constituency in Niigata returned him to the Diet despite the Lockheed scandal. To them, Tanaka was a hero who had brought many public benefits, including the bullet train project connecting Tokyo, to Niigata. The world of personal integrity and freedom seems to be beyond their comprehension, or is too abstract for them to appreciate. There is a Japanese saying, *hana yori dango* (dumplings rather than blossoms). Instead of being blamed for voting for Tanaka, they should be made to realize that life has a fuller meaning when there is a balance between economic gain and socio-political freedom. In many ways, the restrictive situation prevailing today in Japan is the fault of the people, although this may be a result of their ignorance.

Another area where the situation needs improvement is protection of minority rights. People have to realize that this is inextricably related to the expansion of their personal freedom. In the short run, it may be harmful to some of them, since more job opportunities are opened and their chances of getting the jobs they (or their children) desire are reduced. They may even gain pleasure out of discriminating against minorities or in seeing them discriminated against, and have no desire to see an end to it. But to tolerate this situation makes individual rights ambiguous, and demands group conformity of people.

One might argue that to allow people a great deal of freedom can be socially destabilizing and self-defeating. Certainly there are areas in which having a great amount of freedom can lead to problems. Take, for example, sexual behaviour. If the traditional code of sexual behaviour were greatly relaxed, problems would undoubtedly arise. The number of single-parent families would increase as well as the number of illegitimate births and divorces, and this would have serious implications for the discipline and education of children. One can ask whether this is really what people want or whether it is better if the traditional code of sexual behaviour were retained.

In the area of politics, if people keep pressing for political freedom, this may have a detrimental effect on the functioning of government. In a multiethnic country, if minorities demand greater political freedom, this can create problems by dividing the people. Similarly, in a country where democracy is established despite the fact that people are poor and uneducated, manipulation by self-centred politicians may not necessarily bring any of the benefits of democracy to the people.

In the field of education, if too many demands of minority groups are accommodated (for example, as in multiculturalism in the United States), a society may lose its dominant values. Such a liberal attitude towards education may also reduce the effectiveness of the knowledge-enhancing aspect of education and create a large group of functionally illiterate people. It appears that freedom is better guaranteed in a society with a structure and dominant values. A society therefore can not be too free.[10]

History keeps evolving, groping for an elusive equilibrium, which is essentially a balance of economic and socio-political freedom. What this balance is changes over time, adjusting to the experience of the West and the economic challenge of newly industrializing countries in Asia. But clearly Japanese women will become more liberated, minorities will be less discriminated against, and workers' obligations to their companies will become more contractual: they will be freer to enter and leave a network of personal relations, they will enjoy more time with the groups they choose to join to satisfy their non-economic needs, such as the family, they will enjoy greater freedom in expressing their views,[11] and they will enjoy greater opportunities to develop their potential. At present, Japan is a much less liberated country than a typical industrial country in the West, and in this sense, economic development exaggerates Japan's accomplishments.

However, there is no reason to believe that Japan will continue to lag behind the West in bringing about a freer society, especially when we consider that the level of education of most Japanese is high. The Japanese will become increasingly aware that, compared with other countries, their freedom is limited, and they will start questioning the restrictive framework of Japanese society. But Japan will not regard the present Western society as an equilibrium. Since the Japanese have seen the harmful effects of loosening constraints in some areas in the West, for example, sexual behaviour, they will avoid such mistakes and look for a different combination of freedom and constraint. Even in the economic area, a welfare state, which gives greater economic freedom to the poor and low-income groups by loosening the obligation of individual responsibility, turned out to be a big mistake because it deprived people of the incentive to work and left many of them perpetually dependent on welfare payments. Moreover, the experience of Western firms with the uncoupling of productivity with wages and fringe benefits, which has had devastating effects on their competitiveness in the world economy, will make Japanese firms cautious in giving workers greater economic freedom.

Although it is uncertain how Japanese society will evolve, it is possible that, just as Japan alleviated the problem of pollution and brought about the most equitable income distribution among the industrial countries, it will also succeed in expanding the scope of social and political freedom in the future and establish a reasonable balance of various freedoms. In the future, it is in this, rather than in economic areas, that Japan has to excel. At present, Japan's accomplishments, heavily concentrated in the economic area, are one-sided.

1. This paragraph is based on Hosoi Wakizo, *Joko Aishi* [The Pitiful History of Female Workers], Tokyo, Iwanami Shoten, 1954.

2. Tadashi Fukutake, *Japanese Rural Society*, Ithaca, Cornell University Press, 1967, p. 10.

3. The paragraph is based on Yokoyama Gennosuke, *Nihon no Kaso Shakai* [The Lower Strata of Japanese Society], Tokyo, Iwanami Shoten, 1949.

4. Statistical data and historical facts in this section are based on Inoue Kiyoshi, *Nihon Teikoku-shugi no Keisei* [Formation of Japanese Imperialism], Tokyo, Iwanami Shoten, 1968, and Ienaga Saburo, *Taiheiyo Senso* [The Pacific War], Tokyo, Iwanami Shoten, 1968. There are various works in English, on Japanese

imperialism. For example, J. Halliday, *A Political History of Japanese Capitalism*, New York, Pantheon Books, 1975; J. Dower, 'E. H. Norman, Japan and the Uses of History', in J. Dower (ed.), *Origins of the Modern Japanese State: Selected Writings of E. H. Norman*, New York, Pantheon Books, 1975; and J. Dower, *War without Mercy*, New York, Pantheon Books, 1986.

5. Dower, *War without Mercy*, p. 47, and Theodore Friend, *The Blue-Eyed Enemy: Japan against the West in Java and Luzon, 1943–1945*, Princeton, Princeton University Press, 1988, pp. 162–7.

6. Sakata Yoshio, 'Nihon Kindaika no Shuppatsu to Tenkai' [The 'Take-off' and Expansion of Japan's Modernization], *Jinbun Gakuho*, March 1970, p. 15.

7. Even some Marxists historians, notably those who belong to the *Koza* school, admit that Japanese capitalism was still immature and reject the view that the bourgeoisie controlled political and military power in pre-war Japan. They argue that Japanese capitalism was nurtured under the protection and guidance of the government. For example, see Hirano Yoshitaro, *Nihon Shihon-shugi Shakai no Kiko* [The Structure of Capitalist Society in Japan], Tokyo, Iwanami Shoten, 1934, p. 285.

8. For a critical view of economic growth, see R. Mortimer (ed.), *Showcase State: The Illusion of Indonesia's 'Accelerated Modernization'*, London, Angus and Robertson, 1973, Chapter 3.

9. For the power structure of contemporary Japan, see K. van Wolferen, *The Enigma of Japanese Power*, London, Macmillan, 1989.

10. In March 1993, the Japanese court ruled that the Hinomaru is indeed the Japanese flag. The red circle in the middle reminds some people of blood—the sacrifice the government demanded of people during the Pacific War—so they reject it as the national flag. But it is used on various occasions, including the Olympic Games. To form a consensus on this may have been difficult right after the Pacific War, but after about half a century, most Japanese accept it as the national flag. The Ministry of Education, for example, is asking schools to use the Hinomaru on ceremonial occasions. Some oppose this because it exposes children to subconscious nationalist indoctrination. The ministry is taking the stand that a society has to have common values and can not accommodate all minority views. For the view of a Japanese in Okinawa who burnt the Hinomaru during the National Athletic Meet held there, see Norma Field, *In the Realm of a Dying Emperor*, New York, Pantheon, 1991, Chapter 1.

11. The Japanese today enjoy a great deal of freedom in expressing political views, but there are still certain taboos that respectable persons must observe; Communists and leftists are exempted because they have broken these taboos for a long time. If they violate these taboos, they are subject to terrorist attacks by rightists. In 1988, the mayor of Nagasaki created an uproar by saying that the Showa emperor is partly to blame for the Pacific War. He was later wounded in an attack by a rightist. See Field, *In the Realm of a Dying Emperor*, Chapter 3. Clearly, the attitude that the imperial family is above criticism has to change, since it is part of—or used to preserve—the power structure which needs to be modified for a freer society.

# 8
# Lessons for Developing Countries

A person who becomes interested in Japanese economic development is most likely to look for its unique features and ask what their implications will be for his own country. As a non-Western country, Japan is expected to offer a model of development different from that based on the experiences of Western countries. The following discussion will focus on this uniqueness, but it is important to remember that similar chains of causation, as well as phenomena and problems, can be observed in the development process of Western countries as well as Japan. These include the decline of agriculture and the rise of manufacturing industry; changes in the industrial structure, from light to heavy industry and then to knowledge-intensive industry; a change in the composition of exports from agricultural to manufactured goods, and in manufactured goods, from low-value-added to high-value-added goods; booms and recessions; greater equality in the distribution of income; demographic transition; and urbanization. Such similarities may disappoint a person who is looking for a unique model of development. The differences that do exist tend to lie, rather, in the institutional arrangements for bringing about necessary quantitative changes in the economic variables affecting economic growth, such as capital accumulation and export increase.

The following are the highlights of Japanese economic development which attempt to give a somewhat different perspective on the mechanism of economic development. Since they are rarely discussed or highlighted in a typical discourse on economic development, they may be illuminating to a person from a developing country.

1. Technology is a crucial factor in industrialization. Japanese industrialization depended heavily on the country's ability to change major exports from low-value-added goods to high-value-added goods, that is, from textiles to steel and ships, electronic

products, motor cars, and eventually to high-tech products. This required disciplined and educated workers, a good personnel management system, and capital investment, but it also required the ability to develop the necessary technology. Economic development demands the ability to move to a higher value-added product which fetches high prices but which is more difficult to produce. The major component of the ability is technology.

It is not always necessary to compete in pioneering technologies. Japan has not excelled in this area, but has concentrated instead on application technology. Although some people might regard application technology as merely copying or imitating, there is, nevertheless, a wide gap between that sort of technology and no technology at all. In many developing countries today, the technological base is so poorly developed that a factory has to be set up by the plant export from an industrial country. When machines break down, foreign engineers are brought in to repair them. There is no local ability to produce parts, let alone produce machines. Industrialization in such countries is totally dependent on foreign technology. This sort of industrialization can not be the driving force of economic development, and that is why it is aptly called ersatz industrialization.

Until relatively recently, Japanese technology was largely an imitation technology, but it worked to the benefit of the country. It consisted of the ability to understand technological progress in the West, and to introduce the necessary technology for its industrial progress. In many cases, Japanese firms improved on this technology, and created a production system which worked better than the one it had copied from the Western country. In the case of Sony's transistor radio, it was the ability of its technical staff to understand the nature of the transistor as a semiconductor that allowed Sony to triumph. At the time when the transistor was invented, its application to the radio was far from obvious. To see this link required an advanced knowledge of physics.

With the rising popularity of schools of business administration, people tend to think that those with MBAs can run a manufacturing company. Indeed, there are a number of jobs they can do (for example, financial analysis and marketing), but if they go for short-term profits or devalue the importance of R&D, the company's decline will be assured. The basic problem with a number of American companies which have lost their competitive edge is not, however, the people who run them, but a business environment which enabled financial Vikings to raid them. Industrial progress requires not only technical manpower—scientists, engineers, and skilled workers—but also a business environment which encourages manufacturing companies to undertake long-term investment.

2. One unique aspect of Japanese development is its dualistic nature. Since much of modern technology is capital intensive, and the degree of substitution between capital and labour in such technology is limited, it is often introduced with little modification even to countries which have abundant labour but little capital. The modern sector created by such technology co-exists with the traditional small-scale sector in most developing countries. Japan was no exception to this pattern. What is unique to Japan, however, is the large contribution which the traditional sector made to its economic development, for example, earning foreign exchange. Since the present technological situation makes it unlikely that a dualistic structure can be avoided, it is important to make the traditional sector a dynamic force of economic development.

One major problem in doing so is that the traditional sector is isolated from external changes and opportunities. It is not usually up to date with technological changes. It is often ignorant of market opportunities within and outside the country, and even if it wants to take advantage of such opportunities, it lacks adequate finance. These disadvantages can be overcome to a certain extent by developing an institution which can act as an organizer for the traditional sector. A *sogo shosha* (general trading company) and a large assembler in the vertical *keiretsu* are examples of such institutions.

3. Japan has been highly successful in raising the average level of education of its people and minimizing its spread. Economic development is a matter of increasing average productivity. To increase the level of education is one of the most effective ways to do this, for it improves the quality of people who become peasants, workers, managers, and entrepreneurs—the agents of production. A high average level of education with a mixture of highly educated people and badly educated people, as in the case of the United States, is not a desirable situation, because it creates a divisive society. The most desirable situation, as in Japan, is to make efforts to educate all people, so that they can all read and write, know what to do and what not to do, and improve their chances by further learning.

Japan's success in educating its people is partly based on the fact that it is a country of one culture and one language. At the same time, it should be realized that the present level of education did not come about automatically as a result of economic development. The teaching method, the national curriculum, the standard set for each grade by the Ministry of Education, and the care teachers give to slow learners were all contributing factors. People in a developing country tend to look to the United States for an educational model because it has excellent universities and has produced many Nobel Prize winners, but what is more important for developing countries is a good primary and secondary education base, for the rate of return is much higher at that level than at the tertiary level. Japan excels in primary and secondary education.

4. Traditions are constraints on people, and it is a people's natural desire to be free from such traditions. But they were created under certain circumstances to regulate people's behaviour. As these circumstances change, some will no longer be needed, but many others may be still necessary as a restraint on behaviour. Japan has been possibly the most cautious of the industrial countries of today in discarding traditions; this is especially so in the case of traditions relating to the family. Although the code of sexual behaviour has been changing among the younger generations of Japanese, it has nevertheless remained rather traditional in the process of development and has prevented the family from disintegrating. This is the main reason why the number of single-parent families is still small in Japan. Although liberals may say that single parenthood is a matter of choice, it can have detrimental effects on the personality development, discipline, and education of children. Japanese development has depended greatly on the strength of the family.

5. In the process of economic development, modern values and institutions have to be introduced. Modernization need not, however, be inconsistent with tradition. Japan has, in fact, utilized some of its traditional values to build a modern institution. For example, Japanese personnel management relies on such pre-modern values as seniority, submissiveness to authority, personal loyalty, benevolence, and group solidarity. When these were combined with modern practices, such as meritocracy, Japanese personnel management became more effective in raising productivity than Western management which is based largely on modern values.

If Confucianism is regarded as a religion, the contribution of a religion to Japanese development can not be overlooked. Confucian emphasis on education as a means of self-improvement had a significant impact on educational progress in the modern period. Its emphasis on such virtues as loyalty and filial piety, which govern personal relations, were incorporated into business management, and also contributed to social stability.

In the case of a less secular religion (some do not accept Confucianism as a religion, but regard it as an ethical system), it may appear harmful to economic development because it requires its adherents to observe certain 'antiproductive' practices (such as fasting during Ramadan), but its effects have to be judged from a broader perspective. As Max Weber argued for Protestantism, religion can rationalize a person's values, and if this rationalization can be directed to the pursuit of economic goals, religion can be conducive to economic development.

6. The Japanese experience should not, however, make one complacent about traditional values and institutions. In a company, many of these values had to be rejected, and the usefulness of those which were retained had to be periodically re-evaluated. Traditional values are retained as long as they contribute to an increase in productivity. One should not be distracted by anthropologists and sociologists who exaggerate the exotic manners and customs which superficially remain in a Japanese company. In principle, business development means innovation. It is only when it is 'functional', that is, it contributes to productivity increase, that traditional values and institutions are retained, and, in some cases, reinforced.

7. A Japanese company's strength lies in its ability to maintain co-operative relations over an extended period. In the company itself, employees, managers, and stockholders co-operate and share its fruits. They are not treated equally, but the power of stock-holders who own the company in the legal sense is greatly curbed. Managers are not simply the agents of stockholders; they retain a great deal of independence. Workers are not freely laid off by management in order to maximize profits. A company is run according to the philosophy that it is a joint venture of workers, managers, and shareholders. The distribution of fruits is not as unequal as in the United States where managers and shareholders get a larger slice because they insist that they be paid opportunity costs. As a result, there is a large gap in compensation between workers and managers, and while the former are laid off, the latter receive large bonuses.

A vertical *keiretsu* works also to the advantage of Japanese productivity because the large assembler and its subcontractors co-operate and share the fruits of co-operation. This situation can change if the large assembler tries to maximize short-term profits by squeezing its subcontractors, because the physical capital of the subcontractors is a fixed (sunk) cost and they will supply parts to the assembler as long as they can cover variable costs. But if this is done, the quality of the parts they supply will deteriorate over time because the necessary investment will not be undertaken, and the *keiretsu* will stop functioning as an effective production organization. Or if a subcontractor is ousted at the whim of the assembler, it damages the trust relations between them, and impairs the smooth functioning of the *keiretsu*. The assembler has to retain the power to oust a non-performing subcontractor in order to maintain or improve the efficiency of the *keiretsu*, but it has to make the criteria objective and understood by its sub-contractors. At the same time, it has to behave in such a way as to win their trust. Keeping trust relations healthy is essential for a successful co-operative arrangement over a long period of time.

8. The establishment of trust relations is essential for supporting business development. If relations are difficult to establish, trans-action costs become high, and many transactions fall through, thus hindering business and economic development. To rely on the court to implement contracts or to make the other side fulfil a business promise is too time-consuming and expensive. While it is necessary to develop the court system to reduce the temptation of people to break promises, it is equally important for society to make people keep them. In Japan, this has been done partly by moral education, but probably more important has been the fact that most people live in a close network of personal relations. When bound by social obligations, it is more difficult to break business promises.

To create a business alliance has been another way of over-coming the problem of getting cheated in business. A *keiretsu* is such an alliance. It is sometimes criticized because it is closed to outsiders, but as a group of companies which have done business together a number of times, it works to reduce transaction costs and promote the co-ordination of various companies which are needed to undertake a joint co-operative project, such as a plant export. Because there is uncertainty as to the trustworthiness of prospective participants in a co-operative project, without a *keiretsu*, transaction costs may become too high, and the project may not eventuate.

9. What triggered Japanese development was not a religious

revolution. After Max Weber, who traced the source of capitalistic development in Western Europe to Protestantism, many scholars looked—unsuccessfully—for something comparable to Protestantism in Japan. Japan, however, has not experienced a religious upheaval for several centuries. Recently, the Confucian hypothesis has become popular, but since Confucianism has been in existence for over two thousand years and its homeland, China, has not yet developed, its effect on economic development can not be compared to that of Protestantism (assuming that Weber's thesis is correct in explaining the rise of capitalism in the West).

In Weber's framework, it was asceticism, not Protestantism, which formed the spirit of capitalism in Western Europe; the latter was important as the source of the former. Asceticism existed in Japan from the very beginning of the modern period, but it was a passive force, and only after the country entered the modern period, was it utilized to advantage.

If Confucianism, ethical movements such as Shingaku and Hotoku, and 'the ways' like bushido are regarded as religions, then one can not deny the impact of religion on Japanese asceticism. Clearly, too much religion—in the sense of trying to be faithful to God in various aspects of life—is not good for promoting economic growth since it reduces the desire of people to improve their material well-being, but too little is not good, either, because asceticism can be best maintained if it is supported by some faith. Religion can give meaning to asceticism and strengthen it in a person's value system. When society starts moving in the direction of economic development for some reasons, asceticism under-scored by religion can become an invaluable ally of economic growth. On the surface, religion may appear to be a negative factor, encouraging the spending of money (for example, on places of worship or pilgrimages) and encroaching on time which could be spent on more productive purposes, but it can also be a powerful positive factor since it can elevate work and frugality to the level of religious duties. In the Japanese case, Confucianism, ethical movements, and bushido played such a role. In fact, it was their strong influence on Tokugawa society which gave rise to a strong work ethic and a high propensity to save in the modern period.

10. The main impetus for Japanese development came from a political movement. The Meiji Restoration, which ushered Japan into the modern period, was a political 'revolution', and Japanese capitalism was born in its aftermath. In the beginning phase of

industrialization, in order to enlighten the people about the new opportunities available, the government set up pilot factories. It later reduced its direct involvement in industrialization, but continued to play an active role in developing education, building an infrastructure, removing market imperfections, and providing public goods, such as law and order—that is, in creating a congenial environment for the market economy. In the post-war period, the government has intervened in the economy to change its structure so that it can take advantage of the new growth potential which has arisen in the world economy. MITI's industrial policy in the 1950s and 1960s which helped the economy shift its centre to heavy industry is a prime example of this.

Free market economists argue that the economy of a developing country performs better without government intervention and that the most helpful thing to do is to liberalize the economy. But the Japanese case shows that it is possible for the economy to improve with government intervention. This is by no means easy, but under certain circumstances, it can be done. The pay-off of this approach is large since the market economy, which has many imperfections and is slow in responding to opportunities, can function much more smoothly under effective government guidance. This has been demonstrated in Korea, Taiwan, and Singapore as well.

11. For a government to promote development, it must be able to draw up a plan which promotes the economic welfare of the general public (not being the captive of vested interests), have the machinery to implement it, and have the will to carry it out even if it is unpopular. The Japanese government was effective in doing this because the political system was authoritarian even though it had a parliamentary system and competent people were attracted to the bureaucracy. In the pre-war period, sovereignty was vested with the emperor, and as his agents, the bureaucrats ran the country. In post-war years, sovereignty was transferred to the people, and the bureaucrats began sharing power with politicians, but having been used to the authoritarian system, people did not exercise their full right and gave politicians and bureaucrats a great deal of independence. It should be pointed out, however, that this did not result in the establishment of an oligarchy which runs the country in the interests of the élite who control government. Politicians and bureaucrats undoubtedly paid attention to their own interests, but economic policy was generally favourable for national economic development.

It is tempting to argue that an authoritarian government is better for economic development, but it is not only the form of government but also its actual working which has to be considered. An authoritarian government can be worse than a democracy if the former is run by people who ignore the interests of the general public but run the government for the interests of a particular group of people, for example, a certain ethnic group, or to perpetuate their power. An authoritarian government tends to perform poorly when there is no prior tradition of authoritarian government.

In the Japanese case, the results are mixed. Economic policy may have promoted economic development, but the pre-war Japanese government came under the control of the military which plunged the country into a destructive war. Under an authoritarian political system, once the country goes in a certain direction, even if people do not want it, it is often difficult to stop the momentum. In the post-war period, the Japanese government has been more concerned with the welfare of people, but this change was not initiated by the Japanese themselves. Although the new right, which emerged as Japan became an industrial giant, tends to deny, or at least to play down the positive effects of the reforms of the occupation period, it was the Allied Powers which destroyed the military, undertook institutional reforms, and installed democracy in Japan. But the post-war 'authoritarian' system has worked relatively well and can be more attractive than a liberal democracy for a developing country for which escape from poverty can be a more pressing problem than protection of such human rights as the freedom of the press.

Advocates of democracy argue that government performance will improve with economic development, but since a democracy does not work well when people are poor and badly educated, it can be a serious stumbling-block to economic development. In contrast, an authoritarian government is appealing because, from the recent experience of NIEs in Asia, it seems to be the most effective type of government in promoting economic development, and because to make an authoritarian government work is easier than to make a democracy work. But as pointed out, there are inherent dangers in an authoritarian government, and to make it work requires certain conditions—conditions which are not necessarily easy to meet. An authoritarian path can be a short-cut, but it entails dangers.

12. Although Japanese development was rapid compared with that of the West, one must keep in mind that economic development

is essentially a slow process. To reach Japan's present level of income from the subsistence level of the 1870s, it took more than a century. Moreover, in the pre-modern period, although the income of most of the population did not rise, there were institutional developments. Meiji development depended on these changes during the pre-modern period, Taisho development on Meiji, pre-war Showa development on Taisho, and post-war Showa development on pre-war Showa, and Heisei development on post-war Showa. That is, the present level of development is the outcome of the successive evolution of the economy in the past few centuries.

Economic development can be hastened, and the best agent for achieving this is probably the government. But economic development requires a dynamic private sector which responds to government initiatives. For this, the attitude of the people must change. They must be educated, and new capitalist institutions must be created, nurtured, and developed. If the government can be the major agent of economic development, a planned economy should work. The reason that it has not worked is that economic development, that is, productivity increase, depends heavily on private initiative, the quality of people, and institutional arrangements for co-ordination. To develop these factors takes time. So, even if a developmental state is born, which is by no means an easy task to accomplish, economic development can not occur over a matter of a few decades.

The Japanese experience shows that economic development can be accelerated. Certainly, it did not take as long for Japan to reach its present standard of living as Western countries. But Japanese development was not achieved in only one or two generations. A developing country, if successful, can develop faster than Japan, as demonstrated by Korea, Taiwan, and Singapore, but it still requires time, especially in a country where the pre-modern tradition is weak. One should not be misled into believing that a government can bring about development in a few decades. Although political leaders in developing countries try to give that impression, it is more constructive for the government and the people to have a longer time horizon and to work steadily for an eventual 'triumph'.

# Glossary

*Daimyo*: A daimyo was the vassal of the shogun, and his domain was called a *han*.

*Dutch learning (rangaku)*: The study of Western science and the West in general during the Tokugawa period. It was so-called, since all such study was based on Dutch books, the Dutch being the only Westerners allowed to trade with Japan during the period of isolation. Dutch learning became popular from about 1740, and its progress in subsequent years prepared Japan for the contact with the West which resumed in earnest in the mid-nineteenth century.

*Edo*: The former name of Tokyo. The Edo castle (now the Imperial Palace) was the headquarters of the Tokugawa shogunate.

*Han*: A *han* was the domain, or fief, granted by the shogun to his vassal, the daimyo. A *han* government had virtual autonomy over internal matters. There were about 270 *han* in the period.

*Land reform*: This refers to the reform carried out in the occupation period. It drastically reduced the proportion of land cultivated by tenants, and the rent of the remaining land cultivated by tenants became only nominal.

*Land tax*: This refers to the first major tax instituted by the Meiji government. It accounted for the bulk of tax revenues in the first few decades of the Meiji era, and also served as a means for the government to channel surpluses from agriculture to industry. Furthermore, since it was a monetary tax (payable only in money), it accelerated the spread of monetary exchange in villages, and thus contributed to capitalist development in rural Japan.

*Matsukata deflation*: The deflation of the early 1880s named after the then Minister of Finance, Matsukata Masayoshi, who was the prime mover behind the policy. It restored the convertibility of paper notes and laid the foundation for financial orthodoxy in subsequent years.

*Meiji era*: The reign of the Meiji Emperor (1868–1911). Similarly, the reign of the succeeding Emperor, Taisho (1912–25), is known as the Taisho era; and that of the Showa Emperor (1926–88), as the Showa era. The reign of the present Emperor (1989– ) is called the Heisei era.

*Meiji Restoration*: This usually refers to the political events of 1868 which removed the Tokugawa family from the position of shogun and returned sovereignty to the emperor, who took the reign name Meiji (meaning 'enlightened rule').

*Occupation period*: The period from September 1945 to March 1952, during which Japan was occupied by the Allied Powers, principally the United States. In September 1951, the San Francisco Peace Treaty was signed, and in April 1952, Japan regained independence.

*Rice tax*: The rice tax comprised the bulk of government revenues in the Tokugawa period. The tax rate was set by the individual domains, and the samurai received their stipends in rice.

*Samurai*: Samurai, or warriors, were the ruling class in the Tokugawa period, and enjoyed various social privileges over other classes. Towards the end of the period, however, the lowest-ranking samurai came under straitened circumstances, causing dissension in the samurai ranks. Altogether, the samurai constituted about 5 per cent of the total population.

*SCAP*: The Supreme Commander for the Allied Powers (SCAP) presided over the Japanese government and directed the reforms of the occupation period. General Douglas MacArthur held the position from September 1945 to April 1951, the crucial years of the period, and left his imprint on the institutions of post-war Japan.

*Shogun*: The shogun was the head of a warrior clan, for example, the Tokugawa family in the case of the Tokugawa period, who was entrusted by the emperor to rule the country. The Tokugawa shogun directly controlled about a quarter of the country's agricultural land and let the rest be governed by his vassals, the daimyos. His government is called the shogunate.

*Tenno*: The Emperor of Japan. In the Meiji Constitution, sovereignty rested with him. After the Pacific War, sovereignty was transferred to the people, and the emperor became the symbol of the country and of the unity of the people. In the post-war Constitution, little political power is vested with him.

*Tokugawa period*: The period (1603–1867) during which the Tokugawa shogun ruled the country.

*Zaibatsu*: A *zaibatsu* is a family-controlled group of companies. A family-controlled holding company owned controlling shares of the companies of the group; they were not listed with a stock exchange. In structure, it is similar to the present-day conglomerate. The four largest *zaibatsu* before the Pacific War were Mitsui, Mitsubishi, Sumitomo, and Yasuda. The *zaibatsu* were dissolved during the occupation period. The Mitsui, Mitsubishi, and Sumitomo groups which exist today should be regarded essentially as a group of independent companies. Though there is intragroup shareholding and these companies can not be regarded as completely independent, there is no holding company which controls them. The bank is usually the most influential company in the group, but it does not have controlling shares of the member companies, and legally, it can not own more than 10 per cent of the shares of another company.

# Chronology

## Late Tokugawa Period

1853    Commodore Matthew C. Perry arrives.

1854    Signing of the Treaty of Kanagawa. The period of isolation ends.

1858    Signing of the Treaties with Five Nations (commercial treaties).

1859    Trade with the West begins.

## Meiji Era

1868    Meiji Restoration.

1869    Institutional reforms begin.

1871    The yen is made the basic unit of money.

1873    Institution of the land tax.

1874    Saga Rebellion—the first armed rebellion against the new government.

The first invasionary expedition, against Taiwan, is sent out.

1876    Compulsory commutation of samurai stipends to government bonds.

1877    Satsuma Rebellion, led by Saigo Takamori.

1881    Matsukata Masayoshi becomes Minister of Finance. The 'Matsukata deflation' begins.

1886    Convertibility of paper notes is restored.

1894    Sino-Japanese War begins.

1895    End of the Sino-Japanese War. Taiwan becomes a Japanese colony.

1897    Gold standard adopted.

1901    Yahata Steel Mill begins production.

1904    Russo-Japanese War begins.

1905    End of the Russo-Japanese War. Russia cedes the southern half of Sakhalin, and recognizes Korea as being within Japan's sphere of interest.

1910    Korea is annexed.

1911    Japan regains tariff autonomy.

## Taisho Era

1914    First World War begins.
1915    Economic boom begins in Japan.
1917    Japan goes off the gold standard by imposing an embargo on gold exports.
1918    First World War ends.
1920    Post-war recession begins.
1923    Kanto earthquake destroys most of Tokyo.

## Showa Era

1927    Financial crisis.
1930    Japan returns to the gold standard (January).
1931    Manchuria Incident.
        The gold standard is abandoned (December).
1937    China Incident, which is usually taken as the beginning of the Pacific War.
        Transition to a mobilization economy begins.
1941    Japan attacks Pearl Harbor and declares war on the Allied Powers (December).
1945    Japan accepts unconditional surrender (August).
        Occupation forces begin arriving (September).
        General Douglas MacArthur, Supreme Commander for the Allied Powers, launches post-war institutional reforms.
1946    A new constitution is proclaimed.
1949    The foreign exchange rate is set at 360 yen per dollar.
1950    Korean Conflict begins and triggers the first economic boom in post-war Japan.
1951    Signing of the San Francisco Peace Treaty.
        Ceasefire of the Korean Conflict.
1952    Japan regains independence (April).
1953    Armistice of the Korean Conflict signed.
1960    The period of high economic growth begins.
1964    *Shinkansen* (bullet train) starts operation between Osaka and Tokyo.
        Olympic Games are held in Tokyo.
1970    Pollution first becomes a serious social issue.
1971    The yen revalued, and the new exchange rate becomes 308 yen per dollar (December).
1973    Flexible exchange rate system adopted. The yen starts to revalue.
        The oil crisis (October), which triggers a major economic recession.
1974    GNP growth becomes negative for the first time in the post-war

period. This ends the high growth period which started around 1960.

1976   The economy recovers from the oil shock. In the next few years, the economy grows at about 5 per cent per annum.

1979   Oil prices begin to rise again, resulting in the second oil crisis.

1980   As the aftermath of the second oil crisis, the growth rate declines to about 4 per cent, and finally stabilizes at a level a little below this in 1981–4.

1983   Japan's per capita income (computed by current exchange rates) becomes the tenth highest in the OECD group. This is Japan's first appearance in the list of the top ten countries.

1985   The Plaza Accord (September). The yen starts to revalue.

1986   The exchange rate becomes 165 yen per dollar (September).

1987   The yen revalues further to about 123 yen per dollar towards the end of the year.

A massive outflow of investment to South-East Asia, looking for cheaper production sites.

1990   The third highest in per capita GNP (measured in current exchange rates) among the industrial countries (after Switzerland and Finland).

1992   Economic recession. The growth rate is small but positive; the worst year since the mid-1970s.

1993   The yen begins to revalue again, to about 113 yen per dollar in early April.

The economy experiences the worst year since 1974. There is no immediate prospect for economic recovery.

# Further Reading

The following is a selective list of works in English for those who wish to read further on the subjects discussed in this book.

### Chapter 1

Nakamura, T., *Economic Growth in Prewar Japan*, New Haven, Yale University Press, 1983.

———, *The Postwar Japanese Economy*, Tokyo, University of Tokyo Press, 1981.

Ohkawa, K. and Rosovsky, H., 'A Century of Japanese Economic Growth', in W. Lockwood (ed.), *The State and Economic Enterprise in Japan*, Princeton, Princeton University Press, 1965.

———, *Japanese Economic Growth*, Stanford, Stanford University Press, 1973, pp. 1–43 and 215–50.

Patrick, H. and Rosovsky, H., 'Japan's Economic Performance: An Overview', in H. Patrick and H. Rosovsky (eds.), *Asia's New Giant*, Washington, Brookings Institution, 1976.

### Chapter 2

*Economic Growth*

Kuznets, S., *Economic Growth of Nations*, Cambridge, Harvard University Press, 1971, Chapter 1.

Ohkawa, K. and Rosovsky, H., *Japanese Economic Growth*, Stanford, Stanford University Press, 1973, Chapter 8.

*Population Growth*

Taueber, I., 'Population and Labor Force in the Industrialization of Japan, 1850–1950', in S. Kuznets et al. (eds.), *Economic Growth: Brazil, India, Japan*, Durham, Duke University Press, 1955.

*Development with One's Own Resources*

Komiya, R., 'Direct Investment in Postwar Japan', in P. Drysdale (ed.), *Direct Investment in Asia and the Pacific*, Canberra, Australian National University Press, 1972.

*Building on Traditions*

Abbeglen, J., *Japanese Factory*, Glencoe, Illinois, Free Press, 1958, Chapter 8.

Nakane, C., *Japanese Society*, Harmondsworth, Penguin Books, 1973.

Nakayama, I., *Industrialization of Japan*, Honolulu, University Press of Hawaii, 1965, pp. 25–63.

*Dualistic Development*

Broadbridge, S., *Industrial Dualism in Japan*, London, Frank Cass and Co., 1966.

Yasuba, Y., 'The Evolution of Dualistic Wage Structure', in H. Patrick (ed.), *Japanese Industrialization and Its Social Consequences*, Berkeley, University of California Press, 1976.

Yoshihara, K., *Sogo Shosha: The Vanguard of the Japanese Economy*, Tokyo, Oxford University Press, 1982, Chapters 5 and 6.

*Government Involvement*

Lockwood, W., *Economic Development of Japan*, Princeton, Princeton University Press, expanded edition, 1968, pp. 499–592.

Rosovsky, H., *Capital Formation in Japan*, Glencoe, Illinois, Free Press, 1961, Chapter 2.

Trezise, P., 'Politics, Government, and Economic Growth in Japan', in H. Patrick and H. Rosovsky (eds.), *Asia's New Giant*, Washington, Brookings Institution, 1976.

**Chapter 3**

Krause, L. and Sekiguchi, S., 'Japan and the World Economy', in H. Patrick and H. Rosovsky (eds.), *Asia's New Giant*, Washington, Brookings Institution, 1976.

Lockwood, W., *Economic Development of Japan*, Princeton, Princeton University Press, expanded edition, 1968, Chapters 6 and 7.

Ohkawa, K. and Rosovsky, H., *Japanese Economic Growth*, Stanford, Stanford University Press, 1973, pp. 173–95.

**Chapter 4**

*Contrast with Thailand*

Embree, J., 'Thailand—A Loosely Structured Social System', *American Anthropologist*, April–June 1950, Vol. 52, pp. 181–93.

*Contrast with South and South-East Asia*

Baran, P., *The Political Economy of Growth*, New York, Monthly Review Press, 1957, pp. 151–61.
Geertz, C., *Agricultural Involution*, Berkeley, University of California Press, 1963, pp. 130–54.

*Contrast with China*

Levy, M., 'Contrasting Factors in the Modernization of China and Japan', *Economic Development and Cultural Change*, 1953–4.
Lockwood, W., 'Japan's Response to the West—the Contrast with China', *World Politics*, October 1956.

*Contrast in General*

Landes, D., 'Japan and Europe: Contrast in Industrialization', in W. Lockwood (ed.), *The State and Economic Enterprise in Japan*, Princeton, Princeton University Press, 1965.
Moore, B., *Social Origins of Dictatorship and Democracy*, Boston, Beacon Press, 1966, Chapters 4 and 5.
Ohkawa, K. and Ranis, G., *Japan and the Developing Countries*, Oxford, Basil Blackwell, 1985.

*Tokugawa Heritage*

Bellah, R., *Tokugawa Religion*, Glencoe, Illinois, Free Press, 1957, Chapters 1 and 7.
Dore, R., *Tokugawa Education*, Berkeley, University of California Press, 1965, Chapters 1 and 10.
Fukutake, T., *Japanese Rural Society*, Ithaca, Cornell University Press, 1972, Part 3.
Hall, J., 'The Nature of Traditional Society: Japan', in R. Ward and D. Rustow (eds.), *Political Modernization in Japan and Turkey*, Princeton, Princeton University Press, 1964.
———, 'The New Look of the Tokugawa History', in J. Hall and M. Jansen (eds.), *Studies in the Institutional History of Early Modern Japan*, Princeton, Princeton University Press, 1967.
Hirschmeier, J. and Yui, T., *The Development of Japanese Business 1600–1980*, 2nd edn., London, George Allen and Unwin, 1981, Chapter 1.
Smith, T. C., *The Agrarian Origins of Modern Japan*, Stanford, Stanford University Press, 1959, pp. 201–13.

## Chapter 5

*The Meiji Restoration and Meiji Reforms*

Beasley, W., *The Meiji Restoration*, Stanford, Stanford University Press, 1972.

Craig, A., *Choshu in the Meiji Restoration*, Cambridge, Harvard University Press, 1961.

Hall, I., *Mori Arinori*, Cambridge, Harvard University Press, 1973.

Jansen, M., *Sakamoto Ryoma and the Meiji Restoration*, Princeton, Princeton University Press, 1961.

Pyle, K., *The New Generation in Meiji Japan*, Stanford, Stanford University Press, 1969.

Rosovsky, H., 'Japan's Transition to Modern Economic Growth, 1868–1885', in H. Rosovsky (ed.), *Industrialization in Two Systems: Essays in Honor of Alexander Gerschenkron*, New York, John Wiley and Sons, 1966.

*Reforms of the Occupation Period*

Cohen, J., *Japan's Economy in War and Reconstruction*, Minneapolis, University of Minnesota Press, 1949.

Dore, R., *Land Reform in Japan*, London, Oxford University Press, 1959.

Duke, B., *Japan's Militant Teachers*, Honolulu, University Press of Hawaii, 1973.

Hadley E., *Anti-Trust in Japan*, Princeton, Princeton University Press, 1969.

Henderson, D. (ed.), *The Constitution of Japan: Its First Twenty Years, 1947–67*, Seattle, University of Washington Press, 1968.

Kawai, K., *Japan's American Interlude*, Chicago, University of Chicago Press, 1960.

Kosaka, M., *A Hundred Million Japanese: The Postwar Experience*, Tokyo, Kodansha, 1972.

Textor, R., *Failure in Japan*, New York, J. Day Co., 1951.

## Chapter 6

*The Quality of People*

Bellah, R., *Tokugawa Religion*, Glencoe, Illinois, Free Press, 1957, Chapters 4–6.

Benedict, R., *The Chrysanthemum and the Sword*, Boston, Houghton Mifflin Co., 1946.

Doi, T., *The Anatomy of Dependence*, Tokyo, Kodansha International, 1973.

Nitobe, I., *Bushido: The Soul of Japan*, Tokyo, Charles E. Tuttle Co., 1969.

Reischauer, E., *The Japanese*, Tokyo, Charles E. Tuttle Co., 1978, Chapters 12–22.

*Education*

Duke, B., *The Japanese School: Lessons for Industrial America*, New York, Praeger, 1986.

Rohlen, T., *Japan's High Schools*, Berkeley, University of California Press, 1983.

White, M., *The Japanese Educational Challenge: A Commitment to Children*, Glencoe, Illinois, Free Press, 1987.

### Management

Abbeglen, J., *Japanese Factory*, Glencoe, Illinois, Free Press, 1958.

Dore, R., *British Factory–Japanese Factory*, Berkeley, University of California Press, 1973.

Halberstam, D., *The Reckoning*, New York, William Morrow and Co., 1986.

Morita, A., *Made in Japan: Akio Morita and Sony*, New York, Weatherhill, 1987.

Ouchi, W., *Theory Z*, New York, Avon Books, 1982.

### Business Alliance

Dore, R., *Taking Japan Seriously: A Confucian Perspective on Leading Economic Issues*, London, Athlone Press, 1987, Chapter 9.

Gerlach, M., *Alliance Capitalism: The Social Organization of Japanese Business*, Berkeley, University of California Press, 1992.

## Chapter 7

### Poverty

Caldarola, C., 'The *Doya-Gai*: A Japanese Version of Skid Row', *Pacific Affairs*, Winter 1968–9.

Chubachi, M. and Taira, K., 'Poverty in Modern Japan', in H. Patrick (ed.), *Japanese Industrialization and Its Social Consequences*, Berkeley, University of California Press, 1976.

### Pollution

Huddel, N. and Reich, M., *Island of Dreams: Environmental Crisis in Japan*, New York, Autumn Press, 1975.

Kelly, D. et al., *The Economic Superpowers and the Environment: The United States, the Soviet Union, and Japan*, San Francisco, W. H. Freeman, 1976.

### Imperialism

Dower, J., 'E. H. Norman, Japan and the Uses of History', in J. Dower (ed.), *Origins of the Modern Japanese State: Selected Writings of E. H. Norman*, New York, Pantheon Books, 1975.

——, *War without Mercy: Race and Power in the Pacific War*, New York, Pantheon Books, 1986.

*The Purpose of Development*

Field, N., *In the Realm of a Dying Emperor: A Portrait of Japan at Century's End*, New York, Pantheon Books, 1991.

Taylor, J., *Shadows of the Rising Sun*, New York, William Morrow and Co., 1983.

Van Wolferen, K., *The Enigma of Japanese Power*, London, Macmillan, 1989.

# Index

## DATE DUE

| | | | |
|---|---|---|---|
| | | | |
| | | | |
| | | | |
| | | | |
| | | | |
| | | | |
| | | | |
| | | | |
| | | | |
| | | | |
| | | | |
| | | | |
| | | | |
| | | | |
| | | | |
| | | | |
| | | | |
| GAYLORD | | | PRINTED IN U.S.A. |